Microsoft
SharePoint 2013 Plain & Simple

Johnathan Lightfoot
Michelle Lopez
Scott Metker

ISBN: 978-0-7356-6700-6

Sixth Printing: June 2016

Printed and bound in the United States.

Microsoft Press books are available through booksellers and distributors worldwide. If you need support related to this book, email Microsoft Press Book Support at *mspinput@microsoft.com*. Please tell us what you think of this book at *http://www .microsoft.com/learning/booksurvey*.

Acquisitions and Developmental Editor: Kenyon Brown
Production Editor: Holly Bauer
Technical Reviewer: Marlene Lanphier
Copyeditor: Bob Russell, Octal Publishing, Inc.
Editorial Production: Rich Kershner, Box Twelve Communications
Indexer: Ellen Troutman Zaig
Cover Design: Twist Creative • Seattle
Cover Composition: Karen Montgomery
Illustrator: S4Carlisle Publishing Services

[2013-09-13]

This book is dedicated to my daughter, Giavrielle Sarahannah Lightfoot.
Do know that this book and all that I do I do for you.

—Johnathan Lightfoot

This book is dedicated to my three beloved blessings, Landon, Gabriella, and Daniella.
No more drawing pictures of Mommy with her laptop!

—Michelle Lopez

This book is dedicated to my family, Shannon, Zoe, and Cole. It might not seem as if I'm
thinking of you when I am up to my elbows in code, but I am. I always am.

—Scott Metker

Contents

Getting started with SharePoint sites. 35

Organizing and managing information 57

14 Security within SharePoint 2013 253

15 Using personal sites and social networking. 275

18

Automating tasks with workflows **377**

Acknowledgments

So many thanks go to Microsoft Press and O'Reilly Media for giving us the opportunity to write this book for you and taking us on this journey. Writing a book requires the assistance and experience of a lot of people. Specifically, thanks so much to our wonderful editor, Kenyon Brown, our brilliant technical reviewer, Marlene Lanphier, our witty copyeditor, Bob Russell of Octal Publishing, Inc., the talented illustrators at S4Carlisle Publishing Services, and our stellar production editor, Holly Bauer, for being so patient and helpful throughout the entire process.

Thank you to GP Strategies, specifically Scott Greenberg, Douglas Sharp, Don Duquette, Bill Finnegan, and Deborah Ung for being so supportive throughout the entire process of getting the book completed.

Thanks go out to my coauthors, Michelle and Scott: your encouragement and work toward the book was outstanding. I am really glad to have had the chance to work with the two of you. Also, thank you to Cary Walker III and Yvonne Sletmoe Wilson over at GP Strategies for your encouragement and listening to my SharePoint ramblings every month. A special thank you to Dux Raymond Sy for giving so much of yourself to the SharePoint Community and for always being a great sounding board to my crazy ideas! And, a big thank you Microsoft's SharePoint Development team for making such a terrific platform to work with and write about.

Finally, I would like to thank Karen Kocher and Karla Shores for asking about Community Portals and Sites.

From Johnathan Lightfoot

First and foremost I want to thank God for the blessings that have been given to me and my family.

A *really* big thank you to my wife, Genevievette—thank you for the encouragement during the long nights and weekends it took to get this book completed. Without your sacrifices, commitment, and dedication, I could not have finished this wonderful journey.

From Michelle Lopez

A huge acknowledgment goes out to my husband, Carlos, for always bringing humor to my long days. Thank you for not giving me too much grief for neglecting you and our beautiful family during this amazing endeavor. To my parents, Dwight and Johnette Phillips, whom I love to make proud; to my sister, Noelle Phillips, who gets me like no one else does; and to my children, who continue to inspire me to make the world a better place. Thank you to Johnathan Lightfoot, for believing in me as much as I believe in me. Thank you to Scott Metker for sharing his dedication and resolve with me, even when in Paris!

I'd also like to thank you, our reader, for choosing this book. I hope you begin, or continue, your journey to become as addicted to SharePoint as I am.

From Scott Metker

I would first like to thank my coauthors, Johnathan Lightfoot and Michelle Lopez, for their assistance in writing this book. It truly was a team effort, and I thank you both for the help.

I would like to thank Mike Yamarik, who has been both personally and professionally supportive throughout my career. Additionally, I would like to thank Gabor Fari for his encouragement and countless introductions to other members of the SharePoint community.

Finally, I would like to thank my wife, Shannon, who has been my partner and supporter for all of my projects. You have made these things possible for us, and I will always support you in the same way.

About this book

With the even greater presence of computers in both our personal and professional lives, we are constantly searching for better ways to accomplish our tasks. Over the past few years, many software packages have been created by developers from all over the world, all designed to make working and collaborating with others easier. One of the largest and most successful of these platforms is Microsoft SharePoint. With the release of SharePoint 2013, we have been presented with even more options and tools for getting our work done more effectively, with less effort. The primary goal of *Microsoft SharePoint 2013 Plain & Simple* is to show you how to use the platform to accomplish this and, in the process, make your life better.

In this section:

- What do you want to do today?
- Written in plain English
- Just essential tasks
- A quick overview
- Who this book is meant for
- A few assumptions
- Adapting task procedures for touchscreens
- A final word (or two)

What do you want to do today?

There are literally tens of thousands of companies and organizations and hundreds of millions of people around the world who use the SharePoint platform. But, when you look at all of the features and functions that it has to offer, you quickly realize that there's no mystery to this.

The SharePoint platform has been deployed throughout the world with enormous success. There is hardly a Fortune 500 company, government agency, or nonprofit organization that does not have a SharePoint solution deployed, experiencing tremendous results with it. We have also seen the platform employed in numerous applications throughout the world. But in the end, it boils down to what do you want to do with it today? This is a question that is still being answered by many.

As such, when this book was written, we did not want to wade into that area of the conversation. Instead, we wanted to concentrate on the most critical tasks that a business user has to accomplish. In doing so, we believe that we have created a book that you will find very helpful as you look to apply SharePoint to the challenge of tackling the day-to-day tasks that you encounter.

This is actually the second SharePoint Plain & Simple book. The first book was quite successful and fulfilled a need expressed by many SharePoint users that was unattended up to that point. This book follows the same premise that was set forth previously: it is a valuable resource that is indeed simple to use, but it also explores topics at depths required by the typical business user.

Written in plain English

When you have been assigned a new task, you want to be able to finish it as quickly as possible with as few roadblocks to overcome as possible. You certainly don't want to be bogged down with a bunch of technical jargon. You also, want to be able to find the information you need as fast as possible without having to read numerous pages that, while helpful in understanding the issue as whole, don't do a lot toward helping you accomplish your goal.

That is what this book is all about: it is written in plain English. This is a no-jargon-zone book! The authors are all very adept with using the SharePoint 2013 platform; in fact, working with computers on the technical side of things is what we do for our day jobs—you can believe us when we say we know, live, breath, and eat jargon. But, we all agreed that for this book we had to strip away the jargon and acronyms and explain the concepts in a way that was easy for anyone to pick up and understand.

This book is formatted to be easy to follow; there is not a single task that takes up more than a few pages to explain. You can look up the task in the index or table of contents, flip to the page and access the information that you are looking for in a step-by-step manner. It's really that easy. You will note that we do not bog you down with the why's and wherefore's: all you need to do to complete your task is to follow the steps.

Each section is also designed to stand on its own. Which means you will not have to flip to other sections of the book to gather all the information that you need. For example, if you want to know how to set up a basic Search Center (see page 302), the section will show you. You don't need to first flip to another section to read introductory information.

On occasion, you will be presented with "See Also" Reader Aids. These are sprinkled throughout the book to provide additional related or follow-up information. They are there to help you to gain a better understanding of the operation you are trying to do as a whole. They are by no means meant to be a blocker for you, though. As an example, if you want to set up a basic Search Center for your site, you can flip to the section and it will tell you how to do it. However, we did include a See Also that will refer you back to the section on metadata. Again, you will be able to set up the basic Search Center, but at the same time, we are trying to show you other sections that can help you to fully understand what you're doing and be of use to you in optimizing your search results.

Just essential tasks...

The SharePoint platform is very large. The number of applications and use case scenarios into which it can be adapted to fulfill is almost endless. The purpose of this book is to show you the more common tasks that you will probably need to perform.

The sections and tasks within this book are organized logically for the types of things for which you will most likely use SharePoint 2013. If this is your first time using the SharePoint platform, you can read the book from cover to cover to become familiar with it. However, if you know exactly what you want to accomplish, just locate the task and follow the steps.

...and the easiest way to do them

As was the case for SharePoint 2010, SharePoint 2013 offers the same ribbon interface as the Microsoft Office 2013 suite of products (you'll find that the ribbon is hidden by default, though). Although there are multiple ways to complete a task in SharePoint, we have given preference to using the ribbon to take advantage of the familiarity that most people have with using it and to further reinforce the consistency this brings to the entire suite of Microsoft applications. With that said, however, there will be times when we will show you ways to do things that do not include the ribbon. In those instances, we are merely trying to show you the easiest way to accomplish your task.

A quick overview

SharePoint is most commonly used in business environments, and installation and support requires a certain level of technical expertise that is beyond the scope of this book to describe. Most likely, your first exposure to SharePoint will be at your workplace where it has been set up and initially configured or supported by your company's IT department, or possibly it is hosted through the Office 365 offering or another third-party vendor. As such, this book does not begin with details of installing or configuring a SharePoint farm. Instead, the materials focus on getting you up to speed by using the features that SharePoint provides to you when it comes to managing information and collaborating with colleagues.

Section 2 covers what's new in SharePoint 2013. This section informs those of you with a pretty good understanding of previous versions of SharePoint about the new and exciting capabilities offered by SharePoint 2013 as well as improvements to existing features.

Section 3 introduces SharePoint sites and quickly ramps you up to speed with using the capabilities of SharePoint 2013. In this section, you will learn how to create and configure a basic SharePoint site and how to customize site themes and navigation menus. You also learn how to save your customizations as a template that you and your coworkers can use to create additional sites.

Section 4 explains how you can enhance the ways that you store and organize content by using content types to differentiate categories of files, site columns to provide additional information on each file, and document templates and workflows to support document automation.

Sections 5 and 6 cover the fundamental use cases for engaging SharePoint 2013 to manage information. You use SharePoint lists and libraries to store and collaborate on documents and other types of information such as calendars and tasks. In Section 5 you learn how to use the ribbon to access the content management of features of SharePoint along with how to customize the views. Section 6 provides even more information about working with documents and records.

Section 7 goes over the more specialized features that SharePoint 2013 offers for working with media files, such as video, audio, and images. This includes how to upload video and audio and optimize the metadata associated with them.

Section 8 covers the change from Workspaces to SkyDrive Pro. You learn what SkyDrive Pro is as well as how to use this powerful feature to manage your documents and share those files with others, whether they're within or outside of your organization.

Section 10 focuses on how to organize people and processes to support project tasks, issues, and discussion lists. You learn how to track dependencies between tasks, including using the Gantt Chart features of SharePoint 2013 along with synchronizing SharePoint 2013 with Microsoft Project 2013.

Section 11 explores one of the basic building blocks of Share-Point: Web Parts. In this section you learn how to use Web Parts to display images, document contents, or even another web-page on a SharePoint page. By using Web Parts, you can create dynamic data-driven webpages. This section shows you how to do just that.

Section 9 is useful if you have corporate policies or industry regulatory guidelines to which you must adhere, this section will cover using Information Management Policy features such as retention and auditing.

Throughout the book, we discuss how to use different Office 2013 applications with SharePoint 2013. In Section 12, however, we tie applications together to realize even greater functional-ity when they are used in conjunction with each other. We cover using SharePoint 2013 with Microsoft Outlook 2013 as well as how to connect your Office 2013 applications to SharePoint so that you are able to work in either application and pull (or push) data between SharePoint 2013 and Office 2013.

Section 13 shows you how to create and publish content by using the Blog site features in SharePoint. Blogs (weB Logs) have become a popular and common-place way to publish business or personal short articles, called posts. This section shows you how to get started with your own blog and how to organize and manage the posts and comments.

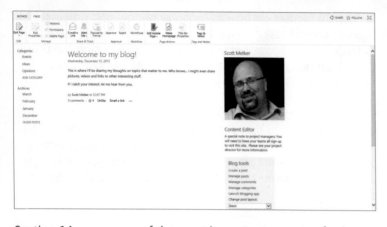

Section 14 covers one of the most important aspects of using SharePoint: security. In this section, we explain how to securely share information, whether it's from broad, high-level access points such as sites and pages, or at a granular level such as lists and libraries or even individual documents.

Section 15 expands on the capabilities you were first introduced to in Section 13, with additional guidance on how to use some of the more advanced social networking features found in SharePoint Server 2013 and SharePoint Online. You learn how to use your My Site to configure a personal profile, upload content, and find people who might be able to assist you with your daily tasks or projects. You also learn to tag content and follow items within your SharePoint environment which might be of interest to you.

Even the most well-organized SharePoint implementation can become difficult to navigate and find information after it begins to grow. Section 16 introduces metadata, folder navigation, and site navigation tools that you can use to help organize information in a more practical way.

Section 17 covers using the new Community Portal and Sites features that became available with SharePoint 2013. This section goes over this feature specifically, with a focus on the administration and use of Community Sites.

Section 18 shows you how to work with and use workflows. We explain what workflows are and how you can use them to automate daily tasks within the SharePoint platform. We also introduce you to another component within the SharePoint family, SharePoint Designer 2013. You learn how easy it is to use this powerful application to automate some of your manual business processes.

Finally, throughout this book, we have presented ways of producing, sharing, and organizing information by using SharePoint 2013. In Section 19, we focus on ways that this information can be discovered, archived, and preserved.

Who this book is meant for

The SharePoint platform has long been known for innovative features and functionality. The SharePoint 2013 platform does not disappoint and carries with it the rich pedigree of its previous iterations. There are literally thousands of operations that can be performed. We must also keep in mind that with the platform being so versatile, it offers numerous areas that can be explored. As such, when it came to writing this book we had to confine our viewpoint to that of the business user.

For the purposes of this book, a business user is defined as someone who is knowledgeable on how to use a computer and the Internet. She is someone whose main job might not be centered on a computer, but her daily tasks do include using a computer. A business user could be an executive, manager, administrative person, operations person, or someone who is a kiosk computer user.

We further limited our discussion to someone who is using the SharePoint 2013 platform to share and collaborate with others. As such, this book does not go into details as to why you would use a certain feature of the platform. The SharePoint platform is vast, so to try to handle all of that in a Plain & Simple series book would be overwhelming. Besides there are a number of other books and online resources to which you can refer to get to a deeper level of understanding of the platform. Again, we wanted to have a book that was usable by as many people as possible.

Therefore, this book is centered on the tasks that can be accomplished by using either the SharePoint Foundation 2013 or Office 365 versions of the platform. There is a SharePoint Server 2013 version, as well. However, it is the SharePoint Foundation 2013 version which is the basis for the Server edition. This means that this book covers the basic functions that you can do with SharePoint. And, if you are using the Server edition of the platform, you will have even more features available to you.

A few assumptions

To write this book, we had to first think about you, our reader. Who are you, what do you already know and more importantly what do you need to know? SharePoint has always been, first and foremost, a web application that was designed for business users to collaborate with others and manage files. You might have been approached to use SharePoint while working on a company project or for sharing documents with colleagues, vendors, or clients. Or, maybe you are a small business owner who is looking to use SharePoint Online to assist your employees with storing and sharing information.

In writing this book, we assumed that you are using a laptop or desktop computer with access to your organization's network or have remote access to a SharePoint implementation over the Internet. We assume that you have a degree of computer literacy and have a basic understanding of how to use your computer, such as turning it on, and starting programs. We also assumed that you are comfortable with using the standard menus and commands of a web browser to open, view, and interact with web applications.

In addition, SharePoint is part of an integrated suite of technologies from Microsoft referred to as the Office System, which includes the Microsoft Office desktop productivity tools (such as Word, Excel, PowerPoint, Outlook and Project, depending on the edition). Although having Microsoft Office 2013 installed—and having some knowledge of how to use the applications—is not necessary to gain benefits from this book, a number of tasks and the entirety of Section 12 make reference to using the integrated features of SharePoint 2013 and Office 2013.

Adapting task procedures for touchscreens

In this book, we provide instructions based on traditional keyboard and mouse input methods. If you're using SharePoint on a touch-enabled device, you might be giving commands by tapping with your finger or with a stylus. If so, substitute a tapping action any time we instruct you to click a user interface element. Also note that when we tell you to enter information in SharePoint, you can do so by typing on a keyboard, tapping in the entry field under discussion to display and use the onscreen keyboard, or even speaking aloud, depending on your computer setup and your personal preferences.

A final word (or two)

Michelle, Scott, and Johnathan (the authors of this book) are all computer professionals whose life-work has focused around making applications and solutions to make the lives of business professionals easier. We believe that computers are in place to assist us and make our lives simpler. This book is nothing more than an extension of this belief system. As such, it has been written to make your learning painless, with easy to-follow steps

and plenty of visual information to help you pick up concepts quickly. Our goals are to give you what you need, make it easy to find and understand, and help you have fun learning to work with SharePoint 2013. The best way to learn is by *doing*, and that is how we hope that you'll use this book.

We have covered over one hundred different tasks within this book. We sincerely hope that you will find the SharePoint 2013 platform enjoyable to use and will want to learn even more. This book only scratches the surface of the possibilities that this great platform can offer. We encourage you to take advantage of additional resources such as SharePoint User Groups, Internet sites, SharePoint Saturday events and other SharePoint books to increase your knowledge of this platform. In doing so, we know that you will find even more creative solutions to the challenges that you face in your organization.

And remember, as the saying goes, "SharePoint—where Sharing *is* the Point."

What's new and improved in SharePoint 2013

With the release of SharePoint 2013, Microsoft has continued the tradition of increasing the functionality of the SharePoint platform by incorporating even more of the features.

This section is where you get your first look at SharePoint 2013 and can see some of the changes that have been implemented. Because the number of changes and upgrades are just too plentiful to go into in any depth within the scope of this book, we will focus on the features that affect the end-user experience.

This section describes the changes and what they mean to you in terms of getting your work done more efficiently. In later sections we delve more deeply into some of the enhancements, showing you how to best utilize these changes to make your life easier.

In this section:

- Creating a new site
- Customizing the interface
- Using the Office Store
- Creating an asset library
- Adding a thumbnail to a video thumbnail
- Using SkyDrive Pro
- Using the timeline feature for tasks
- Mentioning a colleague feature
- Previewing search documents
- Using the Community Site template
- Creating badges
- Using Visual Designer for workflows within SharePoint Designer
- Creating an eDiscovery Center

Creating a new site

Site administrators have a lot of latitude for how they can create a site. With the release of SharePoint 2013, there are yet more options available. Also, the steps involved for creating a new site have been simplified.

Create a new site

1 On the Home page of your site, click the Settings button (the small gear icon next to the name of the logged-on user). On the menu that appears, click Site Contents.

2 On the Site Contents page, in the Subsites section, select the New Subsite link.

(continued on next page)

Shared with...

Edit page

Add a page

Add an app

Site contents ————— 1

Subsites

⊕ new subsite ——————— 2

> **TIP** If you are trying to create a site from a previously saved template, you must select the Custom tab during template selection to see this template.

Create a new site *(continued)*

3 On the New SharePoint Site page, enter a title and description for the site.

4 Enter a URL for the site, relative to the root site.

5 Choose a language for your site.

6 On the Collaboration tab, choose the Team Site template.

7 Choose user permissions for the site.

8 Select navigation options for the site.

9 Click Create.

Site Contents › New SharePoint Site

Title and Description

Title:
Experimental Team Site

Description:
This is a test team site.

— 3

Web Site Address

URL name:
https://techforceconsulting.sharepoint.com/SEMTeamSite/ testsite

— 4

Template Selection

Select a language:
English

— 5

Select a template:

Collaboration   Enterprise   Publishing   Duet Enterprise

Team Site
Blog
Project Site
Community Site

— 6

A place to work together with a group of people.

Permissions

You can give permission to access your new site to the same users who have access to this parent site, or you can give permission to a unique set of users.

Note: If you select **Use same permissions as parent site**, one set of user permissions is shared by both sites. Consequently, you cannot change user permissions on your new site unless you are an administrator of this parent site.

User Permissions:
◉ Use same permissions as parent site
◯ Use unique permissions

— 7

Navigation Inheritance

Use the top link bar from the parent site?
◯ Yes   ◉ No

— 8

Create   Cancel

— 9

Customizing the interface

The chances are good that when you start to use your Share-Point site, you will want to customize a few things to meet the needs of your team. SharePoint 2013 supports a number of out-of-the-box formatting options (as well as supporting

personalization for each option). Using these options, you can set up your site to match your corporate or departmental colors, change layouts, or simply change fonts and logos to your preference.

Customize the look and feel of your site

1 On the Home page of your site, click the Settings button (the small gear icon next to the name of the logged-on user). On the menu that appears, click Site Settings.

2 On the Site Settings page, in the Look And Feel section, click the Change The Look link.

3 On the Change The Look page, click one of the displayed templates.

(continued on next page)

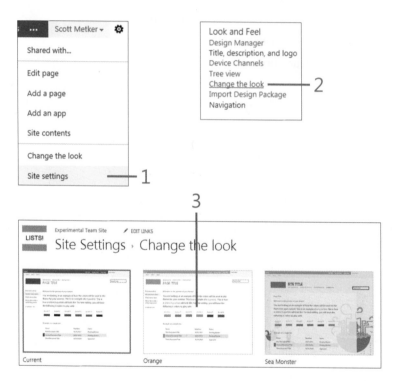

Customize the look and feel of your
site *(continued)*

4 On the Change The Look page for the template you have selected, choose a different color scheme for the template, if you want.

5 Select a non-default site layout for the template, if you want.

6 Select a non-default font for the template, if you want.

7 Click Try It Out.

8 Click Yes, Keep It to save your changes.

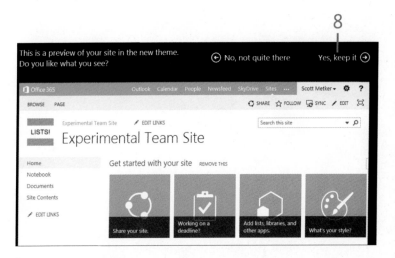

Using the Office Store

Microsoft has incorporated a new application development model in SharePoint 2013 called the *SharePoint app*. Certainly, we've all become familiar with the phrase, "There's an app for that." Well, now SharePoint can say the same. These self-contained web applications can come out of the box or be downloaded from Microsoft's Office Store. Apps provide users with a way to take advantage of existing applications that others have already built rather than building them from scratch. Lists and libraries are apps as well as other useful mini programs.

Perhaps you want to highlight a "Tip of the Day" section on your SharePoint site or implement a Timesheet in which employees can enter their project hours. You can download these apps from the Office Store for free instead of hiring a developer to design and implement it!

Add an app on SharePoint

1 In the upper-right corner of the window, click the Settings button (the small gear icon next to the name of the logged-on user).

2 On the menu that appears, click Add An App.

(continued on next page)

Add an app on SharePoint *(continued)*

3 On the Your Apps page, click the app that you want to add to your site.

4 In the Adding Tasks dialog box, enter a name for the new app.

5 Click Create.

Creating an asset library

An asset library is a SharePoint 2013 app that has been optimized for the storage of digital assets. These assets can include audio, images, and video. The default view for this library presents the assets as thumbnails.

One of the optimizations implemented out of the box is the library's ability to recognize extended metadata information contained with the media, such as author, date taken, people present in the image, resolution of the camera, and comments. The library also has the ability to generate and display a thumbnail image.

Create an asset library

1 On the Quick Launch bar, click the Site Contents link.

2 On the Site Contents page, in the List, libraries And Other Apps section, click the Add An App icon.

(continued on next page)

Create an asset library *(continued)*

3 On the Your Apps page, scroll to the Apps You Can Add section.

4 Select the Assets Library icon.

5 In the Adding Asset Library dialog box, enter a name for the library.

6 Click the Create button.

TRY THIS Create an asset library by using the Asset Library app.

Adding a thumbnail to a video

The asset library has several new features when it comes to working with video files. In the past, you only had the ability to upload a file with an out-of-the-box configuration of SharePoint. Within SharePoint 2013, however, you can also select a frame, an image from your computer, or a web address to use as a thumbnail image for the video. You can also associate related content to a video file. This could be a separate document located in a different library such as a workbook.

Add a thumbnail to a video

1 In the asset library, select the video file with which you want to work.

2 On the ribbon, click the Manage tab.

3 In the Actions group, click the Edit Properties button.

4 In the Edit Properties dialog box, click the Change Thumbnail link.

5 From the three options that appears, click the Capture Thumbnail From Video option.

(continued on next page)

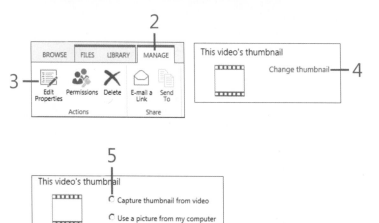

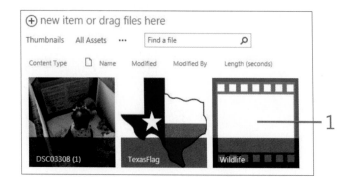

Add a thumbnail to a video *(continued)*

6 In the Video window that opens, click the Play button.

7 Click the Camera icon to capture the image.

8 Click the Save button.

Using SkyDrive Pro

In previous versions of the SharePoint platform there was a feature called Workspaces (or if you are familiar with using the MOSS 2007 version of the platform, it was referred to as Groove). For the SharePoint 2013 platform, Workspaces has been replaced with SkyDrive Pro. Workspaces (or Groove) was a feature that a team could use to share documents on which they were collaborating.

Access SkyDrive Pro

1   On the toolbar at the top of SharePoint site Home page, click the SkyDrive link.

Using the timeline feature for tasks

The graphic timeline view makes it possible for you to see your task dates at a glance.

Use the Timeline view

1 On the ribbon of your Task List page, click the Tasks tab.

2 Select the check box to the left of a task. (Hover over the title to see the check mark option.)

3 On the ribbon, click the Tasks tab and then, in the Actions group, click Add To Timeline.

Mentioning a colleague feature

Many times, when updating the status on your Newsfeed or replying to a Blog Post, you'll reference a colleague's name. Mentioning someone in SharePoint 2013 draws attention to others and alerts those people that you've mentioned them. Newsfeeds will also be updated across the community that someone they're following has been mentioned.

Similarly, when people in your organization mention you in a post, you might want to know that it occurred. If your Newsfeed settings include the option to automatically receive an email when anyone mentions you in a post, you'll be notified in your Inbox. You can also view a history of all posts in which you've been mentioned.

Select a colleague's name

1 On your About Me page, click Newsfeed.

2 In the Start A Conversation box, enter text.

3 Type the "at" symbol (@) and then continue typing to see a list of available colleague names.

4 In the list that appears, click the desired colleague's name.

5 Click Post.

Who has mentioned me?

1 On your About Me page, click Newsfeed.

2 On the Newsfeed page, click Mentions.

Expanding My Tasks settings

After the tasks assigned to you are in one centralized location on your My Tasks page, you can adjust the view options to suit your needs. You might want to view only tasks that have been edited in the last year, or revise the Tasks default timeline range. You can also choose which projects or task lists to include on your page, and synchronize your Tasks with Microsoft Outlook.

Adjust the My Tasks page view

1 On your About Me page, click Tasks.

2 On the ribbon, click the Tasks tab and then, in the Settings group, click Settings.

(continued on next page)

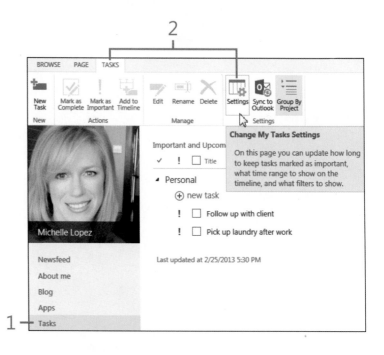

Adjust the My Tasks page view *(continued)*

3 On the My Tasks settings page, update any of the following options: Old Tasks Limit, Upcoming Tasks, Important Tasks, Recently Added Tasks, Default Timeline Range, Automatically Hide Empty Filters, Projects.

4 Click the Save button.

My Tasks

Search everything

Save   Cancel

Old Tasks Limit
☑ Only show the tasks that have been changed within the following number of months:
24

Upcoming Tasks
☑ Only show tasks that were due within this number of days ago:
14
☑ Only show tasks that are due up to this number of days in the future:
14

Important Tasks
☑ Automatically clear importance from a task if it's been marked as important for more than the following number of days:
14

Recently Added Tasks
Number of days a task will stay in the "Recently Added" view:
1

Default Timeline Range
☑ Set a date range for the timeline. To show all tasks, leave the date fields empty.
Start date (number of days before today's date):
7
End date (number of days after today's date):
21

Automatically Hide Empty Filters
☑ Hide a filter which doesn't contain any task for more than the following number of months:
3

Projects
You don't have any tasks from projects right now. When you do, check here to rearrange projects and set default colors for them in the timeline.

Previewing search documents

SharePoint 2013 offers a number of preview options within the search results view. For example, users can quickly preview Microsoft Office documents via the Office Web Apps integration. The same is true for video results.

These features are particularly useful when you are trying to scroll through a number of potentially relevant search results.

Integrated preview makes it possible for you to quickly glance at a document or video and determine if you need to investigate further without opening or downloading the full version of the document.

Preview search documents

1 In the upper-right corner of the window, in the Search box, type a search term and then press Enter to start a search.

2 Hover the mouse over a search result that shows a Microsoft Office document.

3 Navigate within the document by using the preview navigation tools.

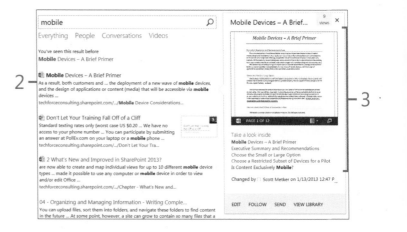

Using the Community Site template

This feature is available to Office 365 and SharePoint Server 2013 editions. It has been included due to its expected popularity and usage. If you are not using Office 365 or SharePoint Server 2013 this section does not apply. If you have a collection of similar Community Sites that are managed by the same group of people, or if you don't have administrative access to create site collections, you can also create a discussion site as a subsite.

Create a discussion site as a subsite

1   On the root site that will contain your community subsite, click the Settings button (the small gear icon next to the name of the logged-on user). On the menu that appears, click Site Contents.

2   On the Site Contents page, in the Subsites section, select the New Subsite link.

(continued on next page)

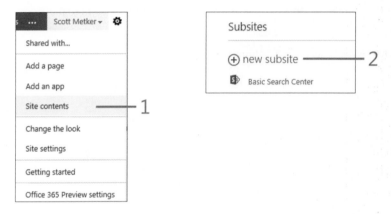

Create a discussion site as a subsite *(continued)*

3 On the New SharePoint Site page, type a title and description for the site.

4 Enter a URL for the site, relative to the root site.

5 Choose a language for your site.

6 On the Collaboration tab, choose the Community Site template.

7 Choose user permissions for the site.

8 Select navigation options for the site.

9 Click Create.

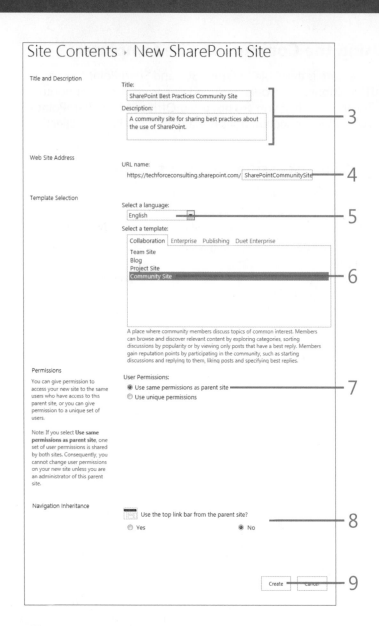

Creating badges

Badges are another new feature with SharePoint 2013. You can create new badges representing special achievements on your site that you or your moderators can award. Badges are a form of *gamification*, which refers to using game-style mechanics and awards in a non–game-playing scenario.

One such example is Microsoft's own SharePoint MVP certification, which is granted to SharePoint pioneers within the Internet community, based upon the breadth and depth of their SharePoint support and evangelism.

Creating a badge

1 On the Home page of your site, in the Community Tools section, click the Create Badges link.

2 On the Badges page, click the New Item link.

3 On the New Badge page, enter a title for your badge.

4 Click the Save button.

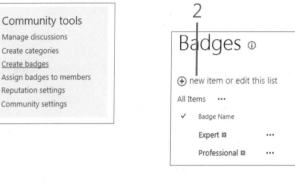

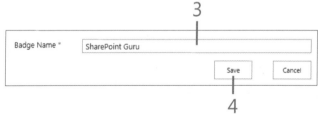

Creating an eDiscovery Center

SharePoint 2013 introduces a new type of site: the eDiscovery Center. An eDiscovery Center is a single site that you can use to organize your discovery and legal-hold activities. You must have at least one eDiscovery Center created to work with legal holds and discovery queries. You can track one or many cases, which represent individual legal or regulatory actions.

The eDiscovery Site template is available to Office 365 and SharePoint Server 2013 editions. It has been included due to its expected popularity and usage. If you are not using Office 365 or SharePoint Server 2013 this section does not apply. In this task, we will walk through the process of using the eDiscovery Site template to create an initial eDiscovery Center in SharePoint 2013.

Create an eDiscovery Center

1 From the Admin Center for your Office 365 instance, at the right end of the toolbar, click the Admin menu.

2 On the menu that appears, click SharePoint.

3 In the SharePoint Admin Center, on the ribbon, click the Site Collection tab, and then click New.

4 On the menu that appears, click Private Site Collection.

(continued on next page)

Create an eDiscovery Center *(continued)*

5 On the New Site Collection page, enter a title for the eDiscovery Center, a URL that will be used to access the site under your main URL, and a language for the new site.

6 Click the Enterprise tab.

7 Select eDiscovery Center.

8 Specify the appropriate Time Zone.

9 Choose the site administrator who will have administrator rights to the site.

10 Select your storage quota and server resource options.

11 Click OK.

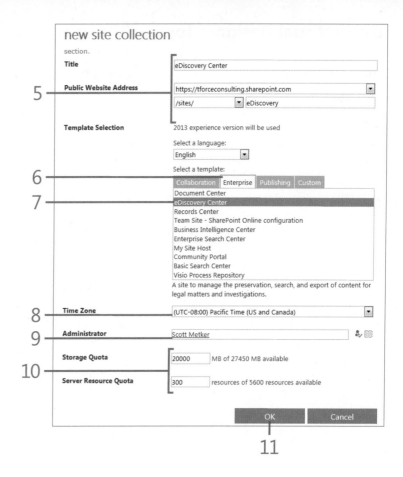

Using Visual Designer for workflows within SharePoint Designer

SharePoint 2013 offers a way of editing workflows by using a flow-chart look and feel based upon integration with Microsoft Visio 2013. You can create complex workflows that you can display and edit using simple visual designers.

Edit a workflow

1 From an open workflow in SharePoint Designer 2013, on the ribbon, click the lower portion of the Views button in the Workflow group.

2 On the menu that opens, select the Visual Designer option.

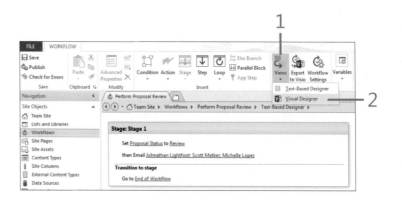

Getting started with SharePoint sites

Microsoft SharePoint 2013 is a web-based platform that supports a number of collaboration-related activities for teams. It includes document management, blogging, project planning, and auditing and security components. In fact, it can be quite difficult to get a sense of all of the features of the application.

A good way to get started with SharePoint is to start working with one of the out-of-the-box SharePoint sites. A SharePoint site is a single website that can be used to organize information that has a common purpose. For example, it might be a team site on which you store documents that your team uses, or it might be a collaboration site where your group stores discussions, questions, and answers.

An immediate benefit to using SharePoint sites is that all of your departmental information is in a single place. You can collaborate, store documents, search for content, and plan projects all from the same site. Gone are the days of having to search through email for file attachments, accessing many different file shares for documents, or trying to guess where the most current version of a document resides.

In this section:

- Understanding sites
- Creating a SharePoint site from a template
- Locating content on a site
- Changing your site's title, description, and logo
- Changing the look and feel of a site
- Changing the navigation tree view settings
- Editing the Quick Launch bar on a nonpublishing site
- Editing the Top Link bar on a nonpublishing site
- Editing publishing site navigation
- Saving a site as a template

Understanding sites

Usually, a SharePoint administrator performs the installation, configuration, and deployment of SharePoint 2013 throughout your organization. Part of this process is establishing something called the *top-level site* (also referred to as a *site collection*). It is through the site collection that subsites (or sites) are created. It is beyond the scope of this book to go into detail about the various SharePoint implementation scenarios; however, remember that once the top-level site is created, subsites can then be created.

Each site has a site administrator (or two) assigned to it. The site administrator's duties can include granting access to the site, creating lists and libraries, and creating additional sites, to name a few. One of the great things about SharePoint is that it gives you the ability to assign various responsibilities to assorted people within your team. After a site administrator has the web address for a site, she can customize the site and apply security settings that permit or deny people access to it.

Access a SharePoint site

1   In your browser, type the web address for the SharePoint site that you want to access and then press Enter.

1

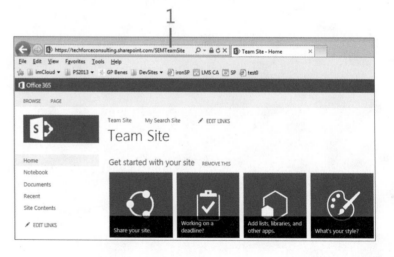

TRY THIS   If you have a SharePoint site that you can access, type the site's web address into your browser bar.

SharePoint 2013 templates

The templates listed in the tables that follow are supplied as part of an out-of-the-box SharePoint installation. You might have additional templates available in your environment if your administrators have installed third-party applications, performed their own development on the site, or simply saved customized templates for common configuration. You might have fewer templates available than are presented here due to your particular licensing of the SharePoint software. Also, some templates might only be used for creating new site collections, which can only be created by certain administrative personnel. If you do not have administrative access, you can ask your IT staff to create a new site collection for those templates which may not be used as subsites.

Template name	Description
Collaboration templates	
Team Site	A site designed for team or work-group interactions, including tracking of documents and a basic newsfeed.
Blog	A site intended for an individual or group to publish blog posts around a particular area.
Developer Site (site collection use only)	A site for developers to work with Office products.

Template name	Description
Project Site	A site intended for managing and collaborating on projects, including tracking status of issues and artifacts related to project deliverables.
Community Site	A site on which members can contribute to discussions based on common interests. This template supports discussions and threaded replies as well as tracking of badges and reputation for site members.
Enterprise templates	
Document Center	A site for managing documents within a corporate enterprise.
eDiscovery Center (site-collection use only)	A template for an eDiscovery Center, where many eDiscovery cases can be created by which designated staff can query for documents subject to legal discovery, initiate legal holds, and create export packages for transmission of discovery-related materials to designated legal personnel.

Template name	Description
Records Center	A template designed for management of regulated documents and for managing routing of files that are changed or deleted that are subject to records retention rules.
Team Site – SharePoint Online configuration	A team site tailored for extension by organization members that supports adding sites and extending the site to external members.
Business Intelligence Center	A site designed for presenting business intelligence reporting capabilities to end users.
Enterprise Search Center (recommended by Microsoft for site-collection use only)	An advanced search center that supports customization of page content and search extensions for page content above and beyond the supplied basic search, people search, conversation search, and video search results pages.
My Site Host (site-collection use only)	A specialized site used for hosting personal profile pages. This site is generally provisioned only by administrative or IT staff.

Template name	Description
Community Portal (site-collection use only)	A site for publicizing and discovering communities.
Basic Search Center (recommended by Microsoft for site-collection use only)	A simplified search center featuring a welcome page, search page, search results page, and advanced search page.
Visio Process Repository	A site used to store and view Visio diagrams.
Publishing templates	
Publishing Portal (site collection use only)	Use this template to create large Internet sites or large intranet portals within companies. Includes access to publishing pages and approval workflows for site content, where authors can submit page changes to approvers prior to releasing on the site.
Enterprise Wiki	Use this for creating wiki sites with easy-to-edit page formats that support authoring by multiple authors. Supports discussions and project management needs.

Template name	Description
Product Catalog (site collection use only)	Used for managing product catalog data
Publishing Site	Used for publishing webpages. The site includes document and image libraries for storing web publishing assets.
Publishing Site with workflow	Used for publishing webpages on a schedule. Only sites with this template can be created under this site.

Creating a SharePoint site from a template

SharePoint 2013 site administrators have a lot of latitude with regard to how they can create a site. They can choose to create a blank site and add different components to it, or they can employ a site template to assist them in creating some of the more common elements of the site. If you have used a template in Microsoft Word, Microsoft Excel, or any other Office program, the concept is the same in SharePoint.

A template is a starting point that you can use to quickly produce a site that has the basics of what your team needs. This saves you time, but it also ensures a certain level of consistency among SharePoint sites throughout your organization. SharePoint 2013 comes with numerous site templates that are ready to be used out of the box.

Create a SharePoint team site

1 On the Home page of your site, click the Settings button (the small gear icon next to the name of the logged-on user). On the menu that appears, click Site Contents.

2 On the Site Contents page, In the Subsites section select the New Subsite link.

(continued on next page)

Create a SharePoint team site (continued)

3 On the New SharePoint Site page, type a title and description for the case.

4 Type a URL for the site, relative to the root site.

5 Choose a language for your site.

6 Choose the Team Site template (located on the Collaboration tab).

7 Choose user permissions for the site.

8 Select navigation options for the site.

9 Click Create.

TIP If you are trying to create a site from a previously saved template, you must select the Custom tab during template selection to see this template.

Site Contents › New SharePoint Site

Title and Description

Title:
Experimental Team Site

Description:
This is a test team site.

— 3

Web Site Address

URL name:
https://techforceconsulting.sharepoint.com/SEMTeamSite/ testsite

— 4

Template Selection

Select a language:
English

— 5

Select a template:

Collaboration | Enterprise Publishing Duet Enterprise

Team Site
Blog
Project Site
Community Site

— 6

A place to work together with a group of people.

Permissions

You can give permission to access your new site to the same users who have access to this parent site, or you can give permission to a unique set of users.

Note: If you select **Use same permissions as parent site**, one set of user permissions is shared by both sites. Consequently, you cannot change user permissions on your new site unless you are an administrator of this parent site.

User Permissions:
● Use same permissions as parent site
○ Use unique permissions

— 7

Navigation Inheritance

Use the top link bar from the parent site?
○ Yes   ● No

— 8

Create   Cancel

— 9

Anatomy of a team site

The Team Site template offers a good sampling of the capabilities in SharePoint 2013. As such, this template is one that you will most likely see deployed in several locations of your organization. The Team Site template includes a newsfeed, document library, and site asset library, already configured and ready for use. With these sites configured, you and your team can quickly set up and begin collaborating on your projects. After you have a team site set up, it's good to go over where everything is located. The following list gives you a brief tour:

- The Top Link bar shows the global navigation that can be inherited from parent sites and makes it possible for you to immediately jump to those other sites.

- The Ribbon bar lets you click and expand the displayed items into a full ribbon bar with additional buttons and functions. In some cases, the ribbon bar is automatically expanded when you click on certain assets in SharePoint.

- The site logo displays a graphic logo that represents your site. Clicking this logo anywhere on the site takes you to the Home page of the site.

- The site title is the title of the site. It can be changed by the site collection owner.

- The Getting Started Web Part shows a tiled menu for rapidly accessing certain maintenance functions on the site. It is intended to assist new users in accessing important site functionality.

- With the Search box, users can enter queries and link to a search site associated with the current site. Searches can be scoped to the current site or the entire SharePoint farm.

- The Share link makes it possible for users to share the site with other users by sending an email and adding selected users to appropriate site permission groups.

- With the Follow link, users can configure the site so that it appears in their My Sites as one that they want follow.

- Using the Sync link, users can synchronize the site content locally to their hard disk (for offline access).

- User can click the Focus link to dismiss the title and navigation elements on the current page to "focus" on the page content.

- The Documents App Part makes it possible for users to view the contents of the documents library that is automatically provisioned when the site is created. Users can also upload new documents to the library directly from the Home page.

- The Newsfeed Web Part makes it possible for users to view recent postings by other users on the Home page as well as allow the current user to submit snippets of plain-text content.

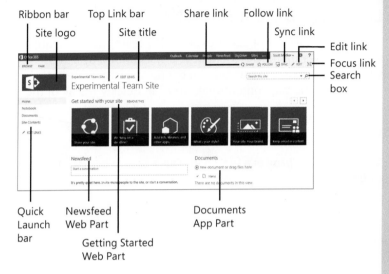

Ribbon bar   Top Link bar   Share link   Follow link

Site logo   Site title   Sync link

Edit link

Focus link

Search box

Quick Launch bar

Newsfeed Web Part

Getting Started Web Part

Documents App Part

Locating content on a site

If you are the owner of a SharePoint 2013 team site, there are two primary areas of the site that you will commonly access while maintaining the site: the site contents and the site settings. Using the site contents link, you can quickly see all of the libraries, applications, and lists on the site as well as any subsites located under the current site. You can also use the site settings link to access the administrative menus with which you configure and maintain the site.

View site contents

1 On the Home page of a site, on the Quick Launch bar, click the Site Contents link.

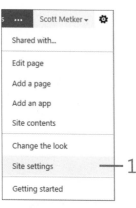

View site settings

1 On the Home page of your site, click the Settings button (the small gear icon next to the name of the logged-on user). On the menu that appears, click Site Settings.

Changing your site's title, description, and logo

One of the simplest formatting changes that you can make to your SharePoint 2013 site is to change its title, description, or logo. There is a separate link on the Site Settings page specifically designed for this change. Both the title and description fields are featured in pages throughout the site, and they can appear within search results, as well.

Change a site title, description, and logo

1 On the Home page of your site, click the Settings button (the small gear icon next to the name of the logged-on user). On the menu that appears, click Site Settings.

2 On the Site Settings page, in the Look And Feel section, click the Title, Description, And Logo link.

(continued on next page)

```
       ...     Scott Metker ▾    ⚙

   Shared with...

   Edit page

   Add a page

   Add an app

   Site contents

   Change the look

   Site settings ──────── 1
```

```
Site Settings

Users and Permissions            Look and Feel
People and groups                Design Manager
Site permissions                 Title, description, and logo ── 2
Site app permissions             Device Channels
                                 Tree view
                                 Change the look
Web Designer Galleries           Import Design Package
Site columns                     Navigation
Site content types
Master pages
Composed looks
```

Change a site title, description, and logo *(continued)*

3 On the Title, Description, And Logo page, verify or change the title entry, as desired.

4 Verify or change the description of your site.

5 In the Logo And Description section, click the From Computer link.

6 In the Add A Document dialog box, click the browse button and locate the file on your computer to upload as the new logo.

7 Click OK to dismiss the dialog box.

8 Click OK to save your title, description, and logo changes.

Site Settings › Title, Description, and Logo

Title and Description
Type a title and description for your site.

Title:
Experimental Team Site —————— 3

Description:
This is a test team site. —————— 4

Logo and Description
Associate a logo with this site. Add an optional description for the image. Note: If the file location has a local relative address, for example, /_layouts/images/logo.gif, you must copy the graphics file to that location on each front-end Web server.

Insert Logo:
FROM COMPUTER | FROM SHAREPOINT —————— 5

Enter a description (used as alternative text for the picture):

Web Site Address
Users can navigate to your site by typing the Web site address (URL) into their browser. You can enter the last part of the address. You should keep it short and easy to remember.

For example,
https://techforceconsulting.sharepoint.com/SEMTeam.../sitename

URL name:
https://techforceconsulting.sharepoint.com/SEMTeam.../ testsite

OK   Cancel —————— 8

Add a document   ×

Choose a file   C:\Users\smetker2\Pictures\Category Images\Lists.jpg Browse... —————— 6
                       ☑ Overwrite existing files

Destination Folder   /   Choose Folder...

                                            OK   Cancel —————— 7

Changing the look and feel of a site

The chances are good that when you start to use your SharePoint site, you will want to customize a few things to meet the specific needs of your team. Fortunately, SharePoint 2013 supports a number of out-of-the-box formatting options (as well as supporting personalization to each option). Using these options, you can tailor your site match your corporate or departmental colors, change layouts, or simply change fonts and logos.

Change the look and feel of your site

1 On the Home page of your site, click the Settings button (the small gear icon next to the name of the logged-on user). On the menu that appears, click Site Settings.

2 On the Site Settings page, in the Look And Feel section, click the Change The Look link.

3 On the Change The Look page, click one of the displayed templates.

(continued on next page)

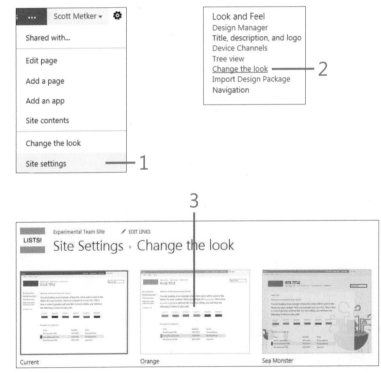

Change the look and feel of your site (continued)

4 On the Change The Look page for the template you selected, choose a different color scheme.

5 Select a non-default site layout for the template, if you want.

6 Select a non-default font for the template, if you want.

7 Click Try It Out.

8 Click Yes, Keep It to save your changes.

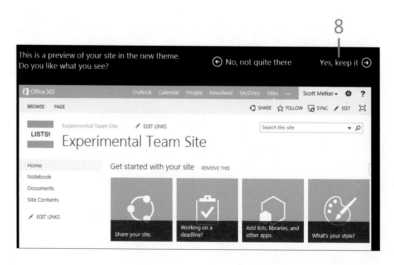

Changing the navigation tree view settings

Depending on the purpose of your SharePoint 2013 site, you might want to modify the default navigation. Normally, SharePoint sites provide a Quick Launch bar for internal navigation and a Top Link bar that inherits from the parent site of the current site (if present). The following options describe how to customize the navigation settings within your site.

Change tree view settings

1 On the Home page of your site, click the Settings button (the small gear icon next to the name of the logged-on user). On the menu that appears, click Site Settings.

2 On the Site Settings page, in the Look And Feel section, click the Tree View link.

3 On the Tree View page, select the Enable Quick Launch check box to show the Quick Launch bar at the left side of your site.

4 Select the Enable Tree View check box to show a hierarchical, content-based view of your site immediately under the Quick Launch bar.

5 Click OK to save your results.

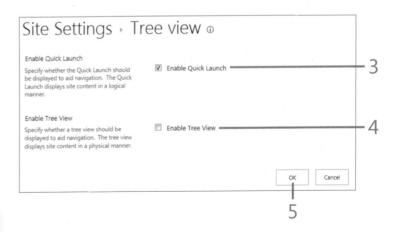

TRY THIS Select and clear the Enable Quick Launch and Enable Tree View check boxes on your site settings and observe the effects on the Home page of your site.

Editing the Quick Launch bar on a nonpublishing site

On nonpublishing sites (sites for which your technical staff have not activated the SharePoint Server Publishing Infrastructure feature), on the Site Settings page, you can edit the Quick Launch bar and Top Link bar separately.

Edit Quick Launch bar on a nonpublishing site

1 On the Home page of your site, click the Settings button (the small gear icon next to the name of the logged-on user). On the menu that appears, click Site Settings.

2 On the Site Settings page, in the Look And Feel section, click the Quick Launch link.

3 On the Quick Launch settings page, you can create another header section (under which additional links can be placed) by clicking the New Heading link. Alternatively, you can proceed to step 6 to create a link under an existing header.

4 On the New Heading page, type the URL and a descriptive label (which will display on the Quick Launch bar) for the heading.

When users click the heading, they are taken to the URL that you entered.

5 Click OK to save your new heading and return to the Quick Launch settings page.

6 On the Quick Launch settings page, you can create a new Navigation Link under an existing heading by clicking New Navigation Link.

(continued on next page)

Edit Quick Launch bar on a nonpublishing site *(continued)*

7 On the New Navigation Link page, enter the URL and a descriptive label (which will be displayed on the Quick Launch bar) for the link.

When users click the link, they are taken to the URL that you entered.

8 Select the existing heading under which this link will be placed.

9 Click OK to save your new heading.

Quick Launch ⋅ New Navigation Link

URL

Type the Web address:

ts/eDiscovery/Style Library

Type the description:

Style Library —————————— 7

Heading

Libraries ▾ ————————————— 8

OK   Cancel ——— 9

✓ **TIP** You can determine that the Publishing Infrastructure feature has not been activated on the root site collection if the Navigation link is available in the Look And Feel section on the Site Settings page.

Editing the Top Link bar on a nonpublishing site

As with the Quick Launch menu on nonpublishing sites, you can also edit the list of linked sites that appears horizontally across the top of your site. This option is only available on sites for which your technical staff has not activated the SharePoint Server Publishing Infrastructure feature.

Edit the Top Link bar on a nonpublishing site

1 On the Home page of your site, click the Settings button (the small gear icon next to the name of the logged-on user). On the menu that appears, click Site Settings.

2 On the Site Settings page, in the Look And Feel section, click the Top Link Bar link.

3 On the Top Link Bar settings page, you can create a new link by clicking the New Navigation Link button.

4 From the New Navigation Link page, type the URL and a descriptive label (which display on the Top Link bar) for the link.

When users click the link, they are taken to the URL that you entered.

5 Click OK to save your new heading.

TIP You can determine that the Publishing Infrastructure feature has not been activated on the root site collection if the Quick Launch and Top Link Bar links are available in the Look And Feel section on the Site Settings page.

Editing publishing site navigation

If your administrative staff has activated the SharePoint Server Publishing Infrastructure feature on your root site collection, you have advanced options for changing your site navigation structure that can also be inherited by subsites. This covers both the Quick Launch bar (on the left side of your site Home page) as well as the Top Link bar (which appears horizontally across the top of your site).

Edit publishing site navigation

1 On the Home page of your site, click the Settings button (the small gear icon next to the name of the logged-on user). On the menu that appears, click Site Settings.

2 On the Site Settings page, in the Look And Feel section, click the Navigation link.

3 On the Navigation Settings page, choose your global navigation options.

These are applied to the Top Link bar that appears horizontally across the top of the Home page of your site.

4 On the Navigation Settings page, choose your current navigation options.

These are applied to the Quick Launch bar that appears vertically on the left side of the Home page of your site.

(continued on next page)

TIP You can determine that the Publishing Infrastructure feature is activated on the root site collection if the Navigation link is available in the Look And Feel section on the Site Settings page.

Site Settings ▸ Navigation Settings ⓘ

Edit publishing site navigation *(continued)*

5 In the Structural Navigation settings section, select the Global Navigation folder to manually add new items to your Top Link bar.

6 You can then use the Add Link button to add additional links.

7 In the Structural Navigation settings section, select the Current Navigation folder to manually add items to the Quick Launch bar.

8 You can then use the Add Link button to add additional links.

9 In the Show And Hide Ribbon section, select whether to allow users to access the Show and Hide ribbon buttons on the toolbar.

10 Click OK to save your results.

Saving a site as a template

After you create a site and set it up the way you want it, you might decide to use it as a template for sites that you create in the future. By saving your newly created site as a template, you can make deploying sites like it much easier because you don't need to re-create them manually.

When you save a site as a template, any lists, libraries, or other objects you have added are also saved. You also have the option of saving some content with the template. For example, maybe in each of your newly created sites you want to have certain forms uploaded to specific libraries during the site creation process.

Save site as a site template

1 On the Home page of your site, click the Settings button (the small gear icon next to the name of the logged-on user). On the menu that appears, click Site Settings.

2 On the Site Settings page, in the Site Actions section, click the Save Site As Template link.

(continued on next page)

Save site as a site template *(continued)*

3 On the Save As Template page, type a file name for your site template.

If you later export the template to a file, this will be the default file name.

4 Type a name and description for the template.

5 If you want to also save all content stored in document libraries on your site in the template, select the Include Content check box.

6 Click OK to save the template.

7 On the Operation Completed Successfully page, click OK.

Site Settings › Save as Template ⓘ

File Name

Enter the name for this template file.

File name:

MyExampleSite ———————————— 3

Name and Description

The name and description of this template will be displayed on the Web site template picker page when users create new Web sites.

Template name:

Example Team Site

Template description:

Used as an example starting team site. ———— 4

Include Content

Include content in your template if you want new Web sites created from this template to include the contents of all lists and document libraries in this Web site. Some customizations, such as custom workflows, are present in the template only if you choose to include content. Including content can increase the size of your template.

Caution: Item security is not maintained in a template. If you have private content in this Web site, enabling this option is not recommended.

☑ Include Content ———————————— 5

OK — Cancel ———— 6

Experimental Team Site › Operation Completed Successfully

The web site has successfully been saved to the solutions gallery. You can now create sites based on this solution.

To manage solutions in the gallery, go to the solution gallery.

To return to the site administration page, click **OK**.

OK ———— 7

Organizing and managing information

If you are used to working with local files and folders or have worked with simple file sharing sites, you will certainly be able to manage your content in Microsoft SharePoint 2013. You can upload files, sort them into folders, and navigate these folders to find content in the future. At some point, however, a site can grow to contain so many files that a simple, folder-based structure is not sufficient to quickly find content, particularly if you have project files spread across many different folders.

In this section, we explain how you can enhance the ways that you store and organize content by using content types to differentiate types of files, site columns to provide additional information on each file, and document templates and workflows to support document automation.

In this section:

- Introduction to SharePoint metadata
- Browsing through site columns
- Creating site columns
- Browsing through content types
- Creating a new content type
- Associating document templates with content types
- Working with workflows

Introduction to SharePoint metadata

As you organize content, a simple method is to add relevant information to the file name or to the name of the folder that contains the file. For example, you might add the company name, document type, and release date of the file to the file name, such as "Contoso - Proposal - May 2013.docx". This can work nicely for a small number of files, but this method becomes difficult to manage for more complex tasks. For example, if you want to find all proposals released in the year 2013, you have no way to quickly find files across multiple companies. In these cases, metadata can be useful for adding additional information to files to help you search, sort, and categorize content. If you have ever used a file folder to store content, you've made use of basic metadata, such as file name, date modified, and size.

SharePoint site columns

In SharePoint, metadata is referred to as site columns. A site column makes it possible for the same piece of metadata to be applied to multiple lists and libraries. When you apply a site column to a list or library, you can define a value for each of the items in that list or library. Additionally, you can add this value to views and further use it to sort or filter large numbers of files. For example, if you define a site column named "Department" and add this column to a document library, you can use this column to sort all files so that you can differentiate between the values "Sales" and "Marketing". These site columns can also be configured to store different types of data, such as text values, date values, and restricted values that can be chosen from a list.

After a site column is defined, you can add it to multiple libraries, which helps support consistency between files located in different libraries. It also makes it possible for users to quickly define new libraries and metadata without entering new columns from scratch on each library.

Site columns appear as data next to each file.

SharePoint content types

You use content types to further organize information across multiple libraries and sites by grouping similar documents into a single category, such as legal documents, memos, or proposals. Because these content types can be used in multiple lists and libraries, documents stored in many different places can be easily classified and treated in a similar way. A content type might define the following behaviors:

- Site columns that will be associated to files that use this content type

- A document template that will be used as a starting point for all new files of this content type

- Workflows that might be used with files of this content type

- Custom New, Edit, or Display forms that might be used to edit metadata for files or items based on this content type

- Custom Document Information Panel settings (used with Microsoft Office files only) for adding metadata while editing the files in Office

- Information management policies (for auditing, expiring, and associating barcodes and labels to documents automatically)

Using content types, your team can manage and organize your information and documents in a consistent fashion. Because content types can include many site columns, you can use them to quickly apply a set of metadata that will be used to classify the files for a single library. This can save your

team valuable time because content types can be reused across libraries and sites.

You can also add multiple content types to the same library; this means that a user can more easily classify the content in a list or library. Each content type can have different site columns and other associated behaviors so that only the relevant metadata is required when uploading one type of content versus another.

As with site columns, content types are inherited by child sites and can be used throughout a site collection. This makes them a very powerful, time-saving device for classifying documents and metadata.

SharePoint 2013 includes a variety of file and item content types that you can immediately use or extend as the parent content type for new content types that your team might create. The following are lists of the more commonly used content types:

Content type	Description
Community content types	
Category	Used to for community site categories
Community Member	Used to associate a community member to a list
Site Membership	Used to associate a community member to a list

Content type	Description
Digital asset content type	
Audio	Used for audio files
Image	Used for graphic and images
Rich Media Asset	Used for other rich media
Video	Used for video files
Video Rendition	Used for renditions of video files, which are different sizes and encodings of videos that are generated for mobile devices, and so on
Display template content types	
JavaScript Display Template	Used for storing client-side rendering code written by developers to change the display of some controls
Document content types	
Basic Page	Used for basic site pages
Document	Used for site documents. (Typically, this is the main content type that is used as a starting point for building new content types.)
Dublin Core Columns	Used for content tagged by using the Dublin Core Metadata element set (an industry standard for resource discovery)
Form	Used for storing data display and entry forms
Link to a Document	Used for storing external links to documents

Content type	Description
List View Style	Used for list view styles
Master Page	Used for master pages, which are developer resources for applying a consistent look and feel across a SharePoint site
Master Page Preview	Used for master page preview images
Picture	Used for uploaded pictures or images
Web Part Page	Used for site pages containing Web Part zones (where new Web Parts may be added)
Wiki Page	Used for wiki pages, which support community-edited documentation
Document set content types	
Document Set	Used for document sets, which are containers for other types of documents
Folder content types	
Discussion	Used for tracking discussions on discussion boards
Folder	Used for organizing documents within libraries
Summary Task	Used for grouping and describing related tasks
Group work content types	
Circulation	Used for adding a new circulation
Holiday	Used for entering holiday information on calendars

Content type	Description
New Word	Used for entering new words on a list
Official Notice	Used for official notices
Phone Call Memo	Used for recording a memo from a phone call
Resource	Used to describe an asset that can be reserved
Resource Group	Used to group resources
Timecard	Used to record a timecard entry for an employee
Users	Used to associate users to a list
What's New Notification	Used to record a "What's New" notification

List content types

Content type	Description
Announcement	Used for the announcements Web Part, with which announcements can be posted to a page within a site
Comment	Used for comments associated with blog posts
Contact	Used for storing information about a content (for example, First Name, Last Name, Email, and so on)
East Asia Contact	Used for storing information about a content (for example, First Name, Last Name, Email, and so on) using East Asia formatting
Event	Used for describing events that are to be displayed in calendars.

Content type	Description
Issue	Used for tracking issues or problems
Item	Used for basic list items (This is the basic starting point used as the parent for many customized site columns.)
Link	Used for links to other pages or assets
Message	Used for messages
Post	Used for storing blog posts on blog sites
Reservations	Used for reservations of assets within meeting sites
Schedule	Used for scheduling appointments
Schedule and Reservations	Used for both scheduling appointments and reserving assets
Task	Used for storing site tasks
Workflow Task (SharePoint 2013)	Used for storing information about workflow tasks

Special content types

Content type	Description
Unknown Document Type	A special content type first used when documents are first uploaded to SharePoint, and a formal content type has not yet been associated to the file.

Browsing through site columns

You can define site columns in SharePoint 2013 at the site-collection level, and you can add and use them within both lists and document libraries. Sites created under a primary collection can also make use of the same site columns available in the root site. As you explore site columns, you will be able to browse the site columns associated with your site and inspect individual site columns in detail.

Browse through site columns

1 In the upper-right corner of the window, click the Settings icon (the small gear graphic) and then, on the menu that appears, click Site Settings.

2 On the Site Settings page, in the Web Designer Galleries section, click the Site Columns link.

(continued on next page)

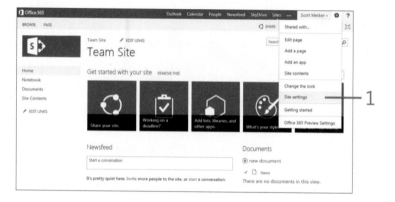

TIP Site columns can be reused throughout a site or any child sites that inherit from the parent site. The site columns that you see within your site might belong to a parent site.

TIP Remember that Site Columns can be inherited from a parent site. This is why you might need to click the Source link to navigate to the parent site if you want to view detail about a particular column. Also, when you click an entry in the Source column, you are taken to the Site Columns page within the parent site, so don't forget to navigate back after you have finished exploring!

Browse through site columns *(continued)*

3 In the Source column, select a site column with a clickable link. If this link is not clickable, you can proceed to step 4.

4 In the Site Column column, click the name of the site column that you want to view.

5 After you finish viewing the column information, scroll to the bottom of the screen and click Cancel to return to your previous view.

Site columns are classified into several groups.

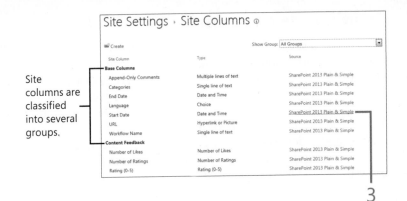

3

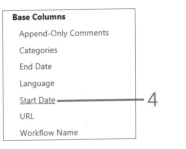

4

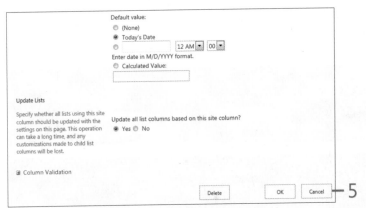

5

TIP Make use of any preconfigured site columns whenever possible (including the out-of-the-box columns). You will save time and make your site more consistent.

TRY THIS Inspect the Language and URL site columns. Examine the differences between these two columns.

Creating site columns

When adding site columns to a SharePoint 2013 list or document library, you should first consider using those that already exist, either out of the box or previously defined by other site users. This supports consistency within a site and makes it easier for users of your site to explore and find content. For example, if you have two columns that have the same meaning, such as "Client" and "Client Name," you make it more difficult for users to choose one of these columns when they search for content or browse through lists on your site.

If you decide to create your own site columns, there is a simple-to-use interface for defining them. In general, we recommend keeping the number of site columns on a site both concise and consistent. Each site column, when associated with a list or library, represents another piece of information that users must enter for each piece of content.

Create site columns

1 On the Site Settings page, in the Web Designer Galleries section, click the Site Columns link, and then, on the Site Columns page, click Create.

(continued on next page)

Site Settings ▸ Site Columns ⓘ

1 — ☐ Create   Show Group: All Groups

Site Column	Type	Source
Base Columns		
Append-Only Comments	Multiple lines of text	SharePoint 2013 Plain & Simple
Categories	Single line of text	SharePoint 2013 Plain & Simple

> **TIP** When you place your new site columns into groups, you make it easier to manage and work with these columns in the future because they will all appear in the same grouping within the list of site columns for your site.

> **TIP** You can store many different types of data in SharePoint site columns. Explore these data types to find those options that work best for your data.

Create site columns *(continued)*

2 Enter a name for the column that you are creating.

3 Click the type of information that this column will store.

4 Pick from an existing group or create a new group in which to organize this column.

5 In the Additional Column Settings section, enter a description of the column and any other appropriate settings.

6 Click OK.

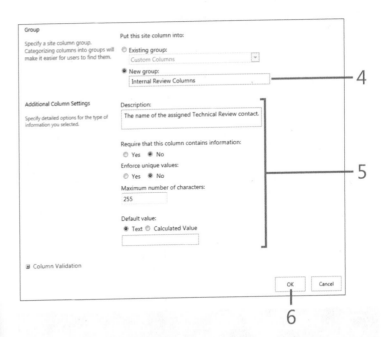

Browsing through content types

To work with SharePoint 2013 content types, you first need to view the existing content types that are available for use. You can use the Site Content Types page to quickly view all content types associated with your site (or its parent sites).

Browse through content types

1 On the Site Settings page, in the Web Designer Galleries section, click Site Content Types.

2 On the Site Content Types page, in the Show Group list box, select a group to view.

3 Select a content type and, if you are able, click the Source link. Otherwise, proceed to the next step.

(continued on next page)

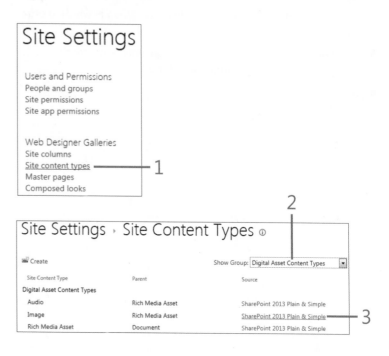

TIP Content types are arranged in groups to help users organize and browse similar content types. You can filter this list by using the Show Groups drop-down list.

Browse through content types *(continued)*

4 Click the Site Content Type column for the content type that you want to browse.

5 Explore the associated columns and other settings for the content type you selected.

Digital Asset Content Types

Audio	Rich Media Asset
Image	Rich Media Asset
Rich Media Asset	Document

4 — Image

Site Content Types › Site Content Type

Site Content Type Information

Name: Image
Description: Upload an image.
Parent: Rich Media Asset
Group: Digital Asset Content Types

Settings

- Name, description, and group
- Advanced settings
- Workflow settings
- Information management policy settings
- Document Information Panel settings
- Delete this site content type

Columns

Name	Type	Status	Source
Name	File	Required	Document
Title	Single line of text	Optional	Item
Preview	Computed	Optional	Rich Media Asset
Keywords	Multiple lines of text	Optional	Rich Media Asset
Thumbnail Preview	Computed	Optional	Rich Media Asset
Picture Size	Computed	Optional	
Comments	Multiple lines of text	Optional	
Author	Single line of text	Optional	
Date Picture Taken	Date and Time	Optional	

5 —

> ✓ **TIP**   You might first need to click a value in the Source column when selecting a content type because that content type is defined in a parent site. Clicking the Source link takes you to the parent site that contains the content type. There you can directly inspect it.

Creating a new content type

In the event that you have a set of documents that you cannot classify by using one of the existing SharePoint content types, you can create your own content type.

Create content type

1 On the Site Content Types page, click Create.

2 On the New Site Content Type page, enter the name and description of the content type.

3 Select a parent content type (you can first select a filtered list from which to choose).

4 Click to choose either a new or existing group in which to place this content type. If you select Existing Group, in the list box, select the group.

5 Click OK.

(continued on next page)

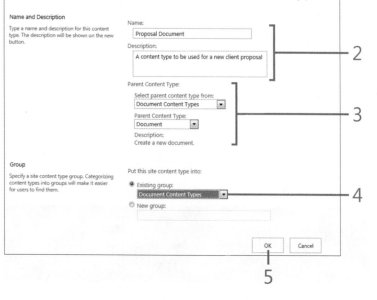

> ⚠ **CAUTION** Use care if you're making changes to content types within a site. Sometimes, you might inadvertently find yourself editing the content types on the parent site or changing a content type that is used by another user or group for a critical business function.

Create content type *(continued)*

6 Click the Add From Existing Site Columns link.

7 In the Select Columns From list box, filter the list of columns. In the Available Columns section, select one or many columns to associate with the content type. Click Add to associate these columns.

8 Click OK.

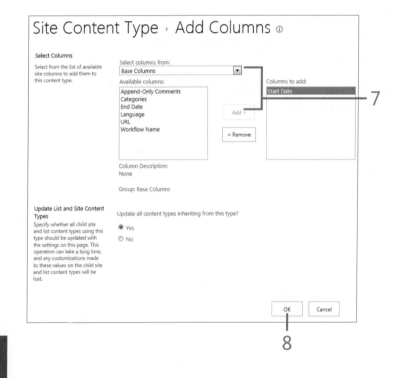

 TIP Enter relevant names, description text, and groups for your new content types to help drive reuse within your site.

TIP For content types that will be associated with file contents (such as Microsoft Office documents), choose to inherit from an existing parent content type such as the "Document" content type.

Associating document templates with content types

A common issue with respect to managing content is enforcing a common look and feel within documents. For example, multiple proposals that are authored by separate departments might have different organizational structure, formatting, and wording.

One way to enforce consistency when using SharePoint 2013 is to upload and associate a document template with your content types. With document templates, users who create new documents based on a content type can have a prepopulated starting point (instead of a blank document). A simple usage is to create the various headers that would be expected in most documents and apply some basic formatting.

Associate a document template with a content type

1 On the Site Content Types page, click the Site Content Type column where you will associate a document template.

2 From the Site Content Types Page, click Advanced Settings.

(continued on next page)

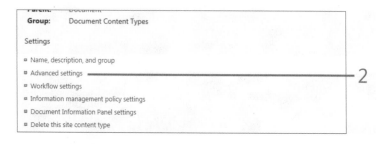

Associate a document template with a content type *(continued)*

3 Prepare and save a Microsoft Word document locally with your desired formatting for new documents based on this content type.

4 Select the Upload A New Document Template option, click Browse, and then select your local document.

5 Click OK to save your changes.

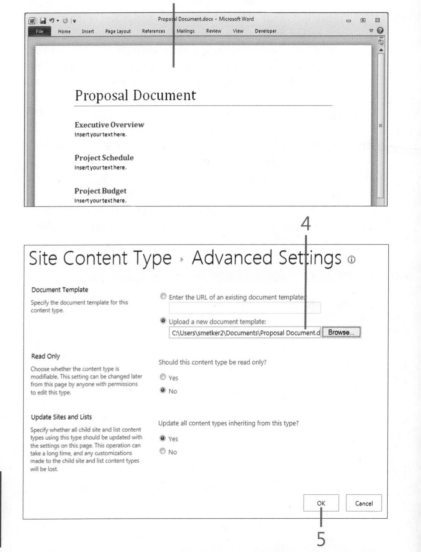

Working with workflows

Within systems that manage content, workflows refer to a series of activities that are applied to a document or item. Content management systems use workflows to automate repetitive tasks such as assigning multiple reviewers to a document and routing the final response back to the originator. In SharePoint 2013, you can assign workflows to list items or documents to automate common tasks, as well.

The advantage of using workflows to automate document tasks is that workflows can include steps to ensure that documents are appropriately processed. For example, if multiple reviewers are assigned to a document within a workflow, the SharePoint workflow can make sure that the next reviewer has received a copy of the document immediately after the

previous reviewer has completed her review. This ensures that documents are not forgotten or misrouted. Also, you can use workflows to send emails during important activities, ensuring that users are reminded that tasks are due.

SharePoint 2013 offers a completely updated workflow experience for users of the Server or Enterprise platforms. Users of SharePoint 2013 Foundation are limited to the workflow functionality that was provided with the previous version, SharePoint 2010. You can use these workflows for basic document routing and notifications of assignees for each workflow task as well as tracking the full history of the document as it is routed and changed within the workflow.

List and library essentials

Organizations rely on accessing pertinent information so they can respond quickly to business needs. Microsoft SharePoint 2013 offers true document-management capabilities and is all about sharing information through apps called lists or libraries.

A list is a collection of like items, such as contact information, calendar events, or inventory items. Similar to a database table, each list contains data that you enter yourself or import from another source. You control how the information is displayed and who has access to either view or manipulate that data. SharePoint provides a central location for team members to access current, accurate, and relevant data.

You can create a custom list that describes the information that you want to capture, or use standard templates that come out of the box. SharePoint 2013 comes with several lists for collecting different kinds of information, such as tasks, announcements, contacts, and links, just to name a few.

In this section:

- Using your apps
- Creating and deleting lists
- Adding and editing list items
- Deleting and restoring list items
- Creating list columns
- Editing and deleting list columns
- Using list and column validation rules
- Sorting and filtering lists
- Creating and selecting a list view
- Sorting or filtering a list view
- Organizing items by using folders

Using your apps

Microsoft has included a new application development model in SharePoint 2013 called the *SharePoint app*. Certainly, we've all become familiar with the phrase, "There's an app for that." Well, now SharePoint can say the same. These self-contained web applications can come out of the box or be downloaded from Microsoft's SharePoint Store. Apps provide users with a way to access existing applications that others have already built rather than building them from scratch. Lists and libraries are apps as well as being other useful mini programs.

Perhaps you want to highlight a "Tip of the Day" section on your SharePoint site or implement a Timesheet in which employees can enter their project hours. You can download these apps from the SharePoint Store for free instead of hiring a developer to design and implement it!

Add an app on SharePoint

1   In the upper-right corner of the window, click the Settings icon (the small gear graphic).

2   On the menu that appears, click Add An App.

3   Click the app that you want to add to your site.

4   Enter a name for the new app.

5   Click Create.

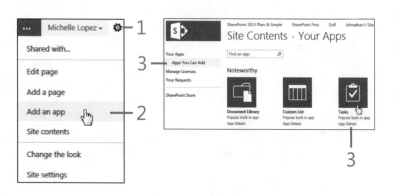

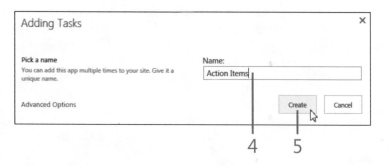

> **TIP**   You can read a brief description of each app by clicking the App Details link, which is located below the app's icon, on the Apps You Can Add page.

Add an app from the SharePoint Store

1 In the upper-right corner of the window, click the Settings icon.

2 On the menu that appears, click Add An App.

3 On the Your Apps page, on the Quick Launch bar, click SharePoint Store.

4 Click the app that you want to add to your site.

5 Click Add It, Buy It, or Try It.

6 If the app requests trust confirmation, follow any instructions that are presented and then click either Trust It or Cancel.

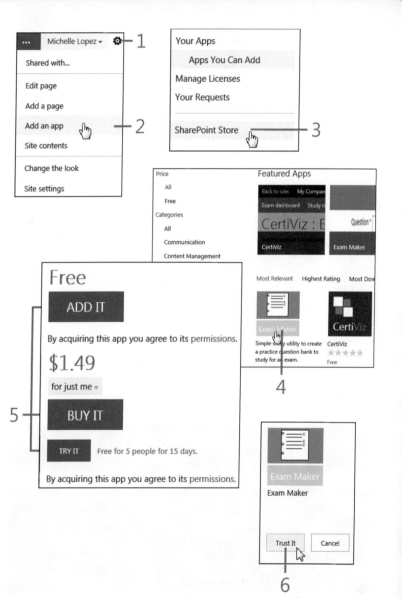

TIP You must be a Site Owner or have Full Control permissions to add apps from either the SharePoint Store or an App Catalog.

Creating and deleting lists

Although SharePoint 2013 provides you with several lists and libraries based on commonly used templates, you'll likely need to customize your list to suit your needs. Perhaps you need a way to display employee vacations or track open issues—SharePoint makes this possible with just a few clicks. To keep your site clean, you'll want to get rid of unused or obsolete lists, as well.

Create a list or library

1   In the upper-right corner of the window, click the Settings icon, and then, on the menu that appears, click Add An App.

2   On the Your Apps page, under the Noteworthy section, select either Document Library or Custom List. For this example, the Custom List app is used.

3   In the Adding Custom List dialog box, enter a name for your list (or library).

4   Click Create.

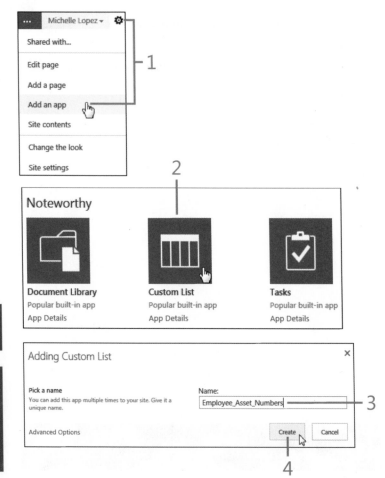

 TIP   A library is actually a list that stores documents instead of information alone.

 TIP   When naming your list, use underscores (_) in place of spaces between words or omit spaces between words altogether. This helps to keep the assigned URL clean. If you want to rename your list after you create it, go to the List Settings and then, in the General Settings section, click List Name, Description And Navigation. There, you can edit the name of your list to include spaces.

Delete a list or library

1 Hover over the list or library that you want to delete and then click the drop-down menu icon (...).

2 On the menu that appears, click the Settings link.

3 On the Settings page, under the Permissions And Management section, click Delete This List (or Delete This Library).

4 In the pop-up message box, click OK to confirm that you want to send the list to the Recycle Bin.

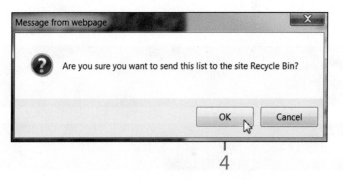

TRY THIS Practice creating a custom list titled New List and then delete it.

Adding and editing list items

After creating a list, you'll want to populate that list with the information for which it was designed. Each row in your SharePoint 2013 list is called a *list item*. SharePoint can support up to 30 million items in one SharePoint list! Depending on your permission level, you can create, edit, and delete items.

You can also attach documents or items to a list item. For instance, it would be practical to attach a menu to a restaurant list or an agenda to a calendar item. By default, SharePoint supports including attachments to list items; however, you can turn off this feature on the Settings page for the list, if you'd like.

Add a list item

1 On the Quick Launch bar, click Site Contents.

2 On the Site Contents page, click the list to which you want to add items.

3 In the list, click New Item.

4 On the list's Edit page, click with the mouse or use the Tab key to move through the item fields, entering data as required or as you see fit.

5 Click Save.

> **TIP** SharePoint automatically assigns a sequential ID number to each new item, eliminating the need for you to assign it manually.

> **TIP** A blue asterisk indicates a required field for which you must provide information before the list item can be saved.

Edit a list item

1 On the Quick Launch bar, click Site Contents.

2 Click the list in which you want to edit items.

3 Click Edit above the list items.

4 Click the mouse or use the Tab key to navigate between and edit the item fields.

5 Click the mouse or use the Tab key to select a different field; the changes are automatically saved.

6 When you're done making changes, click Stop above the list items.

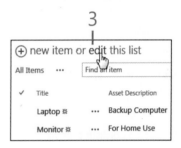

TRY THIS Attach a file to your item by going on the ribbon and clicking Attach File.

TIP Most drop-down commands are also available on the ribbon on the Items tab.

Deleting and restoring list items

It's possible that a user will want to retrieve a deleted item. SharePoint 2013 provides an easy way to restore that deleted item back to its original location.

Deleted items will remain in the site collection's Recycle Bin for 30 days. If you delete an item from your Recycle Bin, you can

request that your Site Collection Administrator restore the item back to its original location for you, as long as the item hasn't exceeded 30 days from the original deletion date.

Delete a list item

1 On the Quick Launch bar, click Site Contents.

2 Click the list from which you want to delete items.

3 Hover over the item that you want to delete and then click the menu drop-down icon (...).

4 On the menu that appears, click Delete Item.

5 In the pop-up message box, click OK to confirm that you want to send the item to the Recycle Bin.

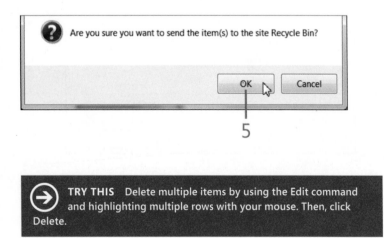

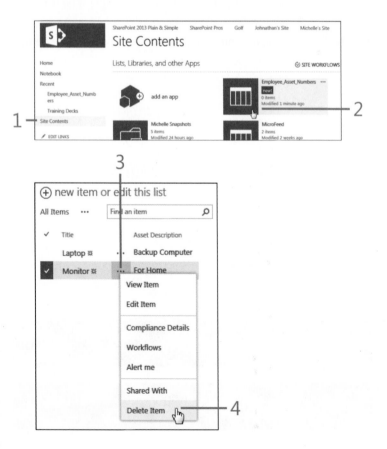

> **TRY THIS** Delete multiple items by using the Edit command and highlighting multiple rows with your mouse. Then, click Delete.

Restore a deleted item

1 On the Quick Launch bar, click Site Contents.

2 On the right side of the Site Contents page, click Recycle Bin.

3 On the Recycle Bin page, select the check box to the left of the item that you want to restore.

4 Click Restore Selection.

TRY THIS Delete a list or library and then restore it.

Creating list columns

SharePoint 2013 provides several templates for common list types, such as Announcements, Calendar, Contacts, and Tasks. These templates can be used and then customized so that you don't have to create a new list from scratch. Create additional columns to suit your list or library's purpose.

Create a column

1 In a list, above the list items, click Edit.

2 To the right of the column headings, click the Add button (the "+" sign).

3 On the menu that appears, click More Column Types.

4 In the Column Name text box, enter a name for the column.

5 Choose the type of information that the new column will store.

(continued on next page)

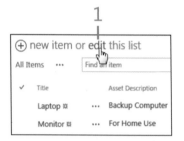

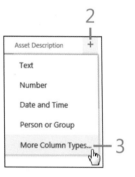

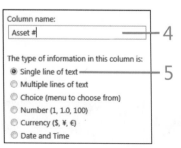

TIP To work with columns, you must have Designer or Full Control permissions.

TRY THIS SharePoint includes several predefined columns. Instead of creating a new column, choose to add from existing site columns when editing list column settings.

Create a column *(continued)*

6 In the Additional Column Settings dialog box, you can also optionally edit the following column settings:

- **Description**   What you enter here displays under the field
  when the user is editing the form.

- **Require That This Column Contains Information**   Select Yes
  to require data to be entered in this field.

- **Enforce Unique Values**   Select Yes to require that each value
  in this column be unique in this list.

- **Maximum Number Of Characters**   This determines the maximum number of characters that can be entered in this field.

- **Default Value**   Any text entered here will be the default
  column entry when a new item is created.

- **Add To Default View**   Select this check box to add this column
  to the default view of this list.

- **Column Validation**   Use rules to accept or reject information
  entered in this column based on defined criteria.

7 Click OK.

Editing and deleting list columns

After you've created new columns for your list or library in SharePoint 2013, you might change your mind about the column name or data type. You might want to require that information is entered in a field or include a different default value. You can also delete columns that are no longer necessary.

Edit column settings

1 On the List tab, in the Settings group, click List Settings.

2 On the List Settings page, in the Columns section, click a column title.

3 Make the desired Column changes and click OK.

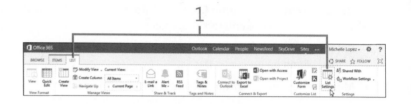

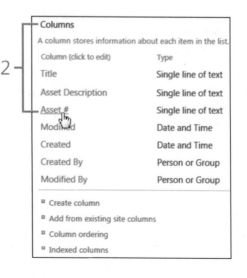

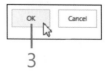

> ⚠ **CAUTION** If you change your mind about the Type for a column, you'll find that not all Types are available when you go back to edit it. In this case, your only alternative is to delete the column and create a new one with the correct Type.

Delete a list column

1 On the List tab, in the Settings group, click List Settings.

2 On the List Settings page, in the Columns section, click a column title.

3 Click Delete.

4 In the pop-up message box asking you to confirm the deletion, click OK.

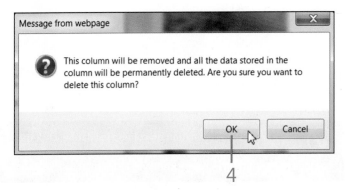

> **✓ TIP** The Title column included in SharePoint lists is a required column, it cannot be deleted. If the Delete button is not displayed in the settings for the column, this indicates that the column is a required column in this list.

> **⚠ CAUTION** Deleting a column also deletes the data in that column. Before deleting a column, consider exporting the list to Microsoft Excel to back up the information. This can be done by clicking Export To Excel in the Connect & Export group of the List's ribbon.

Using list and column validation rules

Being that we're human, entries are bound to contain formatting errors. A SharePoint 2013 feature uses validation rules to accept or reject the entered information based on defined criteria. Rejected information needs to be corrected by the user before the item can be saved in the list. Validation rules exist on individual columns as well as the list level. SharePoint evaluates column rules before evaluating list level rules.

Validation rules are only available on the following column types: Single Line Of Text, Choice, Number, Currency, and Date/Time.

Add a validation rule to a column

1 On the Library tab, in the Settings group, click Library Settings (or List Settings on the List tab).

2 On the Library Settings page, in the Columns section, click a column title.

3 Scroll down to Column Validation and click the plus sign (+) icon next to Column Validation to expand the section.

(continued on next page)

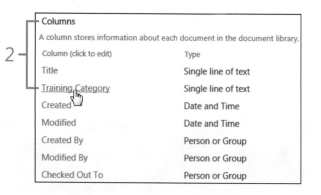

TIP For more information on column validation, click the SharePoint Help button (the question mark in the upper-right corner of a site) and then type **formula** as a search phrase.

Add a validation rule to a column *(continued)*

4 In the Formula text box, enter a validation formula.

5 In the User Message text box, enter a message to display if the information entered in the field is not valid.

6 Click OK.

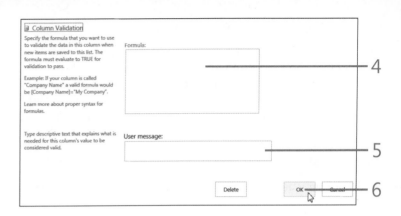

Add a validation rule to a list

1 On the List tab, in the Settings group, click List Settings.

2 On the List Settings page, in the General Settings section, click Validation Settings.

3 In the Formula text box, enter a validation formula.

4 In the User Message text box, enter a message to display if the information entered in the field is not valid.

5 Click Save.

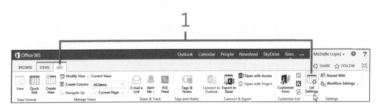

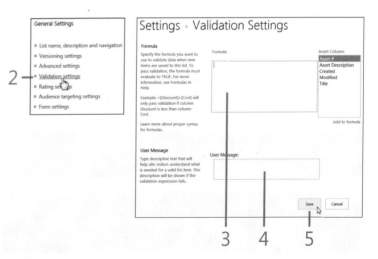

Sorting and filtering lists

Information in lists can be organized and displayed by using views. Views can be created and modified to specify which fields are displayed, the column order, how they are sorted, and whether the information is filtered and/or grouped. SharePoint 2013 provides several formats for displaying views, as well, such as Standard and Datasheet views. Standard views support dynamic sorting and filtering directly in the column headers, whereas Datasheet views give users the option to enter data as a batch instead of entering one list item at a time. Here, you'll learn how to manually sort or filter a Standard view.

Sort a list

1 Hover your mouse pointer over the title of the column by which you want to sort.

2 Click the drop-down arrow to the right of the column title.

3 On the menu that appears, click either Ascending (A on Top) or Descending (Z on Top).

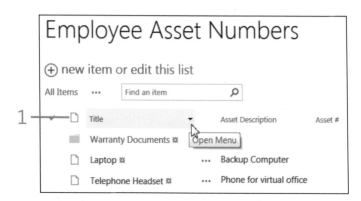

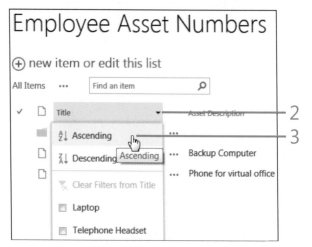

SEE ALSO To sort on more than one column, you need to configure a list view. See "Create a list view" on page 90.

TIP If a column is sorted, a small up arrow or down arrow (depending on whether the column is sorted in ascending or descending order) displays to the right of the column title.

Filter a list

1 Hover your mouse pointer over the title of the column that you want to filter.

2 Click the drop-down arrow to the right of the column title.

3 On the menu that appears, select the check boxes adjacent to the information that you want to include in the filter.

4 Click Close.

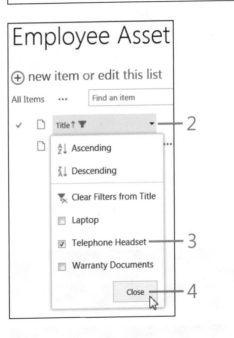

> **TIP** If a column is filtered, a small funnel icon displays to the right of the column title.

> **TRY THIS** Clear the column filters by clicking the small funnel icon and then, on the menu that appears, click Clear Filters From column.

Creating and selecting a list view

SharePoint 2013 provides users with flexible ways to display their list information by using views. You control which fields appear in each list, the field order, as well as filtering or sorting on multiple columns. Additionally, information can be grouped to collapse or expand for a treelike view. Users can determine whether their configured views are available to all users or just themselves, and can be defined for mobile devices. If a preferred view of the list data already exists but is not the default view, SharePoint 2013 makes it easy to switch to that view.

Create a list view

1 Click the drop-down menu icon (...) above the list headings.

2 On the menu that appears, click Create View.

3 On the View Type page, click Standard View.

(continued on next page)

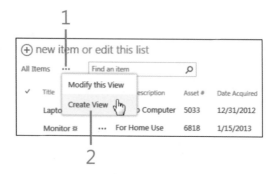

TIP Only include relevant columns to reduce the amount of columns visible on your screen. All fields are visible when you click the link to the item.

TIP Instead of creating a new view from scratch, use the Start From An Existing View option when choosing to create a new view and make modifications.

Create a list view *(continued)*

4 On the Create View page, in the View Name text box, enter a unique name for the view.

5 Select the Make This The Default View check box to make this new view the default view.

6 In the View Audience section, choose to make the view Personal (for your use only) or Public (available to all site users).

7 In the Columns section, you can perform two activities:

- Select the check box adjacent to the columns that you want to display in the view; clear the check boxes adjacent to the columns that you want to hide.

- Order the columns sequentially from left to right by selecting numbers in the Position From Left column.

8 At the top or bottom of the page, click OK.

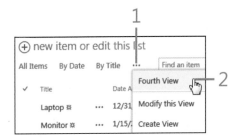

Select a list view

1 Click the drop-down menu icon (...) above the list headings.

2 On the menu that appears, click the view that you want to display.

TIP Three view links are available above the list's columns, available for quick toggling.

Sorting or filtering a list view

If you find yourself continuously filtering the default view to meet your needs, why not eliminate that time by creating alternate views that you'll access often? Here, you'll learn how to modify views by using the sort and filter features.

Sort a list view

1 Click the drop-down menu icon (...) above the list headings.

2 On the menu that appears, click Modify This View.

3 In the Sort section, you can perform two activities:

- Click the drop-down list and select the First Sort By The Column.

- Select whether you want that sorted column in ascending or descending order.

4 If you don't want folders to appear before items, select the Sort Only By Specified Criteria check box.

5 At the top or bottom of the page, click OK.

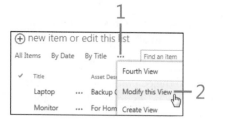

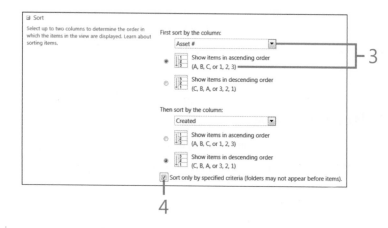

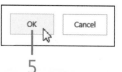

✅ **TIP** Folders will appear before list items by default. If the Sort Only By Specified Criteria option is selected, the folders will appear in the assigned sort order along with the items.

Filter a list view

1 Click the drop-down menu icon (...) above the list headings.

2 On the menu that appears, click Modify This View.

3 In the Filter section, click the Show Items Only When The Following Is True option.

4 To enter filter criteria, do the following:

- Select a column on which to filter from the first drop-down menu.

- Select a condition from the second drop-down menu.

- Enter a value in the text box.

5 Select And or Or to enter additional filter criteria.

6 To filter on more than two criteria, click Show More Columns.

7 At the top or bottom of the page, click OK.

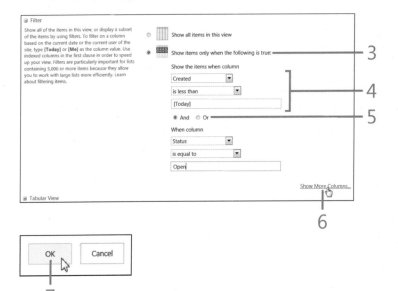

TRY THIS Filter on items by using the Created By criterion and then enter the value [Me].

Organizing items by using folders

In SharePoint 2013, you can create folders to organize your lists, similar to creating folders on your computer. However, for the purposes of organizing information, adding a folder in a list can interrupt the display of the captured information.

You could use SharePoint to organize a Class Schedule listing different Classes, Class Times, and Costs to view at a glance. It would be helpful to have a folder for Class Descriptions for this scenario. Preparing an efficient organizational strategy ahead of time to locate, process, and manage your information is always a best practice.

Create a folder

1 On the Quick Launch bar, click Site Contents.

2 On the Site Contents page, locate the list or library in which you want to create a folder.

3 On the ribbon, click the Items tab of a list, or the Files tab of a library.

4 Click New Folder.

5 In the Create A New Folder dialog box, enter a folder name.

6 Click Save.

> **TIP** If the New Folder option isn't available, the feature needs to be turned on. On the Library Settings tab, click Advanced Settings and then, under the Folders section, click Yes.

Working with documents

Organizations are initially introduced to SharePoint through document management, which continues to be one of SharePoint's many strengths. This section introduces common uses of document libraries, including uploading multiple documents, checking them out and back in again, document IDs, and document sets.

In this section, we'll explain some of the most common ways to use document libraries like uploading multiple documents, and checking documents out for editing. We'll also address how to utilize document IDs and configure document sets on a site.

In this section:

- Managing documents with a document library
- Customizing document templates
- Uploading multiple documents
- Requiring and displaying document check out
- Checking documents in and out
- Configuring documents with document IDs
- Using document IDs
- Moving documents
- Copying or sharing documents
- Configuring document sets on a site
- Configuring document sets on a document library

Managing documents with a document library

The key difference between a SharePoint 2013 library and a list is that libraries are designed to manage files as well as the information attributed to those files. A library can contain a hierarchy of folders and files. It's common for SharePoint sites to contain several document libraries that store different file types such as training guides, financial reports, presentations, and pictures.

Create a document library

1 In the upper-right corner of the window, click the Settings icon (the small gear graphic).

2 On the menu that appears, click Add An App.

3 On the Your Apps page, under the Noteworthy section, click the Document Library icon.

(continued on next page)

Create a document library *(continued)*

4 In the Adding Document Library dialog box, in the Name text box, enter a name for the new library.

5 Click Create.

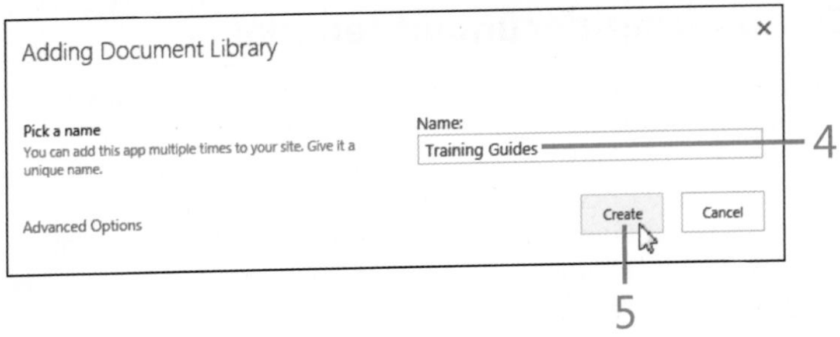

Adding Document Library

Pick a name
You can add this app multiple times to your site. Give it a unique name.

Name:
Training Guides ———— 4

Advanced Options

Create   Cancel

5

Customizing document templates

When a new document library is created, several file types, or content types, are available when you create a new document from the SharePoint 2013 menu. You can choose an empty Microsoft Word document, a Microsoft Excel workbook, a Microsoft PowerPoint presentation, a Microsoft OneNote notebook, or an Excel Survey. You can also select a New Folder.

Instead of creating a commonly used format from scratch, or copying an existing file and then modifying it, with SharePoint, you can customize document defaults and document templates that are available in your library.

Modify the document template for a document library

1 On the Quick Launch bar, select a document library or click Site Contents to locate a library.

2 On the ribbon, click the Library tab.

3 In the Settings group, click Library Settings.

4 On the Library Settings page, in the General Settings section, click Advanced Settings.

5 On the Advanced Settings page, in the Document Template section, click Edit Template.

(continued on next page)

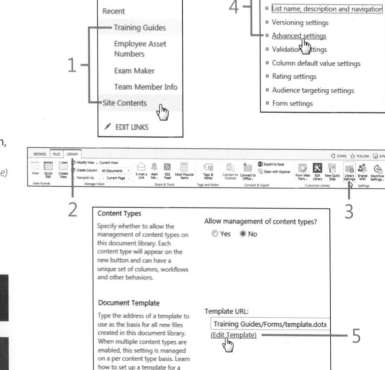

> ✓ **TIP** There can be only one default New Document. Create additional content types to use multiple templates.

> 🔍 **SEE ALSO** For more information about using multiple content types, see Section 4, "Organizing and managing information."

Modify the document template for a document library *(continued)*

6 Make your desired changes to the template.

7 Save the template.

8 Close the application.

9 Click OK.

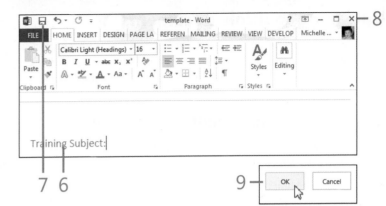

Modify the document template for a content type

1 In the upper-right corner of the window, click the Settings icon.

2 On the menu that appears, click Site Settings.

3 On the Site Settings page, in the Web Designer Galleries section, click Site Content Types.

4 On the Site Content Types page, in the Document Content Types section, click Document.

5 On the Site Content Type page, click Advanced Settings.

6 On the Advanced Settings page, in the Document Template section, click either the Enter The URL Of An Existing Document Template option or the Upload A New Document Template option.

7 Click OK.

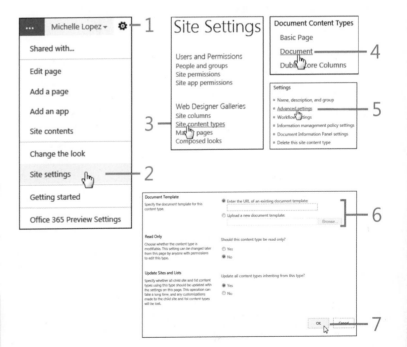

> ⚠ **CAUTION** Changing an existing content type applies that change to that content type across the entire site collection. Creating and customizing a new content type is recommended.

Uploading multiple documents

SharePoint 2013 users will undoubtedly need to upload or move multiple documents to other locations, such as local hard disks, network file shares, or other SharePoint locations. SharePoint lets you drag files directly to your library or upload documents by using Explorer on the Library's ribbon.

Drag multiple documents to a library

1   On the Quick Launch bar or in Site Contents, click the library to which you want to add documents.

2   Right-click the Start button.

3   Click Open Windows Explorer.

4   Browse to the folder that contains the files you want to move.

5   Select the files and drag them to the SharePoint library.

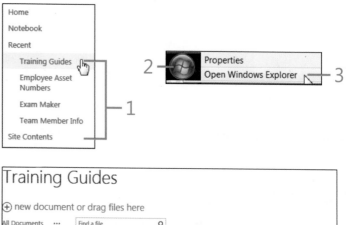

Upload multiple files with Explorer

1 On the ribbon of your document library, click the Library tab.

2 In the Connect & Export group, click Open With Explorer.

3 Drag files to the Explorer folder.

4 Close the Explorer window.

5 Click the Refresh icon in your browser.

Requiring and displaying document check out

SharePoint 2013 is a collaborative platform with which several users can store and share documents with other team members. It's likely that more than one user will attempt to open and edit a document at the same time. SharePoint makes it possible for users to lock a document by checking it out so that only one person can edit the document at a time. Changes made to a document when it is checked out cannot be seen by other users until it is checked back in.

Requiring users to check out documents prior to editing them can be configured in the library settings. An optional comment can also be added when the document is checked in, which can be viewed in the document's history.

Require document check out on a library

1. On the ribbon of your document library, click the Library tab.

2. In the Settings group, click Library Settings.

3. On the Library Settings page, in the General Settings section, click Versioning Settings.

4. In the Require Documents To Be Checked Out Before They Can Be Edited section, click the Yes option.

5. Click OK.

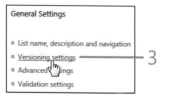

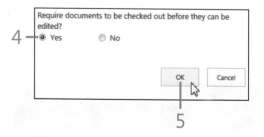

Display the check out status in a document library

1 On the Quick Launch bar or in Site Contents, select the document library with which you want to work.

2 Click the menu drop-down icon (...) above the list headings.

3 On the menu that appears, click Modify This View.

4 On the Edit View page, select the Checked Out To check box.

5 Click OK.

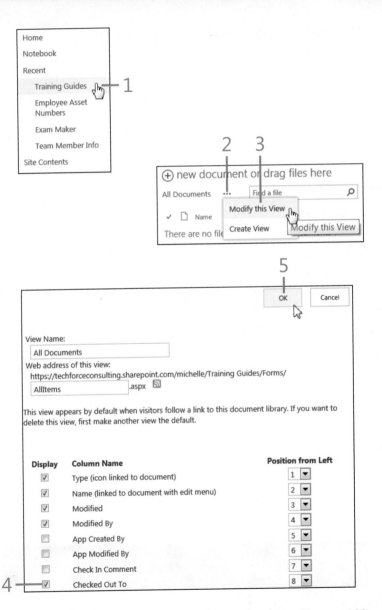

Checking documents in and out

Checking out a SharePoint 2013 document ensures that you are the only one making edits to it. When you're finished making edits, check in the document so that other users can view the changes you made. Even if the document is saved, if it is still checked out, the most recent changes will not be visible to other users.

Check out a document

1 On the Quick Launch bar or in Site Contents, select the document library with which you want to work.

2 Click to the left of one or more documents to select it; a check mark will indicate it's selected. (Hover over the title to see the check mark option.)

3 On the ribbon, click the Files tab.

4 In the Open & Check Out group, click Check Out.

5 In the pop-up message box that appears, click OK.

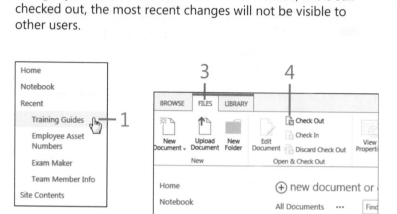

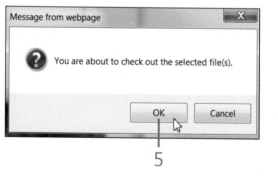

Tip

TIP When a document is checked out, its icon displays an outward-pointing white arrow within a green box.

Check in a document

1 Click to add a check mark to the left of one or more document titles that display the green checked-out icon.

2 On the ribbon, click the Files tab.

3 In the Open & Check Out group, click Check In.

4 In the Check In dialog box, click Yes or No to keep the file checked out after checking it in.

5 In the Comments text box, enter optional comments to include in the document's version history.

6 Click OK.

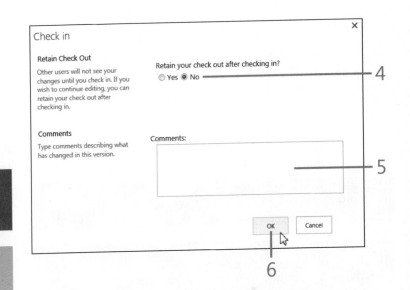

> ✓ **TIP** Checking in a document but retaining its Checked Out status makes it possible for others to see your recent changes while you continue to work on it.

> ⚠ **CAUTION** Selecting Discard Check Out will cancel any changes that you made since your last Check In. Check In often to ensure that the changes you make are saved.

Configuring documents with document IDs

SharePoint 2013 utilizes a feature called document ID, which automatically generates and assigns a unique number to each document. Each document ID is stored as information about that document and can be used to locate that document anywhere in the site collection. In the tasks that follow, you will see how to set up this feature in your site collection.

Turn on the document ID service

1 In the upper-right corner of the page, click the Settings icon.

2 On the menu that appears, click Site Settings.

3 On the Site Settings page, in the Site Collection Administration section, click Site Collection Features.

4 Click the Activate button for Document ID Service.

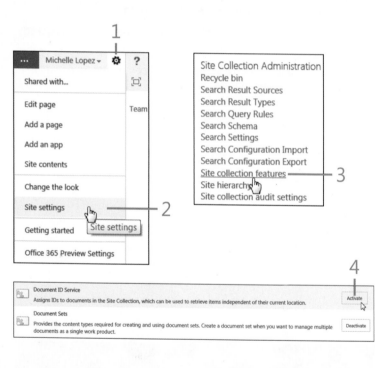

 TIP   To enable any services, you must work in the top-level site of the site collection and have the appropriate permissions.

 TIP   You might not immediately see document IDs associated with your documents. Activation of the Document ID Service is completed by an automated SharePoint process.

Configure document ID settings

1   In the upper-right corner of the page, click the Settings icon.

2   On the menu that appears, click Site Settings.

3   On the Site Settings page, in the Site Collection Administration section, click Document ID Settings.

4   On the Document ID Settings page, perform the following:

- To enable auto-generated IDs, select the Assign Document IDs check box.

- To assign a prefix to new document IDs in the site collection, in the Begin IDs With The Following Characters text box, type the characters that you want to use as a prefix.

- To apply the new prefix to existing documents in the site collection, select the Reset All Document IDs In This Site Collection To Begin With These Characters check box.

5   Click OK.

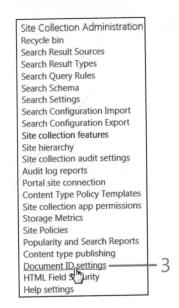

Using document IDs

Document IDs are useful for locating documents that are out of order or have been moved. By adding a Search By Document ID Web Part to your SharePoint 2013 page, you make it easy for users to find a document quickly.

Locate the document ID on a document

1 Click to add a check mark to the left of a document title. (Hover over the title to see the check mark option.)

2 On the Files tab, in the Manage group, click View Properties.

3 In the properties dialog box for the document, click the Document ID value to open the document. (Take note of the Document ID; you will use it in the next task.)

4 Click Close to close the properties dialog box.

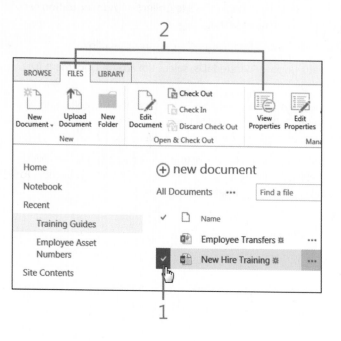

Use the Find By Document ID Web Part

1. On the ribbon of your home page, click the Page tab.

2. In the Edit group, click the Edit button.

3. On the ribbon, click the Insert tab.

4. In the Parts group, click Web Part.

5. In the Categories list box, click Search.

6. In the Parts list box, select Find By Document ID.

7. Click Add to insert the Web Part onto the page.

8. On the Format Text tab, in the Edit group, click the Save button.

9. Enter a Document ID in the Find By Document ID text box.

10. Click the Find icon to search for the document.

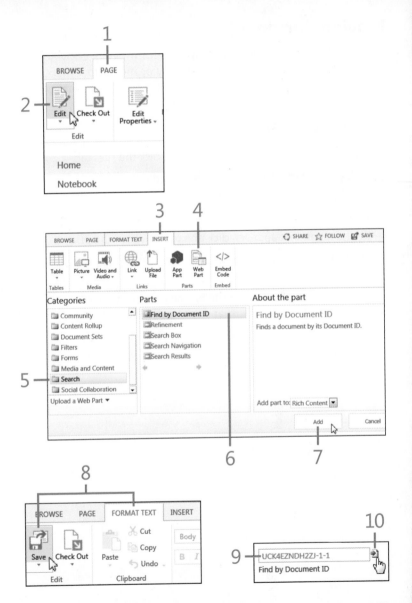

Moving documents

SharePoint 2013 provides many options for moving, copying, or sharing documents on your site. To copy or move documents between document libraries or across sites and site collections, use the Send To menu. You can also download a copy of a document to your local computer or share a link to it via email.

Use the Send To menu

1 On the ribbon of your document library, click the Files tab.

2 Click to add a check mark to the left of a document. (Hover over the title to see the check mark option.)

3 On the ribbon, in the Copies group, click Send To.

4 On the menu that appears, click one of the following options:

- To move or copy the document to another library or site, click Other Location.

- To create a collaboration site for the document, click Create Document Workspace. That document is automatically copied to the workspace.

Add a custom Send To location

1 On the Library tab of your document library, click Library Settings.

2 On the Settings page, in the General Settings section, click Advanced Settings.

3 On the Advanced Settings page, in the Custom Send To Destination section, enter a destination name and URL to another document library.

4 Click OK.

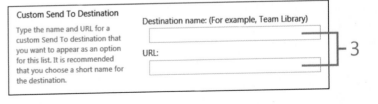

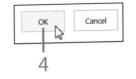

Copying or sharing documents

If you want to work on a SharePoint 2013 document at a later point in time or location at which you know you won't have internet access, you might want to download a copy of it to your local computer beforehand and then upload your updated document when you're back on line.

Also, it's very common to send a document's link to someone via email to let them know its location or invite them to edit it.

Download a copy of a document

1 On the ribbon of your document library, click the Files tab.

2 Click to add a check mark to the left of a document title. (Hover over the title to see the check mark option.)

3 On the ribbon, click Download A Copy.

4 Click Save.

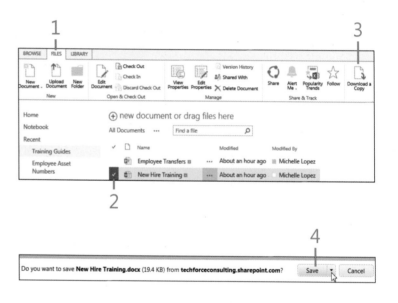

> **⚠ CAUTION** A downloaded copy on your local computer will not remain synchronized with the version on SharePoint.

Share a document

1 On the ribbon of your document library, click the Files tab.

2 Click to add a check mark to the left of a document title. (Hover over the title to see the check mark option.)

3 On the ribbon, click Share.

4 In the Invite People text box, add email names or addresses to Invite others to edit or view the document.

5 Enter an optional message to be delivered with the email invitation.

6 Click Share.

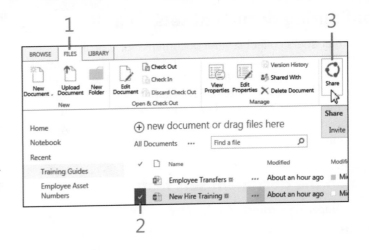

Configuring document sets on a site

Project managers collect several documents for a project: Project Charters, Project Schedules, and Business Requirements. Using document sets, you can organize and manage several items together as a single item. For instance, you might want to change the Status Category of each document to "Complete." With document sets, you can change them all at once instead of one at a time.

Unlike a document library, document sets include a Welcome page that displays metadata or properties common to all documents in the set. The tasks that follow will show you how to turn on the document set feature on your site, configure a document library to support the document set feature, and create a new document set.

Turn on the document sets feature

1 In the upper-right corner of the window, click the Settings icon.

2 On the menu that appears, click Site Settings.

3 On the Site Settings page, in the Site Collection Administration section, click Site Collection Features.

4 Click the Activate button for Document Sets.

Configure document set options

1 In the upper-right corner of the window, click the Settings icon.

2 On the menu that appears, click Site Settings.

3 On the Site Settings page, in the Web Designer Galleries section, click Site Content Types.

4 On the Site Content Types page, in the Document Set Content Types section, click Document Set.

5 On the Site Content Type page, click Document Set settings.

6 On the Document Set Settings page, customize the document as described in the following:

   • Select the available site content types to allow in this document set.

   • Select a default content type and browse to associate a default file to be automatically included in the document set. Additional default files can be included by clicking the Add New Default Content link.

   • Select the Shared check box to share that property value across a document set. Changing the property value on the document set applies that change to all documents within that set.

   • Select which columns to add to the document set's Welcome page.

   • Click Customize The Welcome Page to edit a Web Part Page associated with the content type.

7 Click OK to save changes.

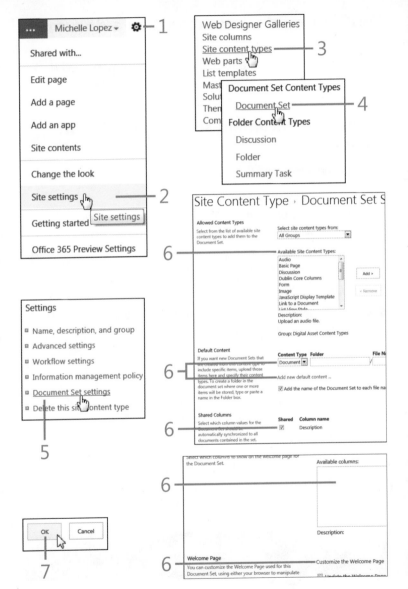

Configuring document sets on a document library

Unlike a document library, document sets include a Welcome page that displays metadata or properties common to all documents in the set. This section will introduce you to enabling the document set feature on your site, show you how to configure a document library to support the document set feature, and demonstrate how to create a new document set.

Enable the document sets on a document library

1 On the ribbon of your document library, click the Library tab.

2 In the Settings group, click Library Settings.

3 On the Settings page, in the General Settings section, click Advanced Settings.

4 On the Advanced Settings page, in the Content Types section, click the Yes option for Allow Management Of Content Types?

5 Click OK.

6 On the Settings page, in the Content Types section, click Add From Existing Site Content Types.

(continued on next page)

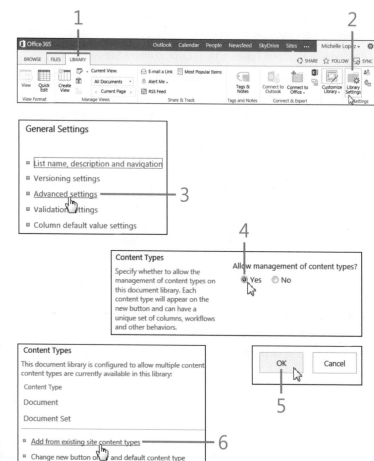

(continued on next page)

> **(→) TRY THIS** Create a custom content type from a document set and add it to a document library.

Enable the document sets on a document library *(continued)*

7 In the Select Site Content Types From list box, select Document Set Content Types.

8 In the Available Site Content Types section, select Document Set and click Add.

9 Click OK.

7 →

Select site content types from:
Document Set Content Types ▾

8 →

Available Site Content Types:

Document Set

Content types to add:

Add >

< Remove

Description:
Create a document set when you want to manage multiple documents as a single work product.

Group: Document Set Content Types

OK   Cancel

9

Create a document set

1 On the ribbon of your document library, click the Files tab.

2 In the New group, click New Document and then, on the menu that appears, click Document Set.

3 In the New Document Set dialog box, enter a name and optional description for the document set.

4 Click Save.

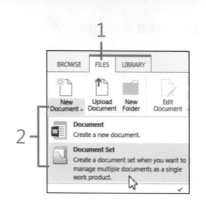

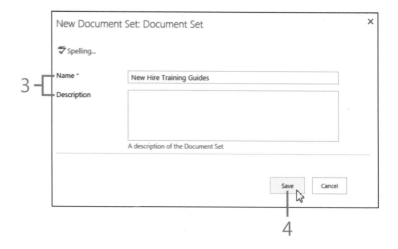

TRY THIS Edit and save a shared property on the Welcome page of the Document Set. The property for each document contained in that set will reflect the update.

Working with media

7

In this section:

- Introducing the Asset Library app
- Uploading and tagging media files
- Tagging media files
- Organizing by using keywords and metadata
- Working with video files
- Using SharePoint assets in Microsoft Office
- Adding media to a SharePoint page

Up to this point, we have only worked with documents as content within the Microsoft SharePoint 2013 platform. But, if your organization is like others, you might find that documents are not the only content sources you have; you probably also have to work with video, audio, and image files.

In previous sections, we have gone into detail about the concept of metadata and how it is used. Recall that metadata is simply information about content (or, put more generically, information about information). When it comes to an image file, some examples of metadata might include the date the picture was taken, the individuals in the image, and GPS coordinates of where the image was taken. You might also hear people refer to metadata as *tags*, as well. In the end, whether the term used is metadata or tags, its primary purpose is to assist in searching for content based on the assigned values.

In this section we will show how to create, configure and work with the improved features within SharePoint 2013—the SharePoint Asset Library app. Using this template, you can store media files by using the expanded feature set, which will also make it possible for you to recognize metadata fields, promote them as columns, facilitate navigation and filtering based on metadata values, and associate related content to media files.

Introducing the Asset Library app

An asset library is a SharePoint 2013 app that has been optimized for the storage of digital assets, which can include audio, image, and video assets. The default view for this library presents the assets in a thumbnail view.

Create an asset library

1 On the Quick Launch bar, click Site Contents.

2 On the Site Contents page, in the Lists, libraries, And Other Apps section, click the Add An App icon.

(continued on next page)

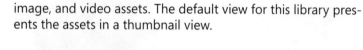

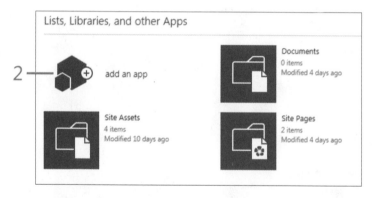

Create an asset library *(continued)*

3 On the Your Apps page, scroll to the Apps You Can Add section.

4 Click the Assets Library icon.

5 In the Adding Asset Library dialog box, in the Name text box, enter a name for the asset library.

6 Click the Create button.

TRY THIS Create an asset library by using the Asset Library app.

Uploading and tagging media files

One of the optimizations implemented out of the box is the library's ability to recognize extended metadata information contained with the media, such as author, date taken, individuals in the image, resolution of the camera, and comments. The SharePoint 2013 library also has the ability to generate and display a thumbnail image.

Upload and tag media files

1 On the Quick Launch bar, click the Site Contents link.

2 On the Site Contents page, in the Lists, libraries, And Other Apps section, click the asset library with which you want to work.

3 In the library, click the New Item link.

(continued on next page)

Upload and tag media files *(continued)*

4 In the Add A Document dialog box, click the Browse button to select a single image to upload

5 Click OK.

6 In the Metadata Input dialog box, fill in the relevant information.

7 Click the Save button.

Add a document   ×

Choose a file   [   ] Browse... ──── 4

Upload files using Windows Explorer instead

☑ Overwrite existing files

OK   Cancel

|
5

Content Type   Image ▼
Upload an image.

Name *   DSC03308 (1)   JPG

Title   [   ]

Keywords   [   ]

For example: scenery, mountains, trees, nature

Comments   [   ]   ── 6

A summary of this asset

Author   [   ]
The primary author

Date Picture Taken 10/8/2011   🗓 1 PM ▼ 45 ▼

Copyright   [   ]

Created at 12/18/2012 9:07 AM by ☐ Johnathan Lightfoot   Save   Cancel
Last modified at 12/18/2012 9:07 AM by ☐ Johnathan Lightfoot

|
7

TIP The preceding steps will assist you when you are uploading single items. If you need to upload multiple items, though, this procedure can be cumbersome. The following task, "Upload multiple files," will assist you.

TRY THIS Upload an image from your computer to the asset library.

Upload multiple files

1 On the Quick Launch bar, click Site Contents.

2 On the Site Contents page, in the Lists, libraries, And Other Apps section, click the asset library with which you want to work.

(continued on next page)

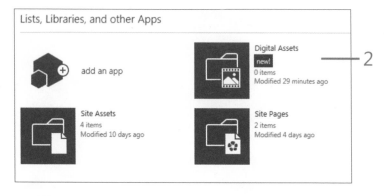

Upload multiple files *(continued)*

3 In another window, navigate to and open and the folder that contains the files that you want to upload in Windows Explorer.

4 Select the files that you want to upload.

5 Drag the files over to the section in SharePoint labeled New Item Or Drag Files Here and release the mouse.

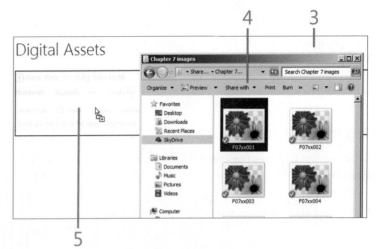

TRY THIS   Upload multiple digital files from your computer.

Tagging media files

You might have noticed that when you use the drag-and-drop method to upload images to SharePoint 2013 that you are not presented with the dialog box prompting you to enter metadata information. This might seem like an inconvenience initially, but can you imagine if you uploaded five, ten, or more images, simultaneously having to go through all of those separate dialog boxes? All is not lost, however. If you need to tag multiple files individually you still have the ability to do so.

Tag media files

1 On the Site Contents page, in the Lists, libraries, And Other Apps section, click the asset library that contains the files you need to tag.

2 Click the file to which you want to add metadata.

(continued on next page)

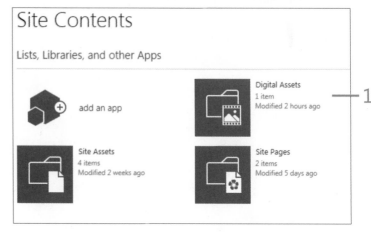

126 Tagging media files: Tag media files

Tag media files *(continued)*

3 On the ribbon, click the View tab and then, in the Manage group, click the Edit Item button.

4 In the Add Content Dialog box, fill in the metadata information for the file.

5 Click the Save button.

Content Type	Image ▾
	Upload an image.

Name *   DSC03308 (1)   .JPG

Title

Keywords

For example: scenery, mountains, trees, nature

Comments

A summary of this asset

Author

The primary author

Date Picture Taken   10/8/2011   📅   1 PM ▾   45 ▾

Copyright

Created at 12/18/2012 9:07 AM by ☐ Johnathan Lightfoot

Last modified at 12/18/2012 9:07 AM by ☐ Johnathan Lightfoot

Save   Cancel

TRY THIS   Tag a few of your digital files.

What are Enterprise Keywords?

Enterprise Keywords are a set of agreed-upon keywords that you can use when tagging content within your organization. By using them, you can work with a set of keywords that are accepted and recognized by everyone within your organization. Enterprise Keywords are different from the keywords listing that you might have used up to this point. The standard keyword list comprises your own tags, which you designated, but when you use it, you can end up using keywords that are not generally acknowledged within your organization. By using the personally selected keywords alone, you might experience problems when others try to locate content based on those keywords.

In the next task, you see how to customize an asset library to use Enterprise Keywords.

Organizing by using keywords and metadata

Media files (audio, image, and video) oftentimes share similar characteristics, such as file formats, size, and so on. SharePoint 2013 is able to use this information to assist you in organizing information and ease the search effort for certain kinds of content.

With SharePoint, you have the ability to extend the capabilities of a standard asset library. Metadata navigation assists you by filtering media files based on metadata.

Enable Enterprise Keywords

1 In the asset library for which you want to enable Enterprise Keywords, on the ribbon, click the Library tab.

2 In the Settings group, click Library Settings.

3 On the Library Settings page, in the Permissions and Management group, click the Enterprise Metadata And Keywords Settings link.

4 On the Enterprise Metadata And Keywords Settings page, select the check box adjacent to Add An Enterprise Keywords Column To This List And Enable Keyword Synchronization.

5 Click the OK button.

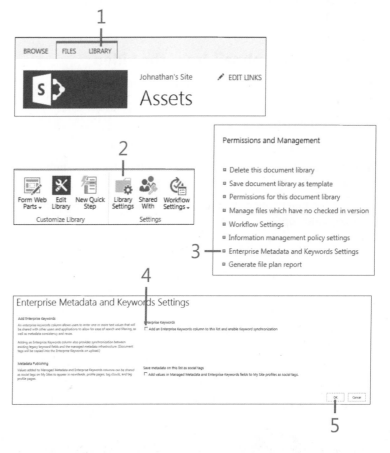

Working with video files

The asset library has several new features for working with video files. In the past, you only had the ability to upload a file with an out-of-the-box configuration of SharePoint. Within SharePoint 2013, however, you can also select a frame, an image from your computer, or a web address to use as the thumbnail image for the video. You can also associate related content to a video file. This could be a separate document located in a different library such as a workbook.

The upload process for a video is the same as if you were going to upload any other type of file. It is when you are shown the metadata dialog box that you can see the differences. In this task, you learn how to choose a thumbnail image for a video and how to associate related files to video files.

Capture a thumbnail from the video

1   In your assets library, select the video file with which you want to work.

2   On the ribbon, click the Manage tab.

3   In the Actions group, click the Edit Properties button.

4   In the the Edit Properties dialog box, click the Change Thumbnail link.

5   From the three options that appear, click the Capture Thumbnail From Video option.

(continued on next page)

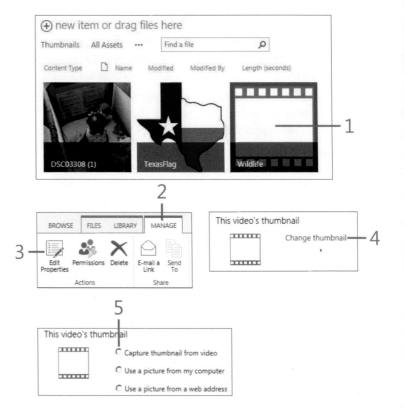

Capture a thumbnail from the video *(continued)*

6 In the video window that opens, click the Play button.

7 Click the Camera icon to capture the image.

8 On the Video Properties page, click Save.

Use an image from your computer as a thumbnail

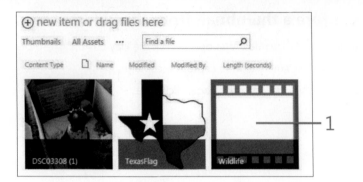

1. In your assets library, select the video file with which you want to work.

2. On the ribbon, click the Manage tab.

3. In the Actions group, click the Edit Properties button.

4. In the Edit Properties dialog box, click the Change Thumbnail link.

5. From the three options that appear, click the Use A Picture From My Computer option.

(continued on next page)

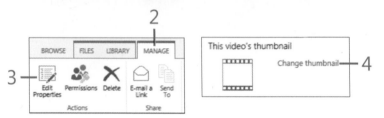

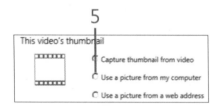

Use an image from your computer as a thumbnail *(continued)*

6 Click the Browse button that appears.

7 In the Choose File To Upload dialog box, select the image that you want to use.

8 Click the Open button.

9 Click the Upload Button.

10 On the Video Properties page, click Save.

Use a picture from a web address (on the Internet) as a thumbnail

1 In your assets library, select the video file with which you want to work.

2 On the ribbon, click the Manage tab.

3 In the Actions group, click the Edit Properties button.

4 In the Edit Properties dialog box, click the Change Thumbnail link.

(continued on next page)

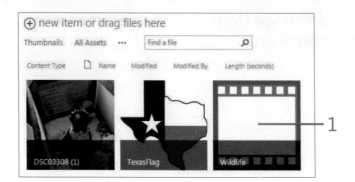

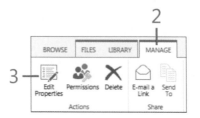

TRY THIS Upload three video files using each of the previous three methods to designate the thumbnail image.

Use a picture from a web address (on the Internet) as a thumbnail *(continued)*

5 From the three options that appears click the Use a picture from a web address option.

6 Type the web address for the image.

7 Click the Preview button.

8 Click the Save button.

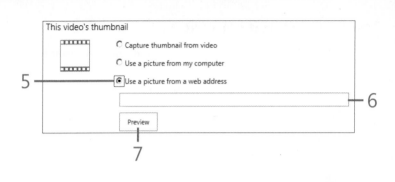

Associate related content to a video file

1 In your assets library, select the video file with which you want to work.

2 In the Related section, click the Add New Item link.

3 In the Add A Document dialog box, click the Browse button.

(continued on next page)

Associate related content to a video
file *(continued)*

4 In the Choose A File To Upload dialog box, select the file that you want to associate with the video.

5 Click the Open button.

6 Click the OK button.

7 Fill out the metadata information.

8 Click Save.

Add a document   ×

Choose a file   C:\Users\Administrator\SkyDrive\Presentations\Don't L   Browse...

Upload files using Windows Explorer instead

☑ Overwrite existing files

OK   Cancel

6

Video Properties

Content Type   Video ▾
                    Upload or link to a video.

Name *   Wildlife

Description

                    A summary of the Video

Owner   Johnathan Lightfoot x
                    The owner of the Video

Show Download Link ☑
                    Specifies whether a button appears on the video player page that allows the user
                    to download the video being played.

Show Embed Link   ☑
                    Specifies whether a button appears on the video player that allows the user to
                    get an embed code for the video being played.

People In Video   Enter names or email addresses...
                    The people appearing in the video.

Created at 12/18/2012 1:22 PM by ☐ Johnathan Lightfoot   Save   Cancel
Last modified at 12/18/2012 1:38 PM by ☐ Johnathan Lightfoot

7

8

Choose File to Upload

Administrator ▸ SkyDrive ▸ Presentations ▸   Search Presentations

Organize ▾   New folder

Favorites   Name ▴   Date modified   Type   Size
  Desktop   📁 GP Sales Conference   10/19/2012 1:31 PM   File folder
  Downloads   📁 GP Webinar Series   10/19/2012 1:31 PM   File folder
  Recent Places   📁 Press   10/19/2012 11:58 AM File folder
  SkyDrive   📁 SPC2011   10/19/2012 1:32 PM   File folder
                       Don't Let Your Training Fall Off of a Cliff   8/29/2012 10:30 AM   Microsoft PowerPoi...   3,533 KB
Libraries   Don't Let Your Training Fall Off of a Cliff   8/29/2012 10:30 AM   Microsoft Word Doc...   18 KB
  Documents   Falling off of the cliff   8/29/2012 10:30 AM   Microsoft PowerPoi...   92 KB
  Music   GDAIS v5   8/29/2012 10:30 AM   Microsoft PowerPoi...   4,915 KB
  Pictures   GP Strategies_SharePointSummitToronto_Pr...   8/29/2012 10:30 AM   Microsoft PowerPoi...   436 KB
  Videos   GP%20Strategies%20Services%20Presenta...   8/29/2012 10:30 AM   Microsoft PowerPoi...   2,574 KB
                       IRONSP - Conference Content Management ...   8/29/2012 10:30 AM   Microsoft PowerPoi...   608 KB
Computer   Prezi Script - SharePoint LMS Integration   8/29/2012 10:30 AM   Microsoft Word Doc...   28 KB
  OS (C:)   SharePoint Summit.pez   5/3/2012 4:04 PM   PEZ File   3,223 KB
  DVD Drive (F:) 15.(

File name: publishing sites   All Files (*.*)

                                                        Open   Cancel

4

5

Using SharePoint assets in Microsoft Office

Today, so much of what we do entails creating and working with documents. In the past, documents typically consisted mainly of text, but now, they increasingly contain images, charts and spreadsheets, as well. Again, in bygone days, to process this type of document usually involved calling upon the services of a professional typesetter. Several years ago Microsoft introduced Microsoft Office, a suite of products that revolutionized desktop

publishing for the masses. Through the Office interface, anyone can incorporate digital assets into documents with ease.

Microsoft SharePoint 2013 carries on the tradition introduced within SharePoint 2010 of providing a tight integration between SharePoint and the Office product line. Thus, assets that are stored in SharePoint can be added into Office documents.

Connect an asset library to Office

1 In your assets library, at the top of the window, click the Library tab.

2 On the ribbon, in the Connect & Export group, click the Connect To Office button.

3 In the pop-up message box that appears, click the Yes Button.

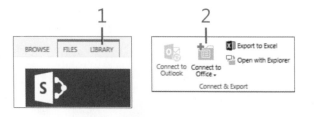

1

2

3

Connect Office to your portal

In order to connect libraries in this site to Microsoft Office, your machine must register the user profile service application used by this site. Doing this will allow Office to display shortcuts to, and synchronize templates from, libraries specified by you and the administrator of the service application. Only click 'Yes' if you trust the site specified below.

https://techforceconsulting-my.sharepoint.com/personal/johnathan_techforceintl_com/

| Yes | No |

→ TRY THIS Connect your asset library to Office.

✓ TIP If you are using an Office 365 instance of SharePoint, you will also need to connect to the service from within Office.

Connect to Office 365

1 Open an Office application, such as Microsoft Word 2013, Microsoft PowerPoint 2013, or Microsoft Excel 2013.

2 Click the File tab to display the Backstage view.

3 Click the Account tab.

4 Click Add A Service.

5 On the menu that opens, point to the Storage option.

6 On the submenu that appears, click Office 365 SharePoint.

7 In the Sign In To Office dialog box, click the Sign In Button.

8 Enter your User ID and Password and then click Sign In.

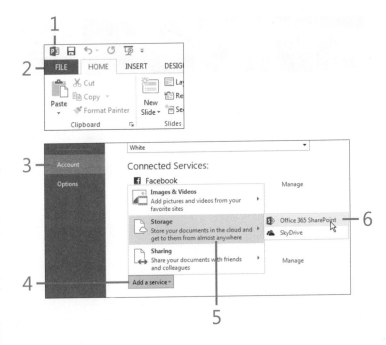

TIP When using Office 365, it can take up to several hours before the Office 365 sites become available for you within Office applications.

Adding media to a SharePoint page

You might have a need to add images to a SharePoint page. In these instances, you will note that SharePoint has provided an easy interface through which you can use do this.

Insert an image from SharePoint

1 Go to the page on which you want to insert an image and then, on the ribbon, click the Page tab.

2 In the Edit group, click the Edit Button.

3 Click in a blank area of the page.

(continued on next page)

Insert an image from SharePoint (continued)

4 Back on the ribbon, click the Insert tab.

5 In the Media group, click the Picture button.

6 On the menu that appears, click From SharePoint.

7 In the Select An Asset dialog box, in the pane on the left, select the image that you want to add from the library in which it resides.

8 Click the Insert button.

9 Click the Save button.

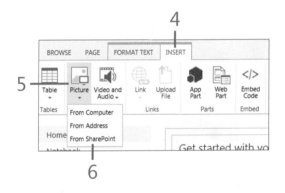

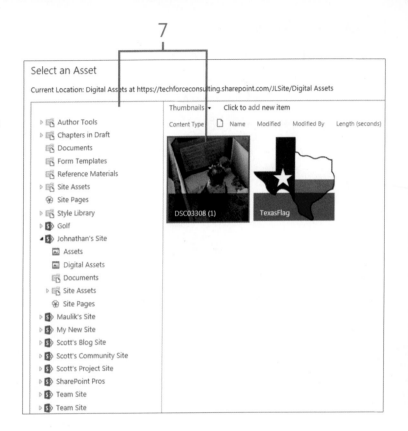

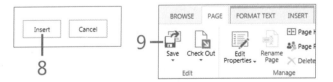

Insert video on a SharePoint page

1 Click an empty area on the SharePoint page.

2 On the ribbon, click the Insert tab.

3 In the Media group, click the Video And Audio button.

4 On the menu that opens, click From SharePoint.

(continued on next page)

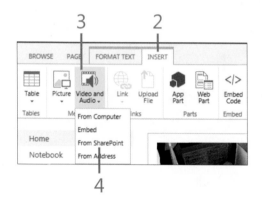

Insert video in a SharePoint page *(continued)*

5 In the Select An Asset dialog box, in the pane on the right, select the video that you want to add from the library (in the left pane) in which it resides.

6 Click the Insert button.

7 Click the Save button.

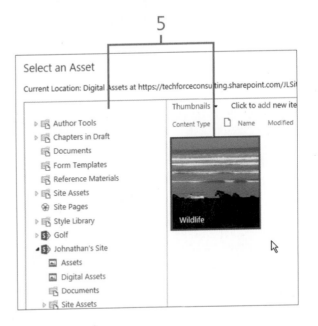

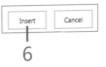

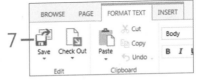

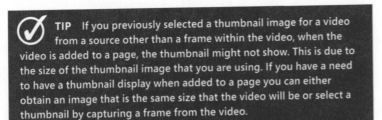

TIP If you previously selected a thumbnail image for a video from a source other than a frame within the video, when the video is added to a page, the thumbnail might not show. This is due to the size of the thumbnail image that you are using. If you have a need to have a thumbnail display when added to a page you can either obtain an image that is the same size that the video will be or select a thumbnail by capturing a frame from the video.

TRY THIS Add a video to an asset library and then add the video to a SharePoint page.

Using SkyDrive Pro

In previous versions of the Microsoft SharePoint platform, there was a feature called Workspaces (or, if you are familiar with using the MOSS 2007 version of the platform, it was referred to as Groove). For the SharePoint 2013 platform, Workspaces has been replaced with SkyDrive Pro. Workspaces (Groove) was a feature that a team could use for sharing documents on which they were collaborating.

This was a peer-to-peer networking feature that was used for downloading libraries to a computer for local storage and usage. This was quite helpful in case you needed to work on documents from a location that didn't have access to the Internet (on a plane, for instance). You were able to download the documents that you wanted to work on ahead of time and then, while you were disconnected from the Internet, you could make changes to the documents. When you were once again connected, the application would automatically upload your changes and synchronize them with the documents in the library (or site).

You might already be familiar with Microsoft's personal storage service called SkyDrive. This is a free cloud-based service available to anyone who sets up a Microsoft Account. SkyDrive gives you the flexibility to access your files, no matter what device you're using.

In this section:

- Accessing your SkyDrive Pro account
- Saving files to SkyDrive Pro
- Saving files to be accessible only to you
- Sharing SkyDrive Pro files
- Following SkyDrive Pro documents
- Locating followed documents by using the newsfeed
- Locating followed documents by using SkyDrive Pro
- Synchronizing SkyDrive Pro to your local computer
- Discontinuing sync between SkyDrive Pro and your local device

What is SkyDrive Pro

You can consider SkyDrive Pro as SkyDrive for business. When you store files on SkyDrive Pro, initially only you have access to them, but you can easily share these files with your coworkers if you choose to. You are also able to access them from your mobile device. Depending on how your organization has set up your SharePoint implementation, the information is either stored on Microsoft's servers (if you are using SharePoint Online) or they are stored on your organization's servers, if you have SharePoint 2013 installed on the premises.

With SkyDrive Pro, you can do the following:

- Store and organize your private documents and other files in a secure location in the cloud or on your company's SharePoint servers

- Share files and folders with other people in your organization and give them permission to review or edit the content

- Synchronize files and folders in your SkyDrive Pro and other SharePoint libraries with your computer or mobile devices so that you can access your content offline

Storing your business files in SkyDrive Pro makes good business sense, because it provides a secure, centralized place to maintain content, find what you need, and share selected items on which you and others can collaborate.

> **TIP** The SkyDrive Pro feature not only replaced Workspaces but it also has taken on the role of serving as the content repository area for your My Site. As such, you now have one convenient place for your documents that are not stored within a team site, and it also doubles as a place where you can share information.

 SEE ALSO For additional information on Using SkyDrive Pro, go to *http://aka.ms/SP2013PS/SkyDrivePro*.

Accessing your SkyDrive Pro account

Each SharePoint 2013 account is set up with a SkyDrive Pro account. Remember that there are two main differences between SkyDrive and SkyDrive Pro:

1. Skydrive is a free online storage option that provides you with a personal library that you can use to to upload and access files form any of your devices.

2. Skydrive Pro provides you with a personal library that you use for business.

Access SkyDrive Pro

1 On the toolbar at the top of your SharePoint site, click the SkyDrive link.

TIP The SkyDrive link that you see at the top of your Office 365 or SharePoint 2013 pages is actually an abbreviation of SkyDrive Pro. This refers to your SkyDrive Pro library, not your personal SkyDrive account that you might have.

TRY THIS Access your SkyDrive Pro account and have a look around. If you have a personal SkyDrive account (the consumer version offered by Microsoft) you will notice that none of the files that you have in your SkyDrive account are present in your SkyDrive Pro account.

Saving files to SkyDrive Pro

You can treat your SkyDrive Pro account as a storage area. (Refer to Section 12, "Using SharePoint with Office 2013," for directions on connecting your SkyDrive Pro library to Microsoft Office.)

When you open SkyDrive Pro initially, you'll notice that you have a folder named Shared With Everyone. As the name implies, anything that you place in this folder is accessible to anyone in your organization by default. (This is similar to the Shared Documents library in SharePoint 2010.) If you store a file in a folder other than the Shared With Everyone folder, it will only be accessible to you by default.

Save files to be shared with everyone

1 On the toolbar at the top of your SharePoint site, click the SkyDrive link.

2 On the SkyDrive page, on the Quick Launch bar, select the library that you want to use for saving files.

3 Follow the instructions in Section 12 for connecting a SharePoint site to Office.

4 Open the Office file that you want to save to the SkyDrive Pro folder (in this example, a Microsoft Excel worksheet) and then, on the ribbon, click the File tab to display the Backstage view.

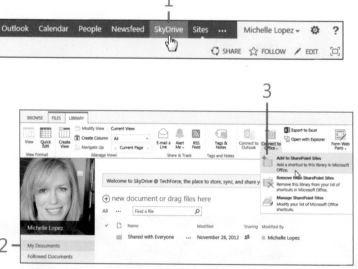

(continued on next page)

TRY THIS Save a few documents to the Shared With Everyone folder. Then, ask one of your colleagues to access the files. He can do this by performing a People Search for your name and then clicking Shared With Everyone.

Save files to be shared with everyone *(continued)*

5 Click the Save As tab.

6 In the Save As section, click Computer.

7 Click Browse.

8 In the Save As dialog box, in the Navigation pane on the left, select the SharePoint Sites folder.

9 Double-click My Site.

10 Double-click Documents.

11 Double-click the Shared With Everyone folder.

12 Type a name for the file.

13 Click Save.

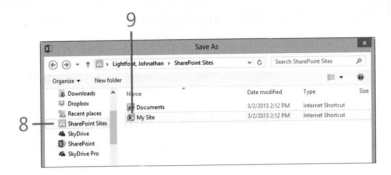

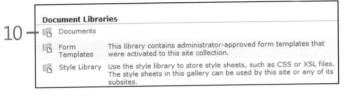

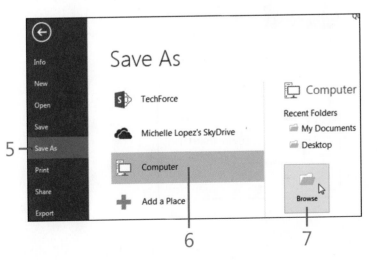

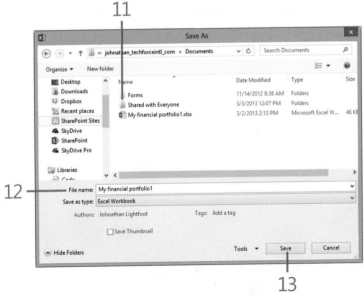

Saving files to be accessible only to you

In the previous task, we went over saving files that anyone can access and open. However, you probably have files that you want to store to which only you should have access. The tasks that follow show you how to save files such that they are accessible only by you. You will also see how you can selectively share these files with certain individuals.

Save files for access only by you

1 On the toolbar at the top of your SharePoint site, click the SkyDrive link.

2 On the SkyDrive page, on the Quick Launch bar, select the library that you want to use for saving files.

3 Follow the instructions in Section 12 for connecting a SharePoint Site to Office.

4 Open the Office file that you want to save (in this example, a Microsoft Excel worksheet) and then, on the ribbon, click the File tab to display the Backstage view.

(continued on next page)

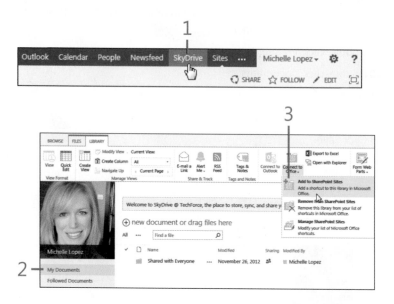

Save files for access only by you *(continued)*

5 Click the Save As tab.

6 In the Save As section, click Computer.

7 Click Browse.

8 In the Save As dialog box, in the Navigation pane on the left, select the SharePoint Sites folder.

9 Double-click My Site.

10 Double-click Documents.

11 Select the location to which you want to save the file.

12 Type a name for the file.

13 Click Save.

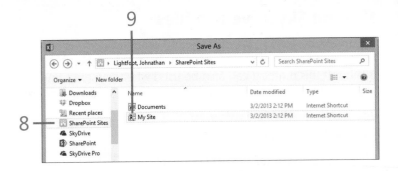

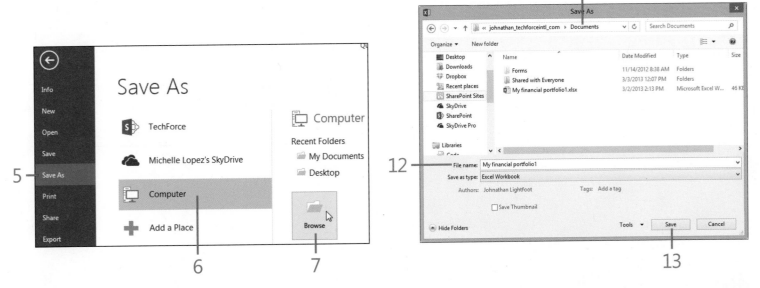

Sharing SkyDrive Pro files

You might be used to saving files and granting permissions to coworkers, permitting or denying them access those files. Although this method can also be used when you are using SkyDrive Pro, you might not want to give access to your entire SkyDrive Pro library. Perhaps you only want to give coworkers access to a specific file, instead. In this case, granting permission to your entire SkyDrive Pro library might seem like overkill.

Share SkyDrive Pro files

1 On the toolbar at the top of your SharePoint site, click the SkyDrive link.

2 On the SkyDrive page, select the file that you want to share with others.

3 Click the More Options ellipsis (...) and then, in the Properties pop-up box that appears, click the Share link.

(continued on next page)

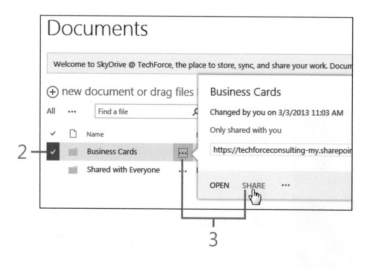

Share SkyDrive Pro files *(continued)*

4 In the Share dialog box, do one of the following:

  a If you want to share the file with coworkers within your company or organization, type their names and then select them from the drop-down selection box that appears.

  b If the people are not within your company, you can type their email address.

  c If you want to share the file with everyone within your organization you can type **Everyone**.

5 To the right of the Invite People text box, chose whether the invitees can edit the document or view it only.

6 Enter a message that will be sent to the invitees.

7 Click Share.

Share 'Business Cards'

🔒 Only shared with you

Invite people

Enter names, email addresses, or 'Everyone'.

Can edit
Can edit
Can view

Include a personal message with this invitation (Optional).

SHOW OPTIONS

Share   Cancel

4 5 6 7

TIP An email invitation will be sent to the people with whom you share the content. If you don't want to send an email to the new people, click Show Options and clear the Send An Email Invitation check box before sharing.

Requiring sign-in

If you would like to share a document with others who might or might not be in your company or organization, clear the Require Sign-In check box. Remember that this is used for the sharing of an individual document and not for folders.

Unlike previous versions of the SharePoint 2013 platform in which you were limited to only being able to share files with coworkers, SkyDrive Pro features provide the ability for you to easily share files with people who are not directly within your organization (vendors, clients, suppliers, and so on). The main concern here, of course, is security. After all, if you are sharing a file with someone in your company, the security is pretty much taken care of through Active Directory. However, if you want to share a document with someone who is not a member of your organization's Active Directory, how do you know that the file will be accessible only to those you have designated? When you enter the email address of someone who is not located within your organization and you require that she sign in, she will have to do so with either a free Microsoft Account or one of your organization's accounts. If she doesn't have either a Microsoft Account or an organizational account, she is offered the opportunity to sign up for a free Microsoft Account.

Keep in mind that any invitations you send outside of your organization expire after seven days. If the individuals you invite do not access the file within that time frame, you will need to resend the invitation to them.

TIP By default, SharePoint sends an email notification to your invitees. If you have another way that you would like to inform them of their access to the file, click the Show Options hyperlink and clear the Send An Email Invitation check box.

TRY THIS Save a file to which you want to restrict access to only you. Then, share the file with one or two other people. If possible have one of them be from outside your organization. Observe the experience each person has when accessing your file.

Following SkyDrive Pro documents

When you share and collaborate on documents with others, you might want to keep abreast of any changes that are made to those documents. With SharePoint 2013 you can do this by "following" those documents. When you follow a document you are in essence elevating this document so that it will appear in your newsfeed. This way, you can receive notifications through your newsfeed when there have been changes made to it. This alleviates from you the burden of having to constantly open a document to check its status.

Follow SkyDrive Pro documents

1 On the toolbar at the top of your SharePoint site, click the SkyDrive link.

2 On the SkyDrive page, click the More Options ellipsis (...) next to the document that you want to follow.

3 In the Properties pop-up box that appears, click Follow.

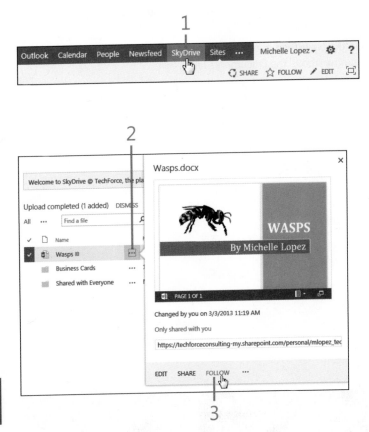

Locating followed documents by using the newsfeed

When you follow documents, you can end up monitoring several that could be located in various sites, libraries, and folders that might not be located on your SkyDrive Pro account.

SharePoint 2013 provides several ways for you to locate all of these files. One of those is through your newsfeed.

Find documents by using the newsfeed

1 On your About Me page, on the Quick Launch bar, click the Newsfeed link.

2 On the Newsfeed page, in the I'm Following section, click the number above the Documents label.

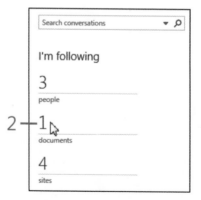

TRY THIS Locate all of the documents you have followed previously through the newsfeed.

Locating followed documents by using SkyDrive Pro

You can also find documents that you are following through the SkyDrive Pro interface.

Find documents by using SkyDrive Pro

1 On the toolbar at the top of your SharePoint site, click the SkyDrive link.

2 On the SkyDrive page, on the Quick Launch bar, click the Followed Documents link.

TRY THIS Locate the documents that you have followed through the SkyDrive Pro interface.

Synchronizing SkyDrive Pro to your local computer

You can synchronize a SkyDrive Pro library to your computer. When you synchronize the files initially, SharePoint automatically recognizes the name and web address of your SkyDrive Pro library. Also, by default it synchronizes your files to C:\Users\ [username]\SkyDrive Pro. After you have synchronized your

SkyDrive Pro library to your computer, you can access a local copy of your files located within your SkyDrive pro account. You are also able to add documents locally to your computer, which will also replicate over to your SkyDrive Pro account the next time you connect to your organization's network.

Synchronize SkyDrive Pro to your local computer

1 In the upper-right corner of your SharePoint Home page, click the Sync button.

2 In the Microsoft SkyDrive Pro dialog box, click the Sync Now button.

(continued on next page)

1

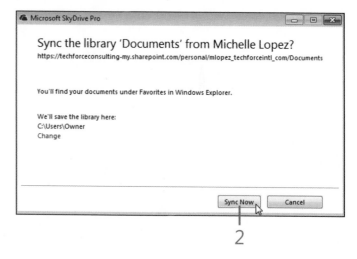

2

> **✓ TIP** To use this feature, you must have Office 2013 (Standard or Professional edition) or an Office 365 subscription with a license for Office applications.

Synchronize SkyDrive Pro to your local computer *(continued)*

3 On the next page of the Microsoft SkyDrive Pro dialog box, click the Show My Files button.

Microsoft SkyDrive Pro

Your files are syncing as we speak. Go take a look and watch them come in.

You can see your files here:
C:\Users\Owner\SkyDrive @ TechForce

Show my files...

3

TRY THIS Synchronize your SkyDrive Pro account to your local computer. Upon completion, view the files on your local computer and drag a file from another location on your computer to your SkyDrive Pro folder on your computer. Notice SharePoint pick up the file and it appears in your SharePoint 2013 SkyDrive Pro library.

Discontinuing sync between SkyDrive Pro and your local device

Being able to synchronize content on your SkyDrive Pro account with your local computer is a great convenience. However, be advised that when you do this you are actually introducing a possible security issue: remember that you are taking a file that is in a secure location and making the file available on your local device. If your computer is compromised—perhaps lost, stolen, or hacked—your synchronized files will then be available to whomever or whatever has compromised your computer.

Also, when you synchronize sites to your local computer you might end up with a site that houses more information than you can store on your local computer. You are able to synchronize up to 20,000 items from your SkyDrive Pro account to your local computer. Each file downloaded can be up to 2 GB in size. So, in theory, you can synchronize up to approximately 39 tera-bytes (TB) of data from your SkyDrive Pro account to your local device. I don't know about you, but I haven't seen many PCs or tablets lately with 39 TB of storage capacity!

Therefore (and not surprisingly), it is considered a best practice to stop synchronizing files, folders, or sites when you no longer require offline access to them.

Discontinue syncing SkyDrive Pro files with your local device

1   In the notification area, at the far right of the taskbar, click the up arrow.

2   Right-click the SkyDrive Pro icon.

3   On the shortcut menu that appears, click Stop Syncing A Folder.

(continued on next page)

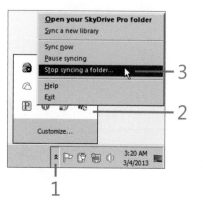

Discontinue synchronizing SkyDrive Pro files with your local device *(continued)*

4 In the Stop Syncing A Folder dialog box, select the item with which you want to stop synchronization.

5 Click Stop Syncing.

6 In the pop-up message box that appears, Click Yes.

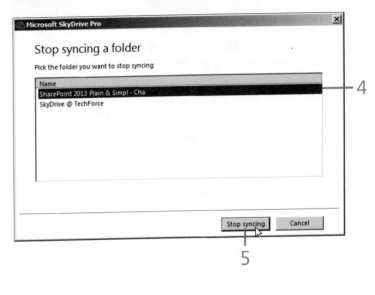

Limits on synchronizing content in SkyDrive Pro

Note the following limitations related to synchronizing libraries to your computer with SkyDrive Pro:

- You can synchronize up to 20,000 items in your
  SkyDrive Pro library, including folders and files.

- If you would like to synchronize libraries other than
  your SkyDrive Pro account, you are limited to 5,000
  items.

- For any library, you can download files up to 2 GB in
  size.

 TRY THIS   Discontinue synchronizing your SkyDrive Pro
account and your local computer.

Using information management policies

9

With Microsoft SharePoint 2013 sites, groups of people can quickly consolidate a large number of files and content. Other sections in this book address methods of categorizing, organizing, and searching this information. Information management policies, however, give you the ability to apply regulatory rules to your content to control aspects such as data retention and disposal of data.

Information management policies are implemented via the application of rules (policies) that are applied to files to help regulate the usage of documents within your organization. Four main types of policies are included with SharePoint 2013: retention, auditing, document label, and document barcode. (The document label and document barcode policies have been deprecated in SharePoint 2013. For more information, see "Introduction to information management policies" on the next page.)

Information management policies are not typically needed for the casual user or by small groups of users with informal rules about how files are created, modified, or deleted. However, if you have corporate policies or industry regulatory guidelines that you must follow, information management policies can help.

In this section:

- Introduction to information management policies
- Accessing site content type information management policies
- Accessing list information management policies
- Creating content type retention policies on a library
- Set library or folder-based retention schedules
- Creating auditing policies
- Viewing an audit report
- Document label and document barcode policies

Introduction to information management policies

Information management policies typically exist to enforce corporate or regulatory policies that apply to the management of content. For example, your company might require the storage of an audit trail listing all users who have ever viewed a particular document. It is important to understand that information management policies have different mechanisms of action. For example, some policies might prevent a user from removing a file, or they might simply log that a user has deleted a file.

Information management policies can be applied across an entire site to a particular content type, or they can be limited to documents within a single library or folder. Unlike other changes to content types or site columns, policies defined at the site-collection level can override any changes at a lower level.

Four types of retention policies can be defined.

Retention

Schedule how content is managed and disposed by specifying a sequence of retention stages. If you specify multiple stages, each stage will occur one after the other in the order they appear on this page.

Note: If the Library and Folder Based Retention feature is active, list administrators can override content type policies with their own retention schedules. To prevent this, deactivate the feature on the site collection.

☐ Enable Retention

Auditing

Specify the events that should be audited for documents and items subject to this policy.

☐ Enable Auditing

Barcodes

Assigns a barcode to each document or item. Optionally, Microsoft Office applications can require users to insert these barcodes into documents.

☐ Enable Barcodes

Labels

You can add a label to a document to ensure that important information about the document is included when it is printed. To specify the label, type the text you want to use in the "Label format" box. You can use any combination of fixed text or document properties, except calculated or built-in properties such as GUID or CreatedBy. To start a new line, use the \n character sequence.

☐ Enable Labels

⚠ **CAUTION**   Document label and barcode policies have been deprecated in SharePoint 2013. It is recommended that you do not use these features if they are made available within your implementation of SharePoint 2013.

Note that some of the information management policies available in Microsoft SharePoint 2013 appear primarily to support previous versions and are not recommended for use in the 2013 version. This includes the document label policies and document barcode policies.

Types of information management policies

The following list provides a brief overview of the four main types of information management policies:

- Retention policies are configured to automatically perform document operations after a particular threshold (typically a date calculation) has been passed. They are used to manage the retention of documents and can be used to ensure that documents meeting designated rules are not deleted from the system. Conversely, these can also force the review or deletion of documents that are too old or have not been recently updated.

- Auditing policies are used to write document activity to a centralized log. They ensure that certain types of document-related activities, such as viewing, editing, or deleting, are recorded permanently. These policies log user activity rather than restrict user actions.

- Document label policies can be used to force users to add labels to Microsoft Office–based documents that include basic document data such as approval dates or document version number. This label can be displayed, for example, in the header or footer of the document.

- Document barcode policies operate in a similar fashion as labels, but they use Office to inject a barcode to uniquely identify the document.

Information management policy inheritance

Information management policies in SharePoint 2013 can be inherited, either from parent content types or from parent folders (if applied to a list). In both cases, it is possible that you will be unable to make any changes to a policy because your site administrator has already made a change at a higher level. In either case, you will either need to remove or edit the policy at the parent object level or talk with your administrator about the best approach to take.

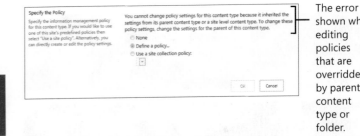

The error shown when editing policies that are overridden by parent content type or folder.

> **✓ TIP** Site Policies might require special activation on your site by an administrator. If you are unable to perform the tips in this section, consult your administrator.

Accessing site content type information management policies

You can view the information management policies that are associated with your root (topmost) site content types. This can help you decide whether there are existing policies in place that will change how you use content types within your lists.

Access site content information management policies

1 In the upper-right corner of the window, click the Settings icon (the small gear graphic) and then, on the menu that appears, click Site Settings.

2 On the Site Settings page, in the Web Designer Galleries section, click Site Content Types.

3 Click the name of the site content type that you want to access.

4 Click Information Management Policy Settings.

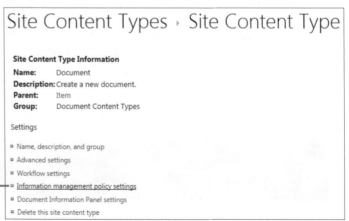

> **TIP** If you are trying to edit a site content type that is inherited from a parent site, you will first need to click on the value under the Source column prior to clicking on the name of the site content type in the Site Content Types column.

> **TRY THIS** Verify that you can access the information management policies for the Document and Basic Page content types.

Accessing list information management policies

In the same way that you can manage information management policies for site content types, you can also access information management policies for a particular SharePoint 2013 list or folder. The difference with this approach is that the policies on a single document library or folder are not used elsewhere on the site and will not impact other users.

When you access information management policy settings at the library level, you have the option to apply retention schedules to all documents in the library rather than to specific content types. Also, information policy settings at the site content type level can be configured to override your local settings. In this case, you will receive a warning noting that you cannot change the settings locally.

Access library-based information management policies

1 In a document library, on the ribbon, click the Library tab.

2 In the settings group, click the Library Settings button.

3 On the Settings page, in the Permissions And Management section, click Information Management Policy Settings.

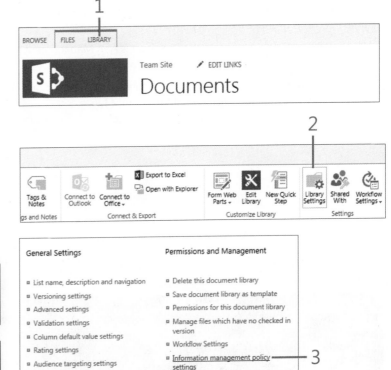

> **TIP** You will generally want to apply list information management rules to document or media libraries because these are the types of content that are regulated by policy.

> **TIP** To make the Library tab available, you must have already navigated to a list or library

Creating content type retention policies on a library

Retention policies cover both the automated retention and expiration of documents. One simple retention policy would be to automatically remove documents from a library that have not been modified in a very long time or to remove previous drafts (older versions) of a document after a period of time.

Content type retention policies can be defined site-wide, or they can be defined within a single library. The steps below cover adding a content type policy to a library.

Create a content type retention policy on a library

1 In a document library, on the ribbon, click the Library tab and then, in the Settings group, click Library Settings.

2 On the Library Settings page, in the Permissions And Management section, click the Information Management Policy Settings link.

3 On the Information Management Policy Settings page, in the Content Type Policies section, click one of the content types.

(continued on next page)

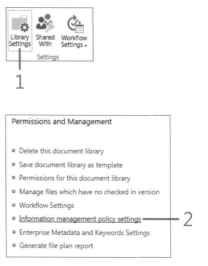

Permissions and Management

- Delete this document library
- Save document library as template
- Permissions for this document library
- Manage files which have no checked in version
- Workflow Settings
- Information management policy settings ———— 2
- Enterprise Metadata and Keywords Settings
- Generate file plan report

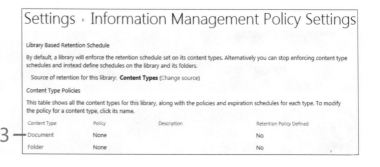

Settings › Information Management Policy Settings

Library Based Retention Schedule

By default, a library will enforce the retention schedule set on its content types. Alternatively you can stop enforcing content type schedules and instead define schedules on the library and its folders.

Source of retention for this library: **Content Types** (Change source)

Content Type Policies

This table shows all the content types for this library, along with the policies and expiration schedules for each type. To modify the policy for a content type, click its name.

Content Type	Policy	Description	Retention Policy Defined
Document	None		No
Folder	None		No

TIP When specifying the date field and duration on a retention stage, you are choosing how long to wait before the retention is triggered. For example, the rule "Modified + 2 Years" indicates the rule will first execute when the record has not been modified for two years.

Create a content type retention policy on a library *(continued)*

4 In the Retention section, select the Enable Retention check box.

5 Click the Add A Retention Stage link.

6 In the Stage Properties dialog box, in the Event section, choose a date field and duration after which the retention policy is executed.

7 In the Action section, choose an action to apply when the stage is executed.

8 In the Recurrence section, choose whether to repeat the stage and duration after which to repeat it.

9 Click OK.

Retention

Schedule how content is managed and disposed by specifying a sequence of retention stages. If you specify multiple stages, each stage will occur one after the other in the order they appear on this page.

☑ Enable Retention

Specify how to manage retention:
Items will not expire until a stage is added.
Add a retention stage...

Stage properties -- Webpage Dialog

https://techforceconsulting.sharepoint.com/SEMTeamSite/_layouts/15/retentionstage

Specify the event that activates this stage and an action that should occur once the stage is activated.

Event

Specify what causes the stage to activate:
◉ This stage is based off a date property on the item

Time Period: Modified ▾ + 2 years ▾

◯ Set by a custom retention formula installed on this server:

Action

When this stage is triggered, perform the following action:

Delete previous drafts ▾

This action will delete all previous drafts of this document.

Recurrence

This stage will execute once according to the event defined above. Use recurrence to force the stage to repeat its action.

☑ Repeat this stage's action until the next stage is activated
After the stage is first triggered, the stage's action will recur forever until the next stage is triggered.

Recurrence period: 2 years ▾

OK | Cancel

> **TIP** You can continue to add additional retention policy stages after the first. For example, after you delete document drafts, you could add a later stage to delete the latest version of a document.

> **TIP** You should only add recurrence to a policy stage if you are going to have a second stage; otherwise, this stage will continue to execute forever, regardless of the trigger event.

Setting library or folder-based retention schedules

When setting retention policies at the library level in SharePoint 2013, you have two options: setting the retention policy on specific content types used within the library or setting the policy on all documents in the library. By setting content type–specific retention policies, you can use different retention policies with the same library (based on the content type of each file). You can use list retention policies for libraries where content types are not enabled or in libraries where you want the same retention policy applied to all documents.

Set library and folder retention policy source

1 In a document library, on the ribbon, click the Library tab and then, in the Settings group, click Library Settings.

2 On the Library Settings page, in the Permissions And Management section, click the Information Management Policy Settings link.

3 On the Information Management Policy Settings page, in the Library Based Retention Schedule section, click the Change Source link.

(continued on next page)

Permissions and Management

- Delete this document library
- Save document library as template
- Permissions for this document library
- Manage files which have no checked in version
- Workflow Settings
- Information management policy settings ——— 2
- Enterprise Metadata and Keywords Settings
- Generate file plan report

Settings › Information Management Policy Settings

Library Based Retention Schedule

By default, a library will enforce the retention schedule set on its content types. Alternatively you can stop enforcing content type schedules and instead define schedules on the library and its folders.

Source of retention for this library: **Content Types** (Change source) ——— 3

Content Type Policies

This table shows all the content types for this library, along with the policies and expiration schedules for each type. To modify the policy for a content type, click its name.

Content Type	Policy	Description	Retention Policy Defined
Document	None		No
Folder	None		No

✓ **TIP** To make the Library tab available, you must have already navigated to a list or library.

✓ **TIP** Library and folder retention policy sources can be defined for the entire library or for individual folders in the library.

Set library and folder retention policy source *(continued)*

4 On the Library Based Retention Schedule page, in the Source Of Retention section, click Libraries And Folders.

5 In the pop-up message box that appears, click OK.

6 On the Library Retention Stage Configuration page, click Add A Retention Stage to add one or more stages.

7 Click OK.

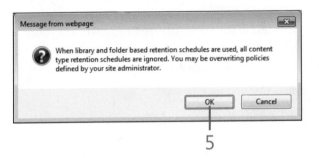

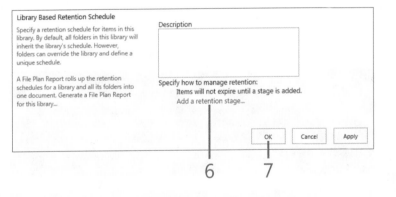

> ⚠ **CAUTION** After you have selected libraries and folders as the retention policy source, any content type policies that you define on the library are ignored.

Creating auditing policies

Auditing policies can be applied to site content types across the entire site collection to ensure that you monitor all files, regardless of where they are used within your site. Alternatively, they can be added only to a single library; however, you will still need to select specific content types to monitor within the library.

Create an audit policy on a site content type

1 Access the Site Content Types – Edit Policy page on a site content type that you want to monitor.

2 Enter descriptive text in the Administrative Description and Policy Statement text boxes.

3 Scroll down and select the Enable Auditing check box.

4 Select the events that you want to audit.

5 Click OK to save your changes.

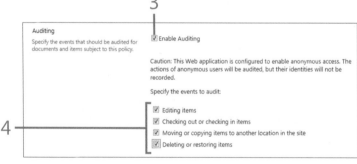

1

Site Content Types ▸ **Edit Policy**

Name and Administrative Description
The name and administrative description are shown to list managers when configuring policies on a list or content type.

Name:
Document

Administrative Description:

Policy Statement
The policy statement is displayed to end users when they open items subject to this policy. The policy statement can explain which policies apply to the content or indicate any special handling or information that users need to be aware of.

Policy Statement:

2

3

Auditing
Specify the events that should be audited for documents and items subject to this policy.

☑ Enable Auditing

Caution: This Web application is configured to enable anonymous access. The actions of anonymous users will be audited, but their identities will not be recorded.

Specify the events to audit:

☑ Editing items
☑ Checking out or checking in items
☑ Moving or copying items to another location in the site
☑ Deleting or restoring items

4

OK   Cancel

5

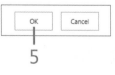

> **TIP** When adding or editing policies, use the Administrative Description and Policy Statement text boxes to describe the policy and provide informative text that can be displayed for users when they edit files. Remember, you will have more success and user adoption when users understand the reasons certain policies have been enacted.

> **SEE ALSO** For information about accessing information management policies on a site content type, see "Accessing site content information management policies" on page 166.

Create an audit policy within a list or library

1   Access the Information Management Policies Settings page for the library that you want to monitor.

2   Select a content type used within the library that you want to monitor.

3   On the Edit Policy page, enter descriptive text in the Administrative Description and Policy Statement text boxes.

4   Scroll down and select the Enable Auditing check box.

5   Select the events that you want to audit.

6   Click OK to save your changes.

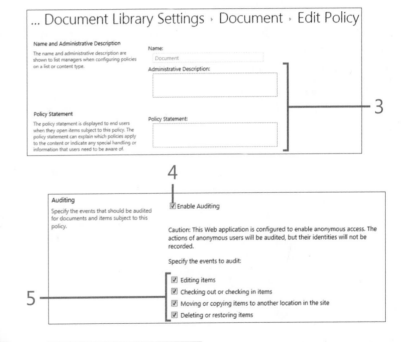

SEE ALSO   For information about accessing information management policies on a list or library, see "Accessing list information management policies" on page 167.

Viewing an audit report

When auditing is configured on a site or library, these events are captured by SharePoint 2013 and can be inspected by anyone with access to the site collection settings. The reports are written to Microsoft Excel–formatted files that contain summary and detail tabs showing the detailed metrics on file accesses and changes.

View an audit report

1 In the upper-right corner of the window, click the Settings icon, and then, on the menu that appears, click Site Settings.

2 On the Site Settings page, in the Site Collection Administration section, click the Go To Top Level Site Settings link. If you are already at the top site, skip this step.

3 Click the Audit Log Reports link.

4 On the View Auditing Reports page, select a report to run.

(continued on next page)

View an audit report (continued)

5 Click Browse to specify a location to which to save the report.

6 In the Select List Or Library dialog box, choose a location to which to save the report and click OK.

7 Back on the Run Reports page, click OK.

8 After the report completes, use the Click Here To View The Report link to open the report.

Run Reports › Customize Report ⓘ

File Location
Specify where to save the report once it has been generated.

Save location:
/Shared Documents

Browse…

OK   Cancel

6   5 7

Select List or Library -- Webpage Dialog

https://techforceconsulting.**sharepoint.com**/_layouts/15/PickerTreeView.aspx?title=CbqPii 🔒

Select a list or library. The Web Part will display content from the list or library you select.

☐ Ⓢ SharePoint 2013 Plain & Simple
  ⊞ 📇 Author Tools
  ⊞ 📖 Book Chapters
  ⊞ 📇 Chapters in Draft
  ⊞ 📇 Documents
  ⊞ 📇 Form Templates
  ⊞ 📇 Master Page Gallery
  ⊞ 📇 Reference Materials
  ⊞ 📇 Site Assets
  ⊞ ⊛ Site Pages
  ⊞ 📇 Style Library
  ⊞ 📖 TestList

OK   Cancel

SharePoint 2013 Plain & Simple › Operation Completed

The report has been successfully generated and saved to the location specified.

Click here to view the report.

OK

8

> **TIP** If the report finds no audit data, an error message will be displayed instead of the report link.

Document label and document barcode policies

Document label and barcode policies can require a user to insert a label or barcode before saving or printing documents created on the SharePoint 2013 site. Unfortunately, this feature has been deprecated and is partially disabled in SharePoint 2013.

In some versions of SharePoint 2013, such as the online beta, the policy options for document labels and barcodes exist in the Information Management Policies administrative views, but they should not be relied upon for future usage.

> ⚠️ **CAUTION** Do not rely on the document label or barcode features, even if they are available in your implementation, because the rules are inconsistently applied depending on which authoring tool you are using. For example, the web-based online Office applications do not support this feature and will not force (or even allow) users to generate labels or barcodes.

Organizing people and work

Microsoft SharePoint 2013 provides users with several list templates to assist you with managing people and work. Contact lists are perfect for keeping up to date information for partners or clients. Issue lists can help you with tracking helpdesk incidents, change management requests, or project tasks.

Special features specific to the type of task list are in place automatically. A project tasks list can track dependencies between tasks, include a Gantt Chart of task schedules, and synchronize with Microsoft Project. An events list includes a calendar view to track individual or recurring meetings.

In this section:

- Creating a project schedule by using a tasks list
- Adding tasks
- Viewing tasks in a Gantt Chart
- Adding multiple tasks and subtasks
- Creating a calendar list
- Scheduling events on the calendar
- Using the issue tracking list
- Creating a discussion board
- Participating in a discussion
- Rating discussions
- Connecting a discussion to Microsoft Outlook
- Synchronizing project tasks with Microsoft Project

Creating a project schedule by using a tasks list

Gantt Charts in SharePoint 2013 help managers coordinate project schedules and assign tasks to team members. A SharePoint task list combines the functionality of a standard task list with a Gantt Chart, making it possible for you to display start and end dates and report task progress based on the percentage complete value of the task.

Create a project task list

1 On the Quick Launch bar, click Site Contents.

2 On the Site Contents page, click Add An App.

3 On the Your Apps page, click Tasks.

(continued on next page)

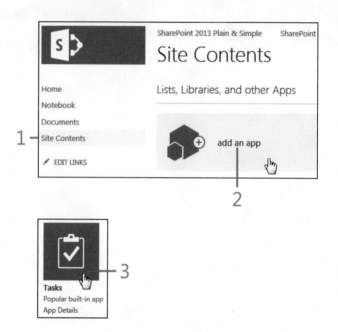

Create a project task list *(continued)*

4 In the Adding Tasks dialog box, enter a name for the new task list.

5 Click Create.

Adding Tasks   ✕

Pick a name   Name:
You can add this app multiple times to your site. Give it a
unique name.   ——— 4

Advanced Options   Create   Cancel

5

Adding tasks

After your task list is created, you can begin populating it with tasks. Tasks in SharePoint 2013 can be a simple checklist or a more complex project in which you can relate tasks to one another or assign predecessors. The graphic timeline view also makes it possible for you to see your task dates at a glance.

Add a task

1 On the Quick Launch bar, under Site Contents, click your task list.

2 On the Task List page, click New Task.

3 On the Task page, enter the Task details.

4 Click the Show More link.

(continued on next page)

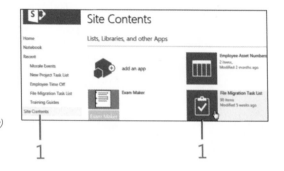

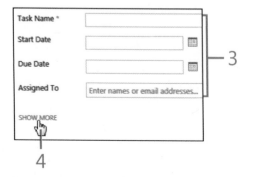

Add a task *(continued)*

5 Enter the task information.

6 Click Save.

> **TIP** Only tasks with a populated date field will show up in the task timeline.

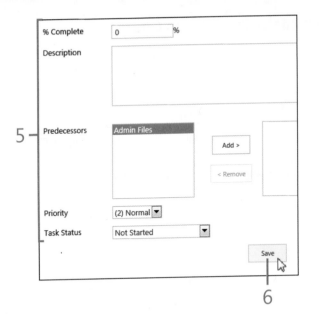

Add a task to a timeline

1 On the ribbon of your Task List page, click the Tasks tab.

2 Select the check box to the left of a task. (Hover over the title to see the check mark option.)

3 On the ribbon, in the Actions group, click Add To Timeline.

> **TIP** Selecting the check box to the left of the column headings will select all tasks.

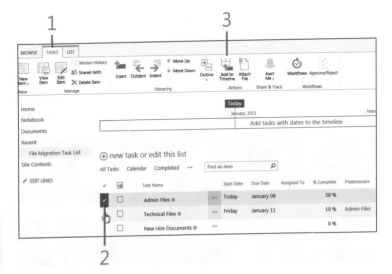

Viewing tasks in a Gantt Chart

Gantt Charts are a common scheduling management tool used to view phases and tasks of a project. SharePoint 2013 uses a timeline and Gantt bars to visually associate the start and end dates of your project's tasks.

View tasks in a Gantt Chart

1 On your Task List page, to the right of the column headings, click the drop-down ellipsis (...).

2 On the menu that appears, choose Gantt Chart.

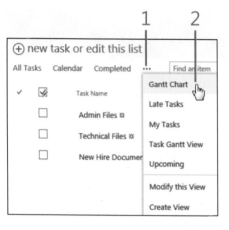

TIP The Gantt Chart View splits the content display and the Gantt chart with a slider. Move the slider to display the columns that you want to see.

SEE ALSO For more information about editing views, see Section 5, "List and library essentials."

Configure Gantt columns

1 In a Gantt Chart view, click the drop-down arrow next to any column heading.

2 On the menu that appears, click Configure Columns.

3 In the Configure Columns dialog box, you can perform any of the following actions:

- Hide or display a column by clearing or selecting the check box next to the column name.

- Change the column display order by selecting a column and clicking Move Up or Move Down.

- Change the width of a column by modifying the Column Width value.

4 Click OK to save your changes.

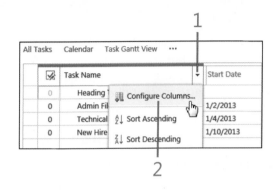

Adding multiple tasks and subtasks

There might be times when you'd like to copy items from Microsoft Excel into a task list, but you don't want to key them one at a time. With SharePoint 2013, you can add entries quickly in the list view, or you can paste content directly.

After tasks are added, you might want to change the way they are displayed or change tasks to subtasks. You can move tasks up or down, indent or outdent them, or delete a task from a list altogether.

Update multiple tasks in a standard view

1 On your Task List page, above the column headings, click Edit.

2 Click a cell to edit its value. Repeat the steps in other cells; changes are saved as soon as you click off the edited row.

TIP Gantt Chart views are already designed as a Quick Edit view, which means you can complete multiple edits directly in the cells.

TRY THIS Order columns in Microsoft Excel to match the columns in a Quick Edit view. Copy the desired cells in Excel, click in the first cell of a new row in your Task List, and then paste!

Add subtasks

1 On the ribbon of your Task List page, click the Tasks tab.

2 Click the check mark option to the left of the desired subtask. (Hover over the title to see the check mark option.)

3 On the ribbon, in the Hierarchy group, click Indent.

TIP You can easily rearrange your tasks by selecting a task and clicking the Move Up or Move Down commands on the ribbon.

TRY THIS Create one subtask directly under a task by clicking its drop-down ellipsis and then, on the menu that appears, click Create Subtask.

Creating a calendar list

SharePoint 2013 calendar lists provide a convenient and visual way for project team members to track project milestones, meetings, and other events. You can display calendar lists in daily, weekly, and monthly views.

Create a calendar list

1 On the Quick Launch bar, click Site Contents.

2 On the Site Contents page, click Add An App.

3 On the Your Apps page, in the Find An App search box, type **Calendar** and click the search button (the magnifying-glass icon).

4 In the search results, click the Calendar icon.

5 In the Adding Calendar dialog box, enter a name for the new calendar.

6 Click Create.

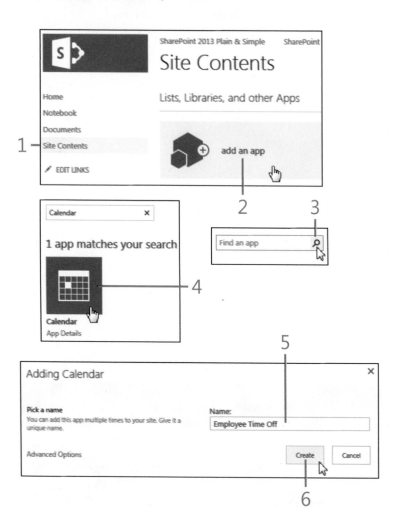

Switch calendar views

1 On the Quick Launch bar, under Site Contents, click your calendar list.

2 On the ribbon, click the Calendar tab.

3 In the Scope group, click any of the following icons to change the calendar view:

- To see events for an individual day, click Day.

- To see events for an entire week, click Week.

- To see events for a calendar month, click Month.

Scheduling events on the calendar

You can add meetings and appointments to a SharePoint 2013 calendar so that all members can see upcoming events, training sessions, or whatever you want to post. You can also view

SharePoint calendars side by side with other Microsoft Outlook calendars or even overlaid on one another.

Schedule an event

1 On the ribbon of your Calendar list, click the Calendar tab.

2 In the Scope group, click Day.

3 On the small calendar to the left, click the date for the event.

4 In the Day pane, drag from the start time to the end time to set the event duration.

5 In the lower-right corner of the highlighted time, click Add.

(continued on next page)

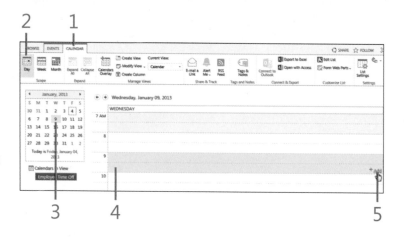

Schedule an event *(continued)*

6 In the New Item dialog box, enter the event details.

7 Click Save to add the event to the calendar.

Employee Time Off - New Item

EDIT

Save | Cancel | Paste | ✂ Cut | 📋 Copy | Attach File | ABC Spelling

Commit | Clipboard | Actions | Spelling

Title *	Discuss Migration Timing
Location	Conference Room
Start Time *	1/9/2013 9 AM 00
End Time *	1/9/2013 10 AM 00
Description	**Agenda** 1. Follow up on last meeting tasks. 2. Assign new tasks.
Category	● Meeting ○ Specify your own value:
All Day Event	☐ Make this an all-day activity that doesn't start or end at a specific hour.
Recurrence	☐ Make this a repeating event.

Save | Cancel

TIP The Description text box supports rich-text formatting, which means that you can create agenda bulleted or numbered lists within it.

TRY THIS Recurring events can be scheduled by checking the box next to Make This A Repeating Event. Create a status meeting that occurs the first Monday of every month.

Using the issue tracking list

Using an issue tracking list in SharePoint 2013 is an excellent method for monitoring several kinds of issues, such as customer support requests, project tasks, and change-management information. With the issue tracking list, you can relate previous issues to new issues as well as track changes via the appending Comments text box.

Create an issue tracking list

1 On the Quick Launch bar, click Site Contents.

2 On the Site Contents page, click Add An App.

3 On the Your Apps page, in the Find An App search box, type **issue tracking** and click the search button (the magnifying-glass icon).

4 In the search results, click the Issue Tracking icon.

5 In the Adding Issue Tracking dialog box, enter a name for the new issue tracker.

6 Click Create.

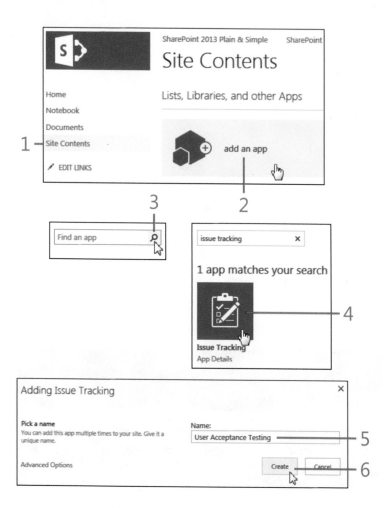

Configure issue categories

1 On the Quick Launch bar, click Site Contents and then click the calendar list.

2 On the ribbon, on the List tab, click List Settings.

3 On the List Settings page, in the Columns section, click Category.

4 Update the Category choices that you want to track.

5 Click OK to save your updated categories.

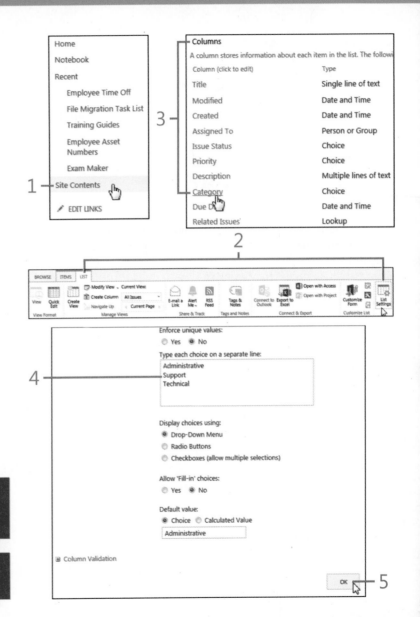

TIP When you edit choice options, the first item in the list becomes the Default value for that field. Update the Default value if necessary or clear it out of the Default value box altogether.

TIP Listing the choice fields in alphabetical order makes it easier for users to find their desired selection.

Creating a discussion board

The discussion board feature in SharePoint 2013 makes it possible for team members to converse in a forum and track all related replies about a specific topic. Participation in discussion boards earn authors achievement points which build their reputation as community members. Reputation statistics like discussions, replies, or best replies are displayed next to the profile name and photo and are added to the newsfeed on the About Me page.

Create a discussion board

1 On the Quick Launch bar, click Site Contents.

2 On the Site Contents page, click Add An App.

3 On the Your Apps page, in the Find An App search box, type **Discussion Board** and click the search button (the magnifying glass icon).

4 In the search results, click the Discussion Board icon.

(continued on next page)

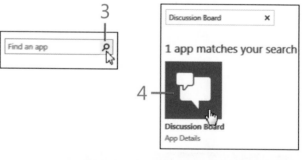

Create a discussion board *(continued)*

5 In the Adding Discussion Board dialog box, enter a name for the new Discussion Board.

6 Click Create.

Participating in a discussion

Participating in discussion boards introduces you to other people with similar interests and skill sets. Your followers' newsfeeds will be notified any time you start a discussion thread or post a reply. You also have the option of turning off the sharing feature in the newsfeed settings of your profile.

Start a discussion thread

1 On the Quick Launch bar, click Site Contents.

2 On the Site Contents page, click a Discussion Board.

3 On the Discussion Board page, click New Discussion.

4 On the Discussion page, add a subject and body for your discussion board.

5 To request answers from other members, select the Question check box.

6 Click Save.

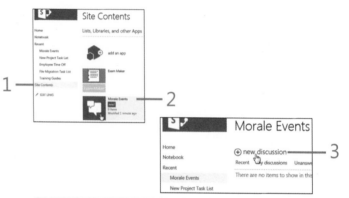

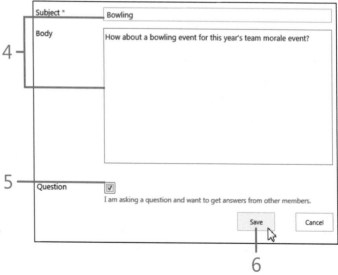

> ✓ **TIP** To participate in a discussion, you must have member permissions.

Reply to a discussion thread

1 On the Discussion Board page, click a subject title.

2 Click the Reply link or click in the Add A Reply text box.

3 Type your response or comments.

4 Click Reply.

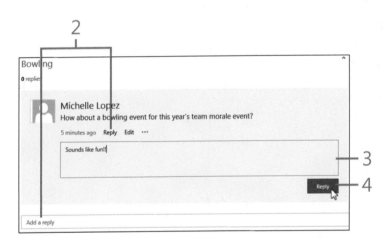

Rating discussions

When you rate a discussion board or a reply, you add to the author's achievement points and help build their reputation rating. Depending on the site's community setup, users can award a post a rating of one to five stars or they can like or unlike posts.

When researching the answer to a question, it's extremely useful to mark any of the replies in a discussion as the "best reply." Best replies will display with a check mark and along with the text "Best Reply" to help locate it easily.

Mark a Best Reply to a post

1 On the Discussion Board page, click a subject title.

2 Click the drop-down ellipsis (...) under the post that you want to mark as the best reply.

3 On the menu that appears, click Best Reply.

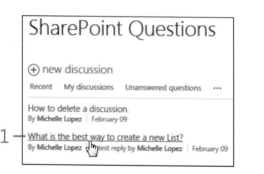

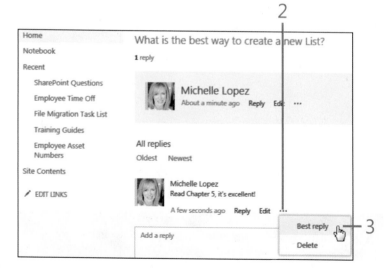

Connecting a discussion to Microsoft Outlook

SharePoint 2013 includes a convenient feature with which you can follow discussions in Outlook instead of accessing the discussion thread directly in SharePoint. The discussions appear just like email messages do!

Connect a discussion thread to Outlook

1 On the Quick Launch bar, click the discussion board.

2 On the ribbon, click the List tab.

3 In the Connect & Export group, click Connect To Outlook.

4 In Outlook, in the Folders pane on the left, expand SharePoint Lists.

5 Click the discussion board name.

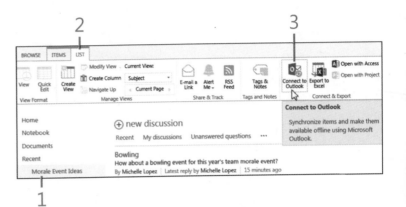

Synchronizing project tasks with Microsoft Project

SharePoint 2013 and Microsoft Project integrate so that project schedules can synchronize with SharePoint project task lists and be updated in both locations. Synchronized columns can be customized so that only some, or all, of the project task fields are included in the synchronization. To perform the following steps, you must have Project 2013 installed on your computer.

Synchronize Project with a tasks list

1 Open a Project file.

2 On the ribbon, click the File tab to display the Backstage view and then click Share.

3 In the Share section, click Sync With SharePoint.

4 In the Sync With SharePoint Tasks List section, click the Go To Save As button.

5 In the Save And Sync section, click Sync With SharePoint.

6 In the Sync With SharePoint Tasks List section, in the Sync With list box, choose New or Existing SharePoint Site. In the Site Address text box, enter the appropriate URL and then click the Verify Site button.

7 In the Task List list box, select the list that you want to sync.

8 Click Save.

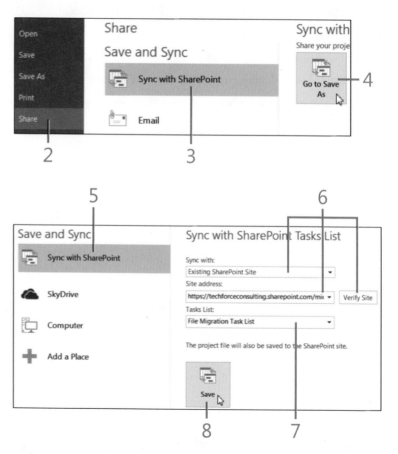

Map synchronization fields

1 On the ribbon of your Microsoft Project file, click the File tab to display the Backstage view and then click Map Fields.

2 In the Map Fields dialog box, fields that are disabled are required fields and cannot be edited. Select the Sync check box in the SharePoint Field row that you want to synchronize.

3 Select a Project Field with which to synchronize. Project Field by default includes a number of text fields (numbered Text1 through Text30) that can be used to map to columns in the SharePoint project tasks list.

4 Click OK.

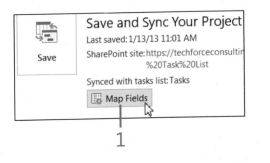

Using Web Parts

Microsoft SharePoint 2013 Web Parts are modular page components that can be used by page authors to add sophisticated, predefined functionality to webpages. For example, you can use Web Parts to add an image or paragraph to the Home page of your site to tell users more about your site. However, Web Parts are not limited to simple page content. If you add a Note Board Web Part to a page on your site, users can enter comments or view the comments made by other users. Using Web Parts, page authors can add incredible functionality to their pages without having to worry about complex web programming requirements.

In this section:

- Available Web Parts
- Adding Web Parts to a wiki page
- Adding Web Parts to a Web Part page
- Adding an App Part to a page
- Editing Web Part properties
- Working with personalized Web Parts on pages
- Targeting Web Parts for an audience

Web Parts and App Parts

Web Parts make it possible for users to add configurable components to pages on a SharePoint site that extend the functionality of the site. Some are simple and are used to only add simple content to a page. This includes the Image Viewer and the Content Editor Web Parts, which you use to add images and static text, respectively, to a page.

The most complex Web Parts perform advanced computations; others can perform searches, query lists, and filter data. Additionally, SharePoint 2013 also introduces the concept of App Parts, which extend the security model of traditional Web Parts. App Parts can be used to interface with external systems. Additionally, all views into lists and libraries now make use of App Parts; this is because lists and libraries are now implemented as Apps.

Categories Web Part   Posts Web Part   Content Editor Web Part

Archives Web Part   Blog Tools Web Part

Web Parts on a page

The accompanying screenshot shows the Home page of a blog site. You can see that most of the content on the page is presented within Web Parts. Web Parts are a critical part of the SharePoint world, and make up much of the dynamically rendered content required for social network–enabled applications such as blogs, on which users can post and interact with data.

Available Web Parts

SharePoint 2013 comes with a variety of out-of-the-box Web Parts that you can use within your sites. You can use them on one or many pages on your site, and they they can configure them on a page-by-page basis. The following tables list some of the more common Web Parts.

Web Parts: Apps Category

Items within this category represent App Parts, which are a new type of Web Part that offer increased security and compartmentalization. As shipped, the primary App Parts available in SharePoint are views of existing libraries. These views make it possible for you to display list or library content on pages outside the document library (for example, displaying the newest documents uploaded to a site). Each of these App Parts is named for the library that they display. For example, you use the Comments App Part to display the Comments library, which contains blog comments added to any blog post on the site.

 TIP As you or your administrator add solutions on your SharePoint site, the available set of Web Parts will increase as new features are enabled. Your site might have additional options already available through third-party and custom software installations.

 TIP Depending on your SharePoint licensing, some of the Web Parts referenced in this section might not be available.

Web Part	Description
Web Parts: Blog	
Blog Archives	Displays quick links for navigating to older blog posts
Blog Notifications	Displays links and instructions for users to track blog changes, either by using SharePoint alerts or by using Real Simple Syndication (RSS)
Blog Tools	Displays the blog tools (only to site owners or administrators) with which you can carry out rapid administration of blog posts
Web Parts: Business Data	
Business Data Actions	Displays actions available from Business Data Connectivity (BDC)
Business Data Connectivity Filter	A filter Web Part that can use values from BDC
Business Data Item	Displays a single item from a data source in BDC
Business Data Item Builder	Reads data from the browser query string and builds a BDC item, which is made available to other Web Parts on the page
Business Data List	Used to display a list of items from a data source

Web Part	Description
Business Data Related List	Used to display items related to a master list
Excel Web Access	Provides a webpage view of a Microsoft Excel workbook
Indicator Details	Displays a status indicator which can be driven by an external data connection
Status List	Shows a list of status indicators for your site or organization
Visio Web Access	Used to display Microsoft Visio drawings on webpages

Web Parts: Community*

About This Community	Displays the site description and other properties of community SharePoint sites
Join	Displays a button that enables nonmembers of a site to join the site, or is invisible if the current user is already a site member
My Membership	Displays the reputation and membership details for the current user of the site

Web Part	Description
Tools	As with a blog site, displays the administrative tools to owners and administrators of a community site
What's Happening	Displays the total number of members, topics, and replies within a community site

Web Part: Content Rollup

Categories	Displays categories in the Site Directory.
Content Query*	Displays content that is aggregated from elsewhere within your site. For example, you can select certain types of content (such as blog posts) and display that information from all webs associated under the current site.
Content Search	Displays content aggregated from multiple site collections by using the search engine. This Web Part is not currently available in the Microsoft Office 365 preview.
Project Summary	Displays project information in a simple view.
Relevant Documents	Displays documents relevant to the current user (for example, documents created, modified, or checked out to the current user).
RSS Viewer	Displays RSS feed data on a page.
Site Aggregator	Displays other sites of your choice.
Sites In Category	Displays sites in the Site Directory that match a specified category.

Web Part	Description
Summary Links**	Allows authors to specify a list of links to associate with the page.
Table Of Contents**	Displays your site navigation.
Term Property	Displays a specified property associated with a Term.
Timeline	Shows a high-level view of a tasks list using a visual timeline.
WSRP Viewer	Displays portlets from websites that use WSRP 1.1. Use this to display externally developed web content on your SharePoint site.
XML Viewer	Displays transformed XML data to the user (the owner of this Web Part can define an XSL transformation on the XML data).

Web Parts: Document Sets

Web Part	Description
Document Set Contents	Displays the content within a document set
Document Set Properties	Displays the properties on a document set

Web Parts: Filters

Web Part	Description
Apply Filters Button	Displays a button with which the user can explicitly apply a filter rather than having each filter applied as the user changes the filter

Web Part	Description
Choice Filter	Filters other Web Parts based on user selections
Current User Filter	Filters other Web Parts based on properties of the current user
Date Filter	Filters other Web Parts based on a user selected date
Page Field Filter	Filters other Web Parts based on information about the current page
Query String (URL) Filter	Filters other Web Parts based on query parameters passed into the current page through the URL
SharePoint List Filter	Filters other Web Parts based on values contained in a SharePoint list
SQL Server Analysis Services Filter	Filters other Web Parts based on values contained within a SQL Server Analysis Services cube
Text Filter	Filters other Web Parts based on user entered text

Web Parts: Forms

Web Part	Description
HTML Form Web Part	Connects a simple HTML form for user data entry to other Web Parts
InfoPath Form Web Part	Connects a Microsoft InfoPath form to the current page

Web Part	Description
Web Parts: Media and Content	
Content Editor	Authors can enter rich text directly onto an area on the page
Get Started With Your Site	Displays a set of Windows 8–styled tiles with common SharePoint actions on your site
Image Viewer	Displays a single image from your site on the current page
Media Web Part	Displays an embedded viewer for displaying media (movies and audio) on the current page
Page Viewer	Displays another webpage within your current page within an IFRAME
Picture Library Slideshow Web Part	Displays a slideshow of images selected from an image library on your site
Script Editor	Authors can embed HTML and JavaScript snippets on the current page
Silverlight Web Part	Authors can embed Microsoft Silverlight applications on the current page. The Silverlight application must be separately uploaded to the site

Web Part	Description
Web Parts: Search	
Find By Document ID	Displays a search form for finding a document by Document ID.
Refinement	Displays a refinement list with which users can refine their current query by common metadata on results. Authors can configure which metadata that users will use to filter the results.
Search Box	Displays a text box in which users can enter their search terms and trigger a search.
Search Navigation	Displays links with which users can navigate between search verticals.
Search Results	Displays the search results and a brief preview of each returned item.
Web Parts: Search Driven-Content*	
Articles	Displays article content from the current site (and other sites) by using the search engine based on a configurable query
Catalog-Item Reuse	Used for the display of managed property information from search content
Items From A Catalog	Displays list items from another list that has been published as a catalog

Web Part	Description
Items Matching a Tag	Displays list items on the current site (or from multiple sites if configured) that match a specified tab
Pictures	Displays pictures from the current site (and other sites) by using the search engine based on a configurable query.
Popular Items	Displays popular items based on the content recommendation feature within SharePoint.
Recently Changed Items	Displays recently changed items from the current site (and other sites) by using the search engine based on a configurable query.
Recommended Items	Displays other recommended items based on the currently viewed object using the content recommendation feature within SharePoint.
Videos	Displays videos from the current site (and other sites) by using the search engine based on a configurable query.
Web Pages	Displays webpages from the current site (and other sites) by using the search engine based on a configurable query.
Wiki Pages	Displays wiki pages from the current site (and other sites) by using the search engine based on a configurable query.

Web Part	Description
Web Parts: Social Collaboration	
Contact Details	Displays details about an author-defined contact on the current page
Note Board	Displays a user-contributable note board, on which users can view or add new comments to the current page
Organization Browser	Displays an interactive view of the organization chart for the company
Site Feed	Contains microblogging conversations on a group site
Site Users	Shows a list of the current users of a site and their current online status (requires integration with Microsoft Outlook and/or Microsoft Lync)
Tag Cloud	Displays popular subjects within your site or organization
User Tasks	Displays a list of tasks for the current user

* Requires the Community features to be enabled on the site

** This Web Part is available only on enterprise publishing sites, on sites with the SharePoint Publishing features enabled.

*** These are not currently available in the online hosted version of Office 365 preview at the time of this publication. They might be added at a later date.

Adding Web Parts to a wiki page

Web Parts can be added whenever you add a page on your SharePoint 2013 site; however, the process is slightly different based on whether you are editing a wiki page or a Web Part page. In both cases, you can determine where you want to insert the Web Part; however, you have a little more flexibility in terms of author layout (and less administrative control over structure) when using wiki pages. With wiki pages, users can layout content by using rich-text style tools, and they can insert items virtually anywhere within the text.

Add a Web Part to a wiki page

1 From a wiki page on a SharePoint site, on the ribbon, click the Page tab.

2 In the Edit group, click the Edit button.

(continued on next page)

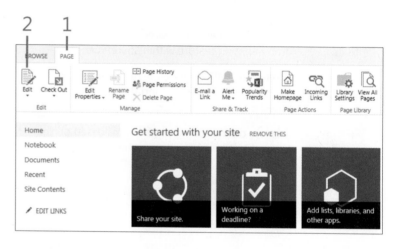

> **TRY THIS** Try adding the Note Board Web Part to the Home page of your site to enable user commenting and collaboration.

Add a Web Part to a wiki page (continued)

3 Find a place in the text on the page and click to place your cursor where you want to insert the Web Part.

4 On the ribbon, click the Insert tab.

5 In the Parts group, click the Web Part button.

6 In the Add A Web Part window that appears, in the Category section, select a category by which to filter the list of Web Parts.

7 In the Parts section, select a Web Part.

8 Click Add.

The Web Part is added to the page at the point where you placed your cursor.

9 Click Save to save your page.

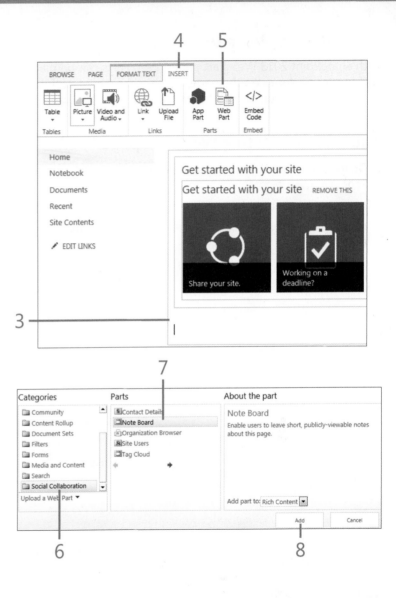

Adding Web Parts to a Web Part page

With SharePoint 2013 Web Part pages, Web Parts can be placed only in specific zones on the page, which makes them useful for scenarios in which administrators need to maintain a tighter control over the look and feel of a site. Users click the Add A Web Part link within available Web Part zones to specify generally where the control should be rendered.

Add a Web Part to a Web Part page

1 On the page that you want to modify, on the ribbon, click the Page tab.

2 In the Edit group, click the Edit Page button.

3 On the page, find an available Web Part zone and click the Add A Web Part link.

(continued on next page)

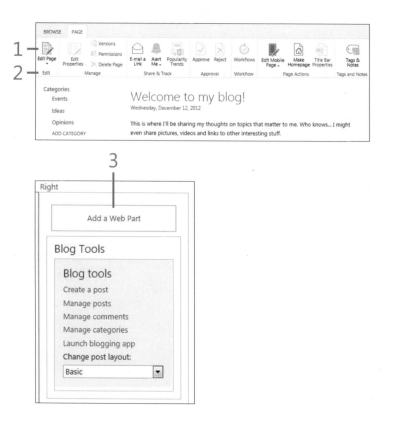

Add a Web Part to a Web Part page *(continued)*

4 In the Add A Web Part window that appears, in the Category section, select a category by which to filter the list of Web Parts.

5 In the Parts section, select a Web Part.

6 Click the Add button.

7 On the ribbon, click the Page tab.

8 Click Stop Editing to save your results.

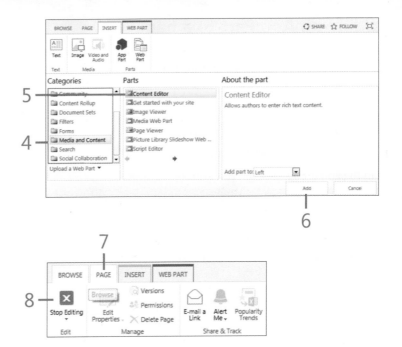

Adding an App Part to a page

With the focus on Apps in SharePoint 2013, each new document library or list is created as a separate application within the site. As a result, if you want to expose a view into a list or document library on the Home page (or any other page) of your site, you will need to make use of the new App Part to show this data.

Add a list to a page

1 On the ribbon tab, click the Page tab.

2 In the Edit group, click the Edit button.

3 Find an insert point on the page and click to place your cursor at this location.

4 On the ribbon, click the Insert tab.

5 In the Parts group, click the App Part button.

(continued on next page)

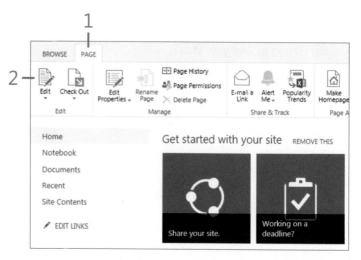

> **TIP** On Web Part pages, you will need to instead click the Add A Web Part links located on the page rather than selecting an insert point and using the Insert App Part link.

> ⚠ **CAUTION** On Publishing pages, you will need to check-in and publish your page before any changes are displayed to other site users.

Add a list to a page *(continued)*

6 In the Parts section of the Add An App Part window that appears, click the name of the App Part that matches the list that you want to add.

7 Click the Add button.

8 Click the Save icon to save your page changes.

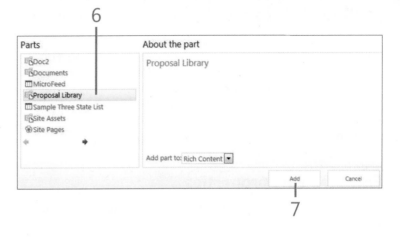

Editing Web Part properties

Many settings on a Web Part can be modified by the page author after the Web Part has been placed on the page. For example, the author can select how the Web Part is framed on the page and how much space is allocated for display of the Web Part. Some Web Parts, such as the Image Viewer Web Part, require that the user specify additional information such as the location of the image to be displayed.

SharePoint provides a standardized tool panel that you can access for viewing and editing the properties for each Web Part. It includes some common properties shared by all Web Parts, such as the Appearance pane, with which you can provide a display title for the Web Part and define its display size in pixels. Additionally, some Web Parts have additional custom fields that you can use to tailor the behavior of the Web Part.

Edit Web Part properties

1 On a page containing a Web Part that you want to configure, on the ribbon, click the Page tab.

2 In the Edit group, click the Edit icon.

3 Locate the Web Part that you want to configure and then, in the upper-right corner, click the Options drop-down arrow.

4 On the menu that appears, click Edit Web Part.

(continued on next page)

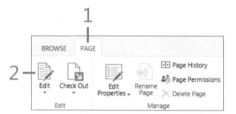

Edit Web Part properties *(continued)*

5 In the Web Part properties dialog box, enter or change any of the visible properties.

6 Expand other sections in the dialog box by clicking the corresponding Expand buttons (the plus signs) next to the section headings.

7 Click OK to save your settings.

Working with personalized Web Parts on pages

Users can also personalize SharePoint 2013 pages, which is particularly powerful when combined with predefined Web Parts. If personalization is enabled on a site, you can add your own Web Parts to a page that are only visible to your account. Thus, users can quickly add items such as links, task reminders, and RSS feeds to their Home page on a site.

After you have personalized a page by adding your own Web Parts, you can switch between your personal view and the view shared by all users by using a few simple menu commands.

Add a Web Part to a personalized page

1 On a Web Part page, in the upper-right corner of the SharePoint window, click your user name.

2 On the menu that appears, click Personalize This Page.

3 Find a Web Part zone on the page and click the Add A Web Part link.

(continued on next page)

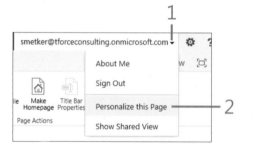

> ➔ **TRY THIS** Try personalizing the Home page of a Blog or Project site, both of which support personalization on the Home Web Page page.

> ✓ **TIP** The personalize pages options are only available for Web Part pages (not wiki pages) and also require permissions to be set up by your administrator. If these options are not available, ask your IT staff about the configuration of the Add\Remove Personal Web Parts option.

Add a Web Part to a personalized page *(continued)*

4 In the Add A Web Part window that appears, in the Category section, select a category by which to filter the available Web Parts.

5 In the Parts section, select a Web Part.

6 Click Add.

7 On the ribbon, click Stop Editing to save the personalized page.

Switch from personal and shared views

1 On a site on which you have already personalized the display, in the upper-right corner of the SharePoint window, click your user name.

2 On the menu that appears, click Show Shared View to display the shared view of the page as viewed by all users.

3 Click your user name to open the menu again.

4 On the menu, click Show Personal View to return to your personalized view of the page.

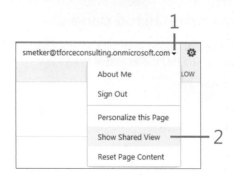

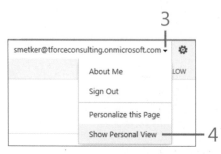

Targeting Web Parts for an audience

Sometimes, you might not want all of the users of your site to see the same Web Parts. SharePoint provides an option called *audience targeting* by which you can specify that certain page components be displayed to selected users and groups. This option is accessed via the Web Part properties dialog box.

When choosing a target audience, you will need to choose from one of the following groups:

- **Global audiences**   Global audiences are populated by audience rules that are set up by your administrator and can be based on organizational reporting relationships as well as other calculations.

- **Distribution/security groups**   Distribution and security groups are based upon list memberships of the user profile service as well as windows security groups imported from the user profile service.

- **SharePoint groups**   SharePoint groups are defined on the local site and can be administered by site collection administrators and other users who have been given permission.

> **TIP**   On sites for which you don't have full administrative privileges, the SharePoint Groups option would be the simplest to administer because you can specify that members of a local group have visibility to a Web Part.

> **TIP**   You can add more than one group to the Target Audiences text box.

Target web parts for an audience

1 On a page that you are editing, select a Web Part and then, in the upper-right corner, click the Options drop-down arrow.

2 On the menu that appears, click Edit Web Part.

3 In the Web Part properties dialog box, expand the Advanced section (click the plus sign).

4 Scroll to the bottom of the Advanced section and click the Browse icon and click the Browse icon for the Target Audience field.

(continued on next page)

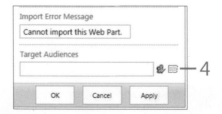

Target web parts for an audience (continued)

5 In the Select Audiences dialog box, choose a group type on which to query. Select from Global Audiences, Distribution/Security Groups, or SharePoint Groups.

6 In the Search box, type a search expression to locate a matching group and then click the Search button (the magnifying-glass icon).

7 Select the appropriate group.

8 Click the Add button to add the group to the Target Audiences text box.

9 Click OK to close the Select Audiences dialog box.

10 In the Web Part properties dialog box, click OK.

5   6

Select Audiences ✕

Find   SharePoint Groups ▾ app 🔍

Name	Alias	Description
Approvers		Members of this group can edit and approve pages, list items, and documents
Designers		Members of this group can edit lists, document libraries, and pages in the site

— 7

◄   ⫶⫶⫶   ►

Add ->   Approvers

OK   Cancel

8   9

Import Error Message

Cannot import this Web Part.

Target Audiences

Approvers   🔖 📇

OK   Cancel   Apply

10

Using SharePoint with Office 2013

Microsoft SharePoint 2013 is a very powerful platform. But, you must also remember that the platform is a part of the overall Microsoft Office 2013 suite of products, as well. With this suite, Microsoft has set up a rich user experience by providing you with servers, desktop applications, and online services. These products are all designed to work seamlessly together. As such, when used in tandem, you have the ability to share, collaborate, create, and manage information within the SharePoint platform.

Office 2013 has been redesigned from previous iterations. And although the changes are significant, the core capability of being able to use SharePoint remains unchanged. You are able to subscribe to individual lists as well as link to SharePoint folders to synchronize documents, which provides you with an improved capability to work with contacts, calendars, and other content.

You are also able to open and save Microsoft Excel, Microsoft PowerPoint, and Microsoft Word documents directly to SharePoint libraries as if they were local storage devices as well as being able to insert media content, which can be stored in SharePoint. Additionally, you can utilize features when working with PowerPoint such as the broadcasting of a presentation to a virtual audience.

In this section:

- Connecting SharePoint libraries to Office
- Connecting SharePoint calendars to Outlook
- Archiving Outlook email in SharePoint
- Importing a spreadsheet into SharePoint
- Exporting data from a SharePoint list to Excel
- Exporting an Excel table to SharePoint
- Connecting Access and SharePoint

Connecting SharePoint libraries to Office

There has been one major change with regard to using Office with SharePoint: the evolution of Workspaces (formerly known as Groove) to SkyDrive Pro. This is available to you as either part of an installation of SharePoint 2013 or as a service if you are using Office365 or a SharePoint Online account. You can organize and store your documents and other files in your personal SkyDrive Pro account. From there you can easily share files and collaborate on documents with others within your company or organization.

Before you can begin to use SharePoint 2013 with Office 2013 products, you need to connect them to one another. When you connect a library to Office, what you are actually doing is adding the library to your SharePoint Sites library in Windows. This is similar to the action you took when you added a mapped drive in older versions of Windows.

Connect a SharePoint library to Office

1 In SharePoint, select the library to which you want to connect Office.

2 On the ribbon, click the Library tab.

3 In the Connect & Export group, click Connect To Office.

4 On the menu that appears, click Add To SharePoint Sites.

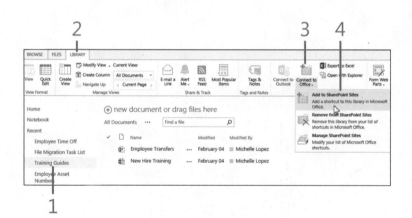

Connecting SharePoint calendars to Outlook

One of the breakthrough features Microsoft has maintained within the SharePoint platform is the ability to connect SharePoint calendars to Outlook. Because Outlook is a common business application that people use for receiving email messages and keeping track of their schedules, the ability to access SharePoint calendars from within Outlook is a great convenience

for those who need to maintain multiple calendars. When you connect a SharePoint calendar to Outlook you have a view into the SharePoint calendar from within Outlook. You can also, add, edit, and delete calendar items within a SharePoint calendar by using the familiar Outlook interface.

Connect a SharePoint calendar to Outlook

1 In SharePoint, select the calendar to which you want to connect in Outlook.

2 On the ribbon, click the Calendar tab.

3 In the Connect & Export group, click Connect To Outlook.

(continued on next page)

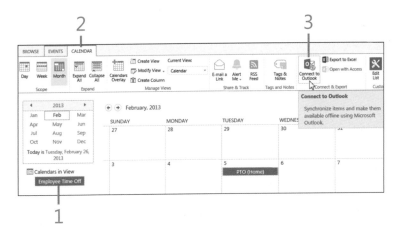

→ **TRY THIS** Connect a SharePoint calendar to Outlook.

Connect a SharePoint calendar to Outlook *(continued)*

4 In the pop-up message box that appears, click Allow.

5 In the next pop-up message box that appears, click the Yes button.

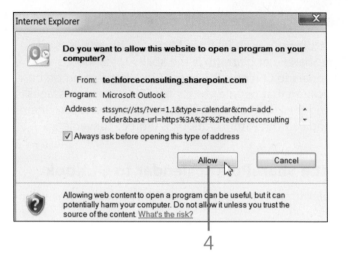

4

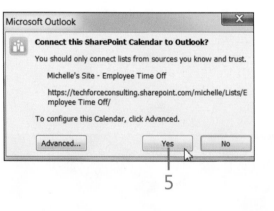

5

> ✓ **TIP** If you are trying to connect a newly created calendar, the option for Connecting To Outlook might not be immediately available. Wait a few minutes and click the refresh button; the option should become available.

Archiving Outlook email in SharePoint

Since the 1990s, business has depended on email. It is the one application with which practically every business professional around the world is very familiar. Despite the increased usage of alternative communication tools, it continues to prevail as the most dominant communication tool that professionals utilize, especially with external customers, vendors, and partners.

As such, it is a common requirement of business professionals to be able to store email messages within SharePoint. By doing so, they are able to not only share the communication with team members but they can turn a mail message into content that

can be collaborated on and included with other content from a project, contract, proposal, and so on.

Although it is easy to simply drag a message from Outlook into a library. It is also easy to store the message as a discussion. The Discussion app is designed specifically to manage threaded conversations, grouped by subject. When an email message is moved to a SharePoint Discussion list, the email body is automatically aggregated into the discussion item as a series of replies. Attachments to any email message are also preserved as attachments on the discussion list item.

Archive Outlook email in SharePoint

1 In SharePoint, on the Quick Launch bar, click Site Contents.

2 On the Site Contents page, click a Discussion Board.

3 Follow the steps in the previous section ("Connecting SharePoint calendars to Outlook") to connect the Discussion Board to Outlook.

(continued on next page)

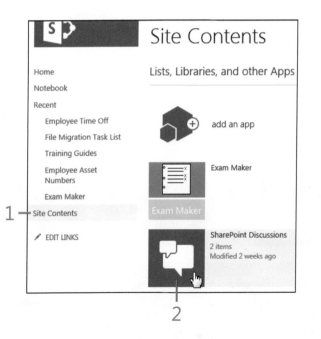

TIP The tasks that follow assume that you have a Discussion list already on your site that you can use. If you do not have a Discussion list available, go to Section 5, "Creating and deleting lists," and refer to the task "Adding an app on SharePoint."

Archive Outlook email in SharePoint *(continued)*

4 In Outlook, on the taskbar, click the Mail option and open an email message in your Inbox.

5 On the ribbon, click the Message tab.

6 In the Move group, click the Move button.

7 On the menu that appears, click the Other Folder option.

8 In the Move Item To dialog box, click a SharePoint Discussion.

9 Click OK.

4

5   6

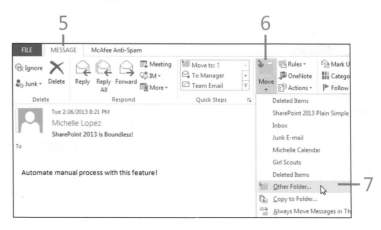

7

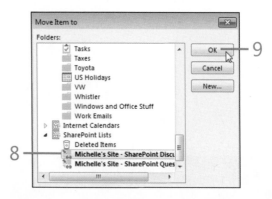

9

8

TIP To see the discussion list on the Site Contents page, you might need to scroll down the list of choices until you see the SharePoint Lists section.

TRY THIS Take any email message and reply to yourself a number of times to create a set of messages with the same subject. Move the message items to the linked discussion list one at a time. Then, review the discussion post to see how the messages were merged into a single one.

Importing a spreadsheet into SharePoint

Spreadsheet programs are mainstays of companies and organizations. They are used throughout the world for anything from organizing and calculating financial information to administrative listings. Excel is the spreadsheet program of choice for the majority of business professionals everywhere. So, it only makes sense that SharePoint 2013 should work very well with it.

Traditionally, Excel spreadsheets were built and saved to a hard disk or some other network storage device. This was not ideal. When you combine the features of both SharePoint and Excel, you are able to use the software in ways that were not possible just a few short years ago, such as using the data within a table to drive a Web Part on a SharePoint site.

Also, the features give you the ability to import and export data from SharePoint lists. You can also use Excel spreadsheets to automatically map and create columns within SharePoint lists to match columns in Excel tables.

You might have a spreadsheet on a shared location that you use with team members. However, if users don't have the Excel application on their computer or if they are trying to access the information through a mobile device, they might not be able to access the file. By using a SharePoint list, however, you are able to avoid these issues. You can also use the information more readily within other lists and libraries. For example, you might want to use a column within the list to populate the choices within another list.

Import a spreadsheet into SharePoint

1   In the upper-right corner of your SharePoint site, click the Settings button (the small gear icon next to the name of the logged-on user).

2   On the menu that appears, click Add An App.

(continued on next page)

TIP   Excel is a very flexible program with some advanced data layout features, including the ability to merge cells. SharePoint can only import tabular-formatted data into lists.

Import a spreadsheet into SharePoint *(continued)*

3 On the Your Apps page, select the Import Spreadsheet Icon.

To find the icon, you might need to scroll through the available apps.

4 On the New page, enter a Name for the list.

5 Enter a Description for the list.

6 Click the Browse button.

(continued on next page)

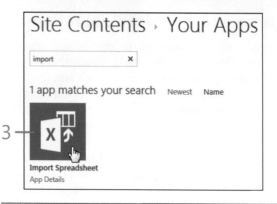

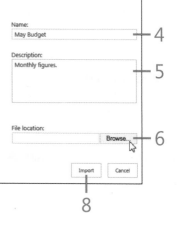

Import a spreadsheet into SharePoint (continued)

7 Double-click the Excel file that you want to import.

8 Back on the New page, click the Import button. (Refer to the screen shot on the previous page.)

9 In Excel, select a range type and range by using one of the following options:

- **Range Of Cells**   In your workbook, select a range by dragging your mouse across a selection of rows and columns.

- **Table Range**   Select a predefined formatted table from the list box.

- **Named Range**   Select a named range of cells from the list box.

10 Click Import.

☒ 06 - Working with Documents	2/15/2013 4:00 PM
☒ Excel2013P&S_Ch05	12/4/2012 1:57 PM
☒ MSPressBooksDeveloper	12/4/2012 1:42 PM
☒ Participate in discussions	2/6/2013 7:01 PM
☒ SharePoint 15 Plain Simple_KB_JL	12/4/2012 1:34 PM
☒ SharePoint2013PS_Ch10_DraftV2	2/6/2013 6:56 PM
☒ Training Metrics	12/28/2012 5:45 PM

Import to Windows SharePoint Services list

Range Type:

Range of Cells

Select Range:

Sheet1!$A$1:$E$8

Import your spreadsheet data as a new Windows SharePoint Services list.

Import   Cancel

Exporting data from a SharePoint list to Excel

SharePoint is a great platform to use for the display of data along with connecting the data to other applications. However, if you need to do extensive analysis of the data within the list, you might encounter some difficulties. Because Excel and SharePoint can operate together, you can take advantage of the powerful data analysis features of Excel to extrapolate needed details. But, you first need to get the data out of the SharePoint list into Excel.

Export data from a SharePoint list to Excel

1 On the Quick Launch bar, click Site Contents or, under Recent, click a list to go to a previously opened list.

2 On the ribbon, click the List tab.

3 In the Connect & Export group, click the Export To Excel button.

4 In the dialog box, click Open.

Excel opens automatically.

5 In the Microsoft Excel Security Notice pop-up message box, click Enable.

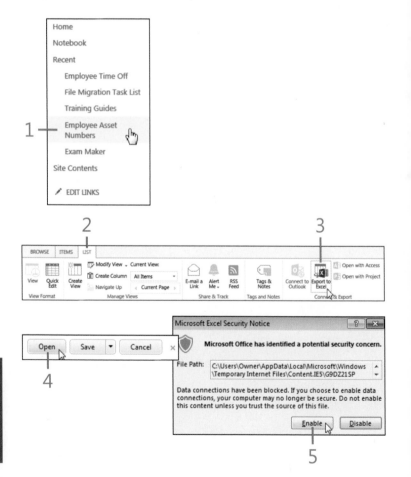

> (→) **TRY THIS** When you export a list to Excel you are given the opportunity to refresh the data from SharePoint when the list is opened. This is due to SharePoint establishing a new data connection between the Excel file and the SharePoint list. On the Design tab in the spreadsheet, explore the options available in the External Table Data group.

Exporting an Excel table to SharePoint

While working within an Excel table, you might want to export the data to SharePoint 2013. In doing so, you are in essence creating a new SharePoint list.

Export an Excel table to SharePoint

1 Open an Excel file that has been formatted as a table and click inside the table.

2 On the ribbon, click the Design tab.

3 In the External Table Data group, click the Export button.

4 On the menu that appears, click Export Table To SharePoint List.

(continued on next page)

TIP If you need to keep the information within Excel synchronized with SharePoint, be sure to select the Create A Read-Only Connection To The New SharePoint List check box.

Export an Excel table to SharePoint *(continued)*

5 On the first page of the Export Table To SharePoint List Wizard that opens, to specify the address to publish to, do either of the following:

- Type the URL to a SharePoint site.

- Select a Quick Link from the list box of sites to which you previously published.

6 Type a name and optional description for the new SharePoint list.

7 Click Next.

8 On page 2 of the wizard, click Finish.

Connecting Access and SharePoint

Microsoft Access is a powerful database tool that, in fact, was also the basis for the datasheet view in previous releases of the SharePoint 2013 platform. Currently, when you select the Quick Edit view on a list within the current SharePoint platform, you are able to do so because of the Access features that have been incorporated into the platform. As a consequence, you can connect a SharePoint list to Access to utilize even more of the tools it offers. One of the more commonly utilized features is the ability to keep information synchronized from both within SharePoint and Access. In doing so, someone could be in Access and update the data, and those changes will show up within the SharePoint list, and vice versa.

Connect Access and SharePoint

1 On the Quick Launch bar, click Site Contents or, under Recent, click a list to go to a previously opened list.

2 On the ribbon, click the List tab.

3 In the Connect & Export group, click the Open With Access button.

4 In the Open In Microsoft Access dialog box, click Browse to select an existing or new database.

5 Choose from two options when exporting the list:

- **Link To Data On The SharePoint Site**   Using this option, you can create a bidirectional link between the Access table and the SharePoint list.

- **Export A Copy Of The Data**   This option exports a copy of the data to an Access table. No link is created by which the data would otherwise remain synchronized between the SharePoint list and the Access table.

6 Click OK.

> ✓ **TIP**   Keep in mind that when you open a list in Access, you are given the choice between creating a copy of the list in Access or creating a link between the list and the table.

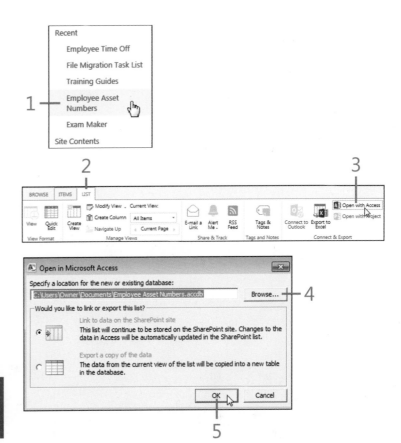

Collaborating with blogs

Blogs are used to publish short articles pertaining to business or personal subjects, called *posts*. The dramatic increase in popularity of blogging has made it common place. Personal blogs usually express an online journal or observations for a network of family and friends. Corporations and other organizations have recognized the value in utilizing blogs to capture and share knowledge as well as strengthen communication and relationships between identified groups such as clients or business partners.

Microsoft SharePoint 2013 incorporates a Blog Site template to include the features that generate collaboration. This section will show you how to get started with your own blog and how to organize and manage the posts and comments.

In this section:

- What's where in a blog site
- Creating a blog site
- Changing your blog picture
- Changing your blog description
- Using categories to organize your blogs
- Managing blog posts
- Managing blog comments
- Subscribing to a blog's RSS feed
- Using desktop blogging tools to publish blog posts

What's where in a blog site

A blog site presents the information that you want to share in an easily accessible fashion. Most series of posts are in reverse chronological order, showing most recent entries on top. SharePoint 2013 blog sites include information about the author and the purpose of the blog itself. Other features include filtering posts by category or calendar month, liking or sharing a link to a post, and subscribing to the blog by using a Real Simple Syndication (RSS) feed or creating an alert.

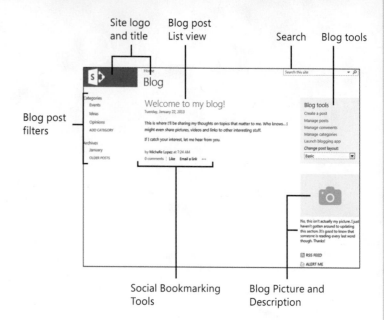

Site logo and title | Blog post List view | Search | Blog tools

Blog post filters

Social Bookmarking Tools | Blog Picture and Description

Creating a blog site

You can create a new blog site in SharePoint 2013 by using the Blog Site template when you're creating a new site or site collection. Typically, this would be created by the SharePoint administrator at your workplace, upon request. If you work at an organization at which you have personal sites, you can create a blog site associated with your personal profile, otherwise known as My Site. The tasks that follow show you how to create a blog site on a SharePoint Team site as well as on your personal My Site.

Create a blog site

1 On the Quick Launch bar, click Site Contents.

2 At the bottom of the Site Contents page, in the Subsites section, click New Subsite.

3 On the New SharePoint Site page, in the Title And Description section, enter a Title for your blog site (optionally, enter a description of the site, if you want). In the Web Site Address section, enter a URL name.

4 In the Select a Template section, click the Collaboration tab and then click Blog.

(continued on next page)

> ⚠️ **CAUTION** If Blog isn't an option on your site, your organization might not allow personal blogging sites. Refer to your company's corporate policy for blogging or contact the SharePoint administrator or Human Resources.

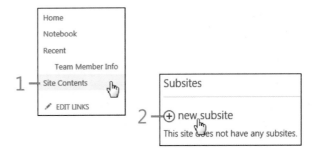

Create a blog site (continued)

5 In the Navigation Inheritance section, under Use The Top Link Bar From The Parent Site, click Yes.

6 Click Create.

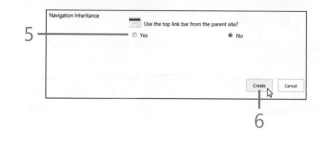

Create a personal blog site from your SharePoint profile

1 In the upper-right corner, click to open the Personal Navigation menu (this is usually indicated by your name).

2 On the menu, click About Me.

3 On the Quick Launch bar, click Blog.

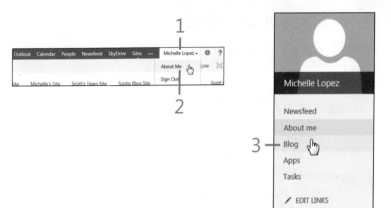

Changing your blog picture

Take a few moments to customize your new SharePoint 2013 blog site before writing posts. Adding a picture or avatar helps your readers to become familiar with who you are, or to connect to the site visually.

Change your blog picture

1 On the ribbon of your blog site, click the Page tab.

2 In the Edit group, click Edit Page.

3 On the lower right of the editable page, in the About This Blog section, click the placeholder image.

4 On the ribbon, click the Image tab.

5 In the Select group, click Change Picture.

6 On the menu that appears, click From Computer.

7 In the Upload Image dialog box, click the Browse button and then, in the Choose File To Upload dialog box that opens, select a picture from your local computer to upload.

(continued on next page)

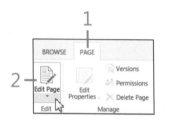

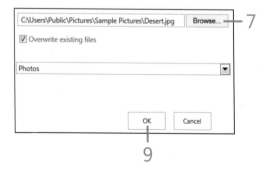

✓ **TIP** You can resize your blog picture by grabbing the picture handles, holding the mouse button down, and then dragging the handles as desired.

Change your blog picture *(continued)*

8 Click Open to confirm the selection.

9 Back in the Upload Image dialog box, click OK. (Refer to the screen shot on the previous page.)

10 In the Photos dialog box, you can add descriptive information about your photo.

11 Click Save.

12 On the Page tab, click Stop Editing.

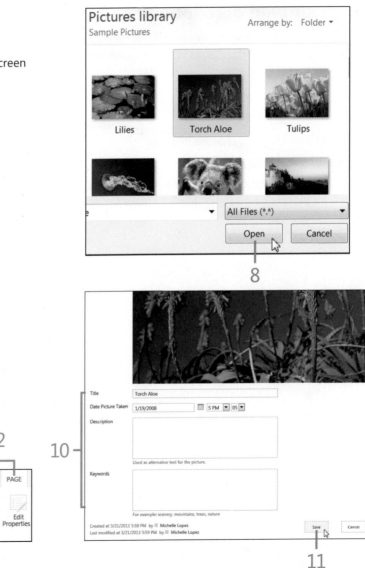

Changing your blog description

You can let your readers know what you plan to write about by adding a blog description. You might want to customize the blog categories by which your topics can be organized.

Change your blog description

1 On the ribbon of your blog site, click the Page tab.

2 In the Edit group, click Edit Page.

3 On the lower right of the editable page, in the About This Blog section, highlight the text below the picture and make the desired changes.

4 On the Page tab, click Stop Editing.

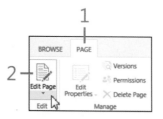

Using categories to organize your blogs

Categories help you to organize your content as well as help your readers to locate the information that interests them. Categorizing your blog content isn't required, but it is useful to separate posts by subjects or topics. SharePoint blog sites come with, but are not limited to, three editable categories: Events, Ideas, and Opinions.

Create a new category

1 On the Quick Launch bar of your blog site, click Add Category.

2 On the Add Category page, in the Title text box, enter the name for your new category.

3 Click Save.

Edit a category

1 In the Blog Tools section of your blog site, click Manage Categories.

2 On the Categories page, click the Edit icon next to the category that you want to edit.

3 Change the name in the Title text box.

4 Click Save.

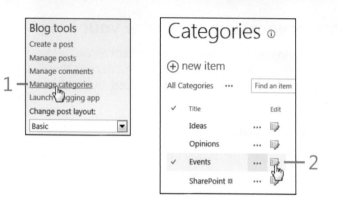

TRY THIS Delete a category by clicking the Delete Item button on the ribbon. Use caution though: deleting a category removes it from all posts to which it was applied.

Managing blog posts

Blog posts share relevant information, promote your expertise, and update colleagues on your activities. Managing your blogs is an essential part of maintaining up-to-date information and keeping your readers well informed.

Create a blog post

1 In the Blog Tools section of your blog site, click Create A Post.

2 On the New Post page, enter your post information.

3 Save the post by using either of the following two methods:

- Click Save As Draft to save the current version. The post will not display to site visitors until it is Published.

- Click Publish to save the post and display it for public viewing. The post will automatically publish on the date that you specified in the Published text box.

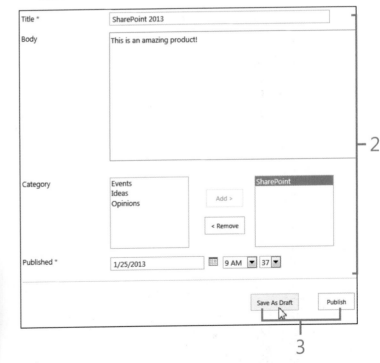

> **TIP** The Save As Draft button will not be an option unless the posts list has the Content Approval option set to Yes in the Versioning Settings on the List Settings page. You can get there by clicking Manage Posts in the Blog Tools section instead of Create A Post.

Publish a blog post that was previously saved as a draft

1 In the Blog Tools section of your blog site, click Manage Posts.

2 On the Posts page, select the check box next to one or more posts whose approval status indicates Pending. (Hover over the items to display the check box.)

3 On the ribbon, click the Items tab and then, in the Workflows group, click Approve/Reject.

4 Click the Approved option.

5 Click OK.

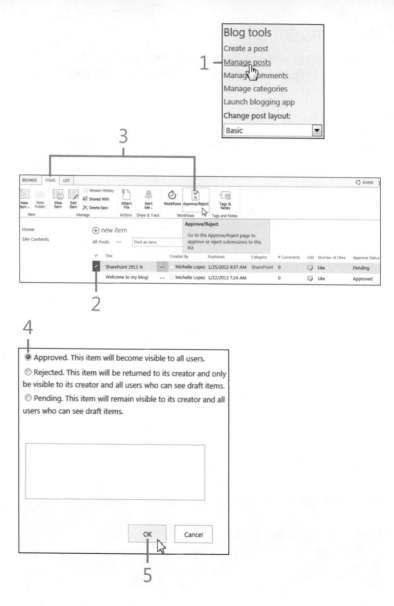

Managing blog comments

Blog comments invite collaboration between you, the author, and your readers. Creating a dialog between the author and viewers enhances the information on the topic.

Add a comment

1 On a blog site, under a blog post, click the Comments link.

2 On the Blog page, in the text box, enter a comment.

3 Click Post.

View, edit, or delete comments

1 In the upper-right Blog Tools section of your blog site, click Manage Comments.

2 On the Comments page, select the check box next to a comment. (Hover over the items to display the check box.)

3 On the ribbon, click the Items tab.

4 In the Manage group, click any of the following options:

- To view comment details, click View Item.

- To edit the comment details, click Edit Item.

- To permanently delete the comment, click Delete Item.

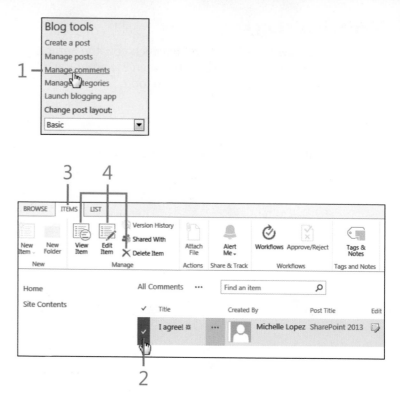

Subscribing to a blog's RSS Feed

RSS (which stands for Really Simple Syndication) Feeds make it possible for content changes to immediately update on the Internet. When you subscribe to an RSS Feed, you or your readers are automatically notified when any changes are made.

Subscribe to RSS

1 On your blog Home page, below the Blog Description, click RSS Feed.

2 On the RSS Feed For Blog Posts page, click the Subscribe To This RSS Feed link.

3 In the Subscribe To This Feed dialog box, click Subscribe to bookmark your feed subscription.

No, this isn't actually my picture. I just haven't gotten around to updating this section. It's good to know that someone is reading every last word though. Thanks!

1 — 🔊 RSS FEED
🗐 ALERT ME

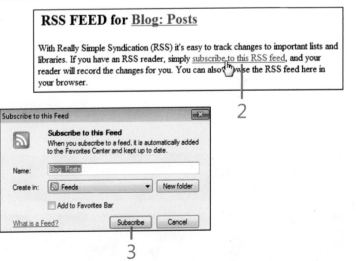

RSS FEED for <u>Blog: Posts</u>

With Really Simple Syndication (RSS) it's easy to track changes to important lists and libraries. If you have an RSS reader, simply <u>subscribe to this RSS feed</u>, and your reader will record the changes for you. You can also browse the RSS feed here in your browser.

2

3

✓ **TIP**   The Alert Me option (below the RSS Feed link) will send your defined changes to your email Inbox.

Using desktop blogging tools to publish blog posts

You can use Microsoft Word and Windows Live Writer to publish to a SharePoint blog site. A blogging tool provides robust options for editing larger posts or working with pictures and other objects that you want to include.

Publish a blog post by using Microsoft Word

1 In the Blog Tools section of your blog site, click Launch Blogging App.

2 In the New SharePoint Blog Account dialog box, click OK to register a new SharePoint blog account with the default settings.

3 In the Account Registration Successful confirmation box, click OK.

4 In the Enter Post Title Here placeholder, type your blog post title.

5 Edit the body of your blog post.

6 On the ribbon, click the Blog Post tab.

7 In the Basic Text group, use the various commands to apply formatting to your post, as desired.

8 In the Blog group, click the Publish button.

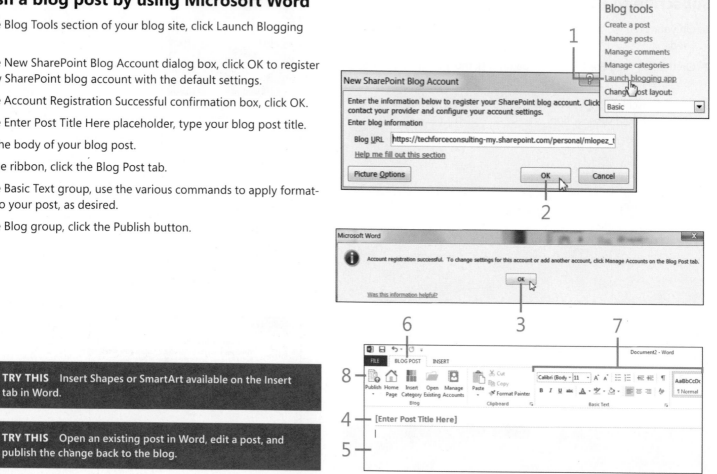

> **TRY THIS** Insert Shapes or SmartArt available on the Insert tab in Word.

> **TRY THIS** Open an existing post in Word, edit a post, and publish the change back to the blog.

Security within SharePoint 2013

14

Securing an organization's information is crucial. Protecting organizational content is a key component to the success of that security.

Microsoft SharePoint 2013 provides proficient security tools to ensure that teams are completely confident that their content is available only to the users to whom they've granted access. Using the SharePoint security model, you can apply access privileges at an overall level such as the site collection, down to an individual level like a single document—not to mention all the levels in between (sites, pages, or lists and libraries).

In this section:

- Understanding SharePoint security
- Adding people to groups
- Creating groups
- Granting permissions to an individual
- Breaking permission inheritance
- Granting access to lists, libraries, and individual items
- Removing security
- Checking permissions
- Editing permissions

Understanding SharePoint security

You can only access SharePoint 2013 if a SharePoint administrator or site owner grants you permission. You can grant permissions to groups of people or to individuals. SharePoint administrators can grant access to Active Directory groups, or Windows network groups, as well.

It is recommended to add individuals to SharePoint groups and then provide access to those groups, rather than directly to individuals. A SharePoint group is a collection of individuals (up to 5,000), and it is much more convenient to manage the applied security settings to a group than to manage individual users.

View site permissions

1   On the Home page, click the Settings button (the small gear icon next to the name of the logged-on user). On the menu that appears, click Site Settings.

2   On the Site Settings page, in the Users And Permissions section, click Site Permissions.

(continued on next page)

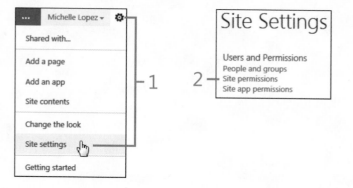

View site permissions *(continued)*

3 On the Permissions page, view the permission levels assigned to each group on the site.

Adding people to groups

A new site can be created to use the same permissions as the parent site or to use unique permissions. Upon creation of a new site with unique permissions, SharePoint 2013 automatically creates three groups: Visitor, Member, and Owner. New groups can be created, and unused groups can be deleted.

Permissions then need to be assigned to groups for them to actually be of use. SharePoint administrators can use permission levels to control what groups or individuals can do within SharePoint. Thirty-three selectable permissions can be mixed and matched in different combinations to define thousands of permission levels.

Permission levels determine what type of activities that group can perform on a site, page, list, library, item, or document. Upon creation of a new team site, SharePoint automatically creates seven permission levels:

Permission level	Definition
Full Control	Users have full control of a site to add, delete, approve, move, and create new sites.
Design	Users can view, add, delete, approve, and customize a SharePoint site.
Edit	Users can add, edit, and delete lists. They can also view, add, update, and delete list items and documents.
Contribute	Users can view, add, update, and delete list items and documents.
Read	Users can view pages and list items. They can also can download document copies.
Limited Access	User can view specific lists, document libraries, list items, folders, or documents when given permission.
View Only	Similar to the Read permission level, but users cannot download items.

Add people to existing groups

1 On the Site Settings page, in the Users And Permissions section, click Site Permissions.

2 On the Permissions page, click the Permissions tab and then, in the Grant group, click Grant Permissions.

3 In the Share dialog box, in the designated text box, enter names, email addresses, or the word "Everyone".

4 Click the Hide Options button.

5 In the Select A Group Or Permission Level list box, select a group name.

6 Click Share.

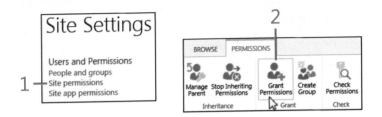

Site Settings

Users and Permissions
People and groups
1 — Site permissions
Site app permissions

BROWSE   PERMISSIONS

Manage   Stop Inheriting   Grant   Create   Check
Parent   Permissions   Permissions   Group   Permissions

Inheritance   Grant   Check

Share 'Michelle's Site'   ×

Invite people to 'Edit'
They'll also get access to the 'SharePoint 2013 Plain & Simple' site and the sites that share permissions with it.

3 — | Enter names, email addresses, or 'Everyone'. |

| Include a personal message with this invitation (Optional). |

4 — HIDE OPTIONS

☑ Send an email invitation

Select a group or permission level

5 — | Members [Edit] |

Share   Cancel — 6

(→) **TRY THIS**   Add yourself to the Members group.

Creating groups

Customizing SharePoint groups makes it possible for your organization to effectively grant access to only the users it specifies.

When you create a group, you can name it, assign it a permission level, and add people to it.

Create a group

1 On the Site Settings page, in the Users And Permissions section, click Site Permissions.

2 On the Permissions page, click the Permissions tab and then, in the Grant group, click Create Group.

(continued on next page)

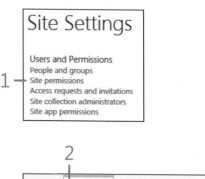

 TIP When necessary, you can assign an existing group as the group owner to allow more than one person to be the group owner.

Create a group *(continued)*

3 On the Create Group page, in the Name text box, enter a name for the group.

4 In the About Me text box, enter a description.

5 Assign a group owner to the group.

6 In the Give Group Permission To This Site section, select a check box corresponding to the permission level that you want to assign to the group.

7 Click Create.

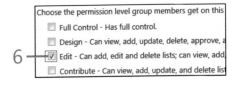

3 ─── Name:
Team Directors

About Me:

4 ───

Group owner:
5 ─── SharePoint Team

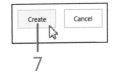

Choose the permission level group members get on this
☐ Full Control - Has full control.
☐ Design - Can view, add, update, delete, approve, a
6 ─── ☑ Edit - Can add, edit and delete lists; can view, add,
☐ Contribute - Can view, add, update, and delete lis

Create   Cancel

7

Granting permissions to an individual

By assigning people to SharePoint 2013 groups, you can see what permissions an individual has and assign those same permissions to someone else simply by adding that person to the same group. Occasionally, however, you might need to assign permissions directly to a user to grant access to a site or its individual items.

Grant permissions to an individual

1   On the Site Settings page, in the Users And Permissions section, click Site Permissions.

2   On the Permissions tab, in the Grant group, click Grant Permissions.

(continued on next page)

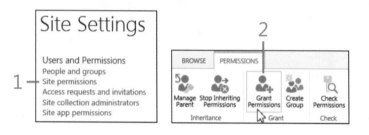

 TIP   It is considered a best practice to manage users within groups instead of individually.

Grant permissions to an individual *(continued)*

3 In the Share dialog box, in the designated text box, enter names, email addresses, or the word "Everyone".

4 Click the Show Options button.

5 In the Select A Group Or Permission Level list box, select a permission level.

6 Click Share.

Invite people to 'Contribute'

Enter names, email addresses, or 'Everyone'.

Include a personal message with this invitation (Optional).

HIDE OPTIONS

☑ Send an email invitation

Select a group or permission level

Contribute

Share   Cancel

Breaking permission inheritance

By default, all children objects (sites, pages, lists, libraries) inherit their permissions from their parent site. Permissions for objects cascade from the parent to the child. For instance, a subsite inherits the permissions of its parent site. A library inherits the permissions of the site in which it is created, and a document inherits the permissions of the library to which it is uploaded. If you want to stop this inheritance and customize permissions, you'll need to break inheritance.

Perhaps you have a site with team information for everyone on your team. By default, everyone who has access to a team library can see the documents in that library. Still, you might want to restrict the Performance Reviews folder to only allow managers to access it. In this case, you would break the inheritance from the parent library so that only the Managers group can see that particular folder.

Break inheritance

1 Select the list or library with which you want to work (for this example, we'll work with a library).

2 On the ribbon, click the Library tab.

3 In the Settings group, click Library Settings.

4 On the Library Settings page, in the Permissions And Management section, click Permissions For This Document Library.

5 On the Permissions tab, in the Inheritance group, click Stop Inheriting Permissions.

(continued on next page)

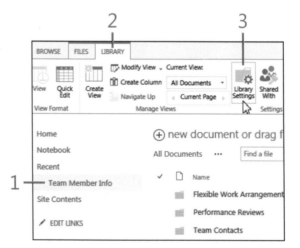

 CAUTION Breaking inheritance prevents future changes to the parent permissions from cascading down to the child item.

TIP It is recommended to inherit permissions whenever possible to avoid burdensome maintenance.

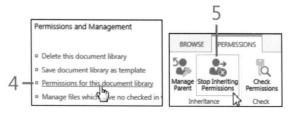

Break inheritance *(continued)*

6 In the pop-up message box that asks you to confirm the change, click OK.

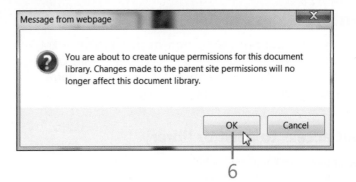

6

Inherit parent permissions

1 Select the list or library with which you want to work (for this example, we'll work with a library). On the ribbon, click the Library tab and then, in the Settings group, click Library Settings.

2 On the Library Settings page, in the Permissions And Management group, click Permissions For This Document Library.

3 On the ribbon, click the Permissions tab and then, in the Inheritance group, click Delete Unique Permissions.

4 In the pop-up message box that asks you to confirm the change, click OK.

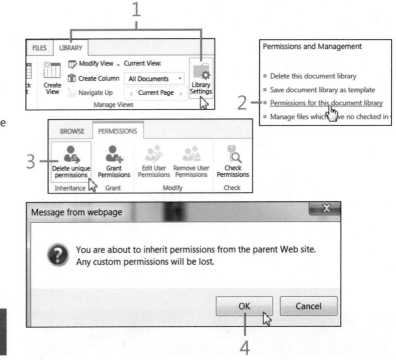

TRY THIS Stop inheriting permissions on a list or library and then configure it to inherit permissions again.

Granting access to lists, libraries, and individual items

When not inheriting permissions from its parent, SharePoint 2013 allows owners to apply unique security at the site collection level, the site level, the library or list level, and to items within a library or list. You might want to grant your department Read access to your site but only allow certain team members to edit documents within the site. SharePoint flexibly accommodates these needs.

Grant access to a list or library

1 Select the list or library with which you want to work (for this example, we'll work with a library).

2 On the ribbon, click the Library tab.

3 In the Settings group, click Library Settings.

4 On the Library Settings page, in the Permissions And Management group, click Permissions For This Document Library.

5 On the Permissions tab, in the Grant group, click Grant Permissions.

(continued on next page)

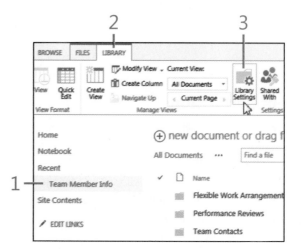

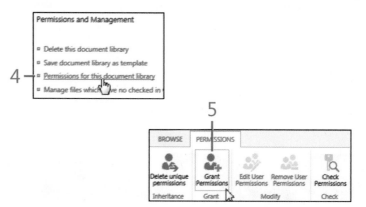

> **TIP** This example assumes that this library does not inherit permissions from its parent.

Grant access to a list or library *(continued)*

6 In the Share dialog box, in the designated text box, enter names, email addresses, or the word "Everyone".

7 Click the Show Options button.

8 In the Select A Permission Level list box, select a permission level.

9 Click Share.

Invite people to 'Contribute'

Enter names, email addresses, or 'Everyone'.

6

Include a personal message with this invitation (Optional).

7 — HIDE OPTIONS

☑ Send an email invitation

Select a group or permission level

8 — Contribute ▼

Share   Cancel — 9

Grant access to individual items

1 Click the drop-down ellipsis to the right of an item in a list or library. (Hover over the item to view the pointing hand.)

2 In the lower-right corner of the Properties box that opens, click the drop-down ellipsis. (Hover over the item to view the pointing hand).

3 On the menu that appears, click Shared With.

4 On the Shared With page, click Advanced.

5 On the Permissions tab, in the Inheritance group, click Stop Inheriting Permissions.

(continued on next page)

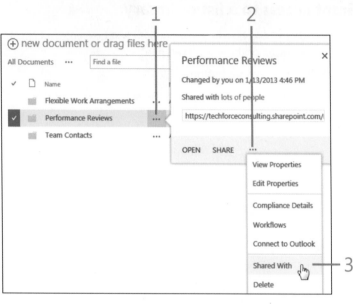

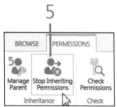

Grant access to individual items *(continued)*

6 In the pop-up message box that asks you to confirm the change, click OK.

7 Back on the ribbon, click Grant Permissions.

8 In the Share dialog box, in the designated text box, enter names, email addresses, or the word "Everyone".

9 Click the Show Options button.

10 In the Select A Permission Level list box, select a permission level.

11 Click Share.

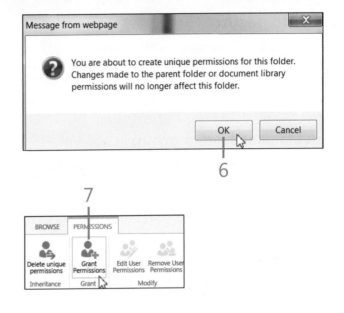

Removing security

Logically, if you'll be granting access to SharePoint 2013, you'll be removing access, as well. Removing users from items or groups involves the same steps as adding users. You'll begin to realize the convenience of managing users in groups as opposed to individually. Removing users from a group can be done in one location instead of each location where they've been added separately.

Remove a user from a group

1 On the Home page, click the Settings button (the small gear icon next to the name of the logged-on user). On the menu that appears, click Site Settings.

2 On the Site Settings page, in the Users And Permissions section, click People And Groups.

3 On the Quick Launch bar, click Groups.

4 Click the name of the group from which you want to remove the user.

(continued on next page)

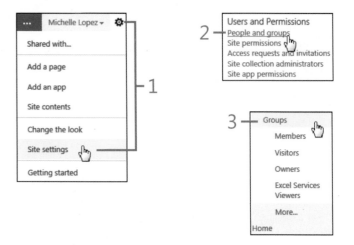

Remove a user from a group *(continued)*

5 Select the check box next to the name of the user whom you want to remove.

6 Click the Actions drop-down arrow.

7 On the menu that appears, click Remove Users From Group.

8 In the pop-up message box that asks you to confirm the change, click OK.

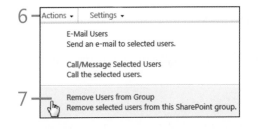

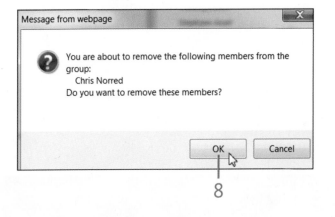

TIP If you don't see the Actions menu, it's because you don't have permissions to edit members of that Group.

Remove a group's site permissions

1 On the Home page, click the Settings button (the small gear icon next to the name of the logged-on user). On the menu that appears, click Site Settings.

2 On the Site Settings page, in the Users And Permissions section, click Site Permissions.

3 Select the check box next to the group from which you want to remove site permissions.

4 On the Permissions tab, in the Modify group, click Remove User Permissions.

5 In the pop-up message box that asks you to confirm the change, click OK.

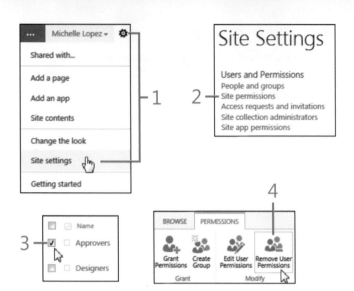

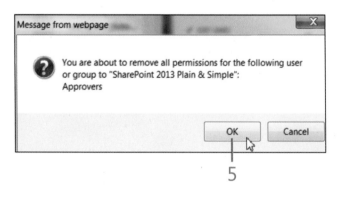

 TIP This example assumes that this library does not inherit permissions from its parent.

CAUTION Removing a group from a site also removes the users within that group from the site.

Editing permissions

Suppose that a project has completed and you no longer want the team to add or edit the project's supporting documents.

The flexibility of SharePoint 2103 gives you the ability to easily make changes to permission level of an individual or a group.

Edit site permissions for an individual or group

1 On the Home page, click the Settings button (the small gear icon next to the name of the logged-on user). On the menu that appears, click Site Settings.

2 On the Site Settings page, in the Users And Permissions section, click Site Permissions.

3 On the Permissions page, if the site is inheriting permissions, click Stop Inheriting Permissions, and then, in the pop-up message box that asks you to confirm the change, click OK.

4 Select the check box next to the group or individual for which you want to edit permissions.

5 Click Edit User Permissions.

6 Clear the current permissions check box and select a different one.

7 Click OK.

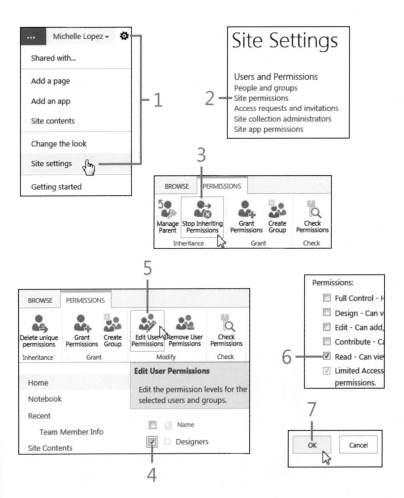

> **TIP** Permissions will default to the highest level of security. Be sure to clear an existing Edit permission level check box if the user/group should only have Read access.

Checking permissions

It can be easy to lose track of who has access to your sites and libraries. You can use the tools on the SharePoint 2013 ribbon to check what permissions are on an entire site or to view a summary of the permissions assigned to a group or individual.

View permissions on a library or list

1 On the Quick Launch bar, click Site Contents.

2 Click the drop-down ellipsis to the right of the library with which you want to work. (Hover over the library for the drop-down indicator to display).

3 On the menu that appears, click Settings.

4 On the Library Settings page, in the Permissions And Management group, click Permissions For This Document Library.

5 On the Permissions tab, review each group name and permission level.

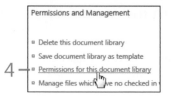

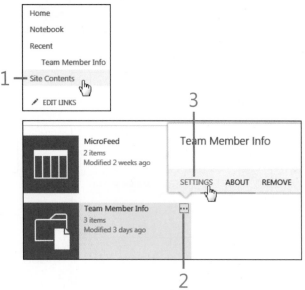

Check permissions for an individual or group

1 On the Home page, click the Settings button (the small gear icon next to the name of the logged-on user). On the menu that appears, click Site Settings.

2 On the Site Settings page, in the Users And Permissions section, click Site Permissions.

3 On the Permissions tab, in the Check group, click Check Permissions.

4 In the Check Permissions dialog box, in the User/Group text box, enter the name of the person or group.

5 Click Check Now.

6 In the Check Permissions dialog box, review the permission level summary.

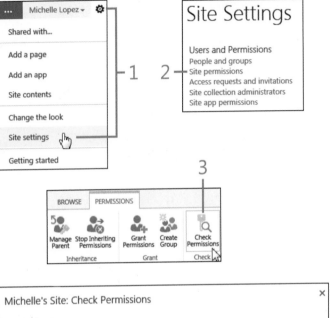

Using personal sites and social networking

If your company or organization provides the feature called My Site, you have your own Microsoft SharePoint 2013 website. You have the ability to store content of interest to you or share it with others. You can also list your interests and areas of expertise, tag content with keywords, share information that others can search for, and make it possible for others to follow your own personal Blog.

In this section:

- Introducing My Site
- Editing your user profile
- Uploading content
- Following people
- Searching for people to follow
- Updating your status
- Using your note board
- Using tags
- Using mentions
- Using tasks
- Customizing tasks views

Introducing My Site

By listing your interests and areas of expertise on your My Site, others can locate you when they're searching for that particular skill set. With My Sites, you can document and blog about your daily observations and invite colleagues to access your content. Likewise, you can follow other colleagues as they share their own content and information.

My Sites include a Newsfeed page for selecting colleagues to follow, topics of interest to tag, and content to track; an About

Me page for managing your profile and activities; a Blog site to promote communication on topics of your choosing; an Apps page to share your own content; and a Tasks page that consolidates all personal tasks with tasks assigned to you across other SharePoint sites.

Open your My Site

1 On the Home page, in the upper-right corner, click your name and then, on the menu that appears, click About Me.

1

| Outlook | Calendar | People | Newsfeed | SkyDrive | Sites | ... | Michelle Lopez ▾ |

SH   About Me

Michelle's Site   Scott's Team Site   Scotts Blog Site   Sc   Sign Out

TIP Check whether your organization has policies regarding what content can be stored and shared online.

Editing your user profile

The user profiles associated with SharePoint 2013 My Sites give you the opportunity to discover and utilize the expertise of people within your organization. In addition, you can showcase your own skills and interests.

When SharePoint is initially deployed, your My Site user profile has undergone minimal customization. So, when you first access your My Site, be sure to update it so that the details you make available to others are helpful and informative.

Edit your user profile

1 On the About Me page, click Edit Your Profile.

2 On the Edit Details page, click any of the following headings to update your information:

- Basic Information
- Contact Information
- Details
- Newsfeed Settings
- Language And Region

3 Click Save All And Close.

TRY THIS Edit your user profile with your current information.

TIP You might want to keep some information private, such as your home phone number. You can adjust shared settings in your profile in the upper-right corner, in the Who Can See This? section.

Uploading content

SharePoint 2013 automatically creates a document library on your My Site called Documents. It also creates a folder within that library called Shared With Everyone, the contents of which is available to read by everyone except external users. Anything outside of the Shared With Everyone folder will be private unless it is intentionally shared by you by editing the content's permissions. Likewise, when viewing colleagues' My Sites, their public documents can be viewed in their Shared With Everyone folder located in their documents library.

Upload public content to your My Site

1 On your About Me page, on the Quick Launch bar, click Apps.

2 On the Site Contents page, click Documents.

3 On the Documents page, click the Shared With Everyone folder.

(continued on next page)

Upload public content to your My Site *(continued)*

4 On the Shared With Everyone page, click New Document.

5 On the menu that opens, click Upload Existing File.

6 In the Add A Document dialog box, click Browse.

7 Select the file that you want to upload.

8 Click Open.

9 Click OK.

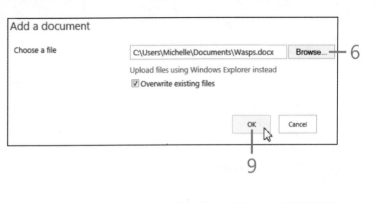

Following people

Following people makes it possible for you to easily link to colleagues, coworkers, industry leaders, or people with whom you share common interests. With SharePoint 2013, you can stay up to date on a person's blogs, insights, tags, and information.

You can follow your colleagues, but you might come across a newsfeed and want to follow someone who shared an interesting post. Your content and opinions can also be followed to promote dynamic connections between yourself and others.

Follow a person

1   Click on a Blog or Community site.

2   Under a blog post, click a person's name.

3   On that person's About Me page, click Follow This Person or click Follow *Name*, where *Name* would be the actual name of the individual whose My Site you're on.

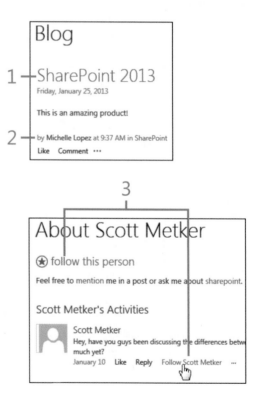

Stop following a person

1 On your About Me page, on the Quick Launch bar, click Newsfeed.

2 On the Newsfeed page, in the I'm Following section, click the number displayed above the People label.

3 On the People I'm Following page, click the drop-down ellipsis (...) next to the name of the person whom you want to stop following.

4 On the menu that appears, click Stop Following.

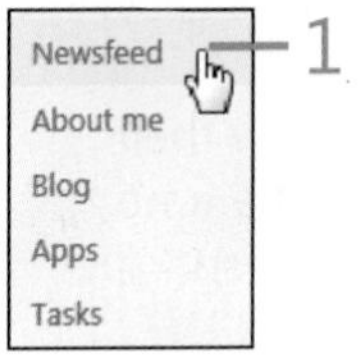

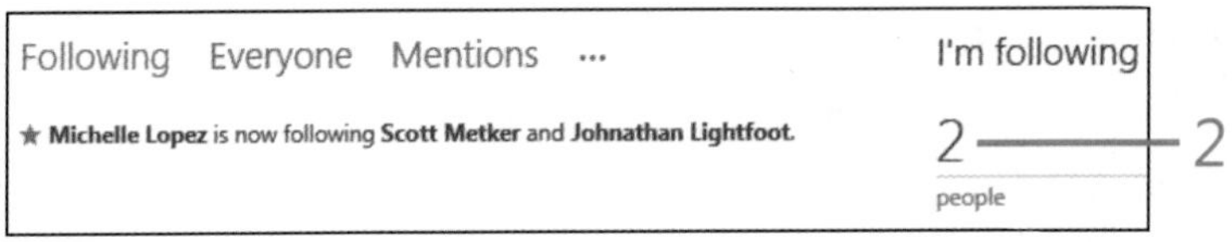

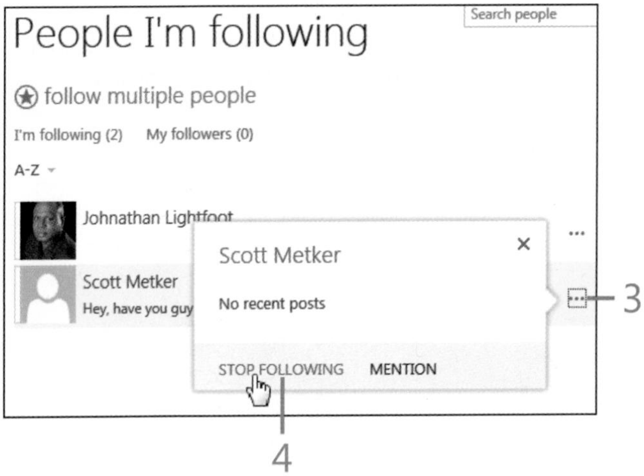

Newsfeed — 1
About me
Blog
Apps
Tasks

Following   Everyone   Mentions   ···   I'm following
★ **Michelle Lopez** is now following **Scott Metker** and **Johnathan Lightfoot.**   2 — 2
                                                                        people

People I'm following   Search people

⊛ follow multiple people

I'm following (2)   My followers (0)

A-Z ▾

Johnathan Lightfoot   ···

Scott Metker   ✕
Scott Metker
Hey, have you guy   No recent posts   ⊞ — 3

                     STOP FOLLOWING   MENTION

                            4

✓ **TIP** You can see who is following you by clicking My Followers.

Searching for people to follow

Searching for people is simple when you already know their name or want to search for more than one person at a time. Sometimes you might be looking for someone with a specific skill set or expertise but don't yet know the person's name. In this case, you can search on keywords and let SharePoint 2013 find the people who retain that desired knowledge.

Search for a person by name

1 On your About Me page, click Newsfeed.

2 On the Newsfeed page, in the I'm Following section, click the number displayed above the People label.

3 On the People I'm Following page, click Follow.

4 In the Follow People dialog box, type the names of people whom you want to add. (SharePoint searches and displays possible matches as you type.)

5 Click the Follow button.

Newsfeed — 1
About me
Blog
Apps
Tasks

Following   Everyone   Mentions   ...   I'm following

★ **Michelle Lopez** is now following **Scott Metker** and **Johnathan Lightfoot**.   2 — 2

people

3

People I'm following

⊛ follow multiple people

I'm following (3)   My followers (0)

Follow People   ✕

Follow people to get updates about them in your newsfeed.

4 — Johnathan Lightfoot x   dan|

Dan Park
Vice President NA Sales
Showing 1 result

Follow   Cancel

5

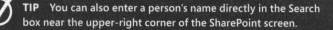

TIP You can also enter a person's name directly in the Search box near the upper-right corner of the SharePoint screen.

Search for a person by keyword

1 On the About Me page, in the Search Everything field located in the upper-right corner, click the drop-down arrow.

2 On the menu that appears, click People.

3 In the Search People field, enter a keyword on which to search.

4 Click the Search button (the magnifying-glass icon).

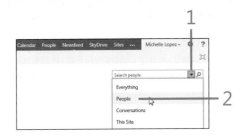

Updating your status

Updating your status keeps others abreast of your current activities. SharePoint aims to provide a platform for users to update their status in a business context. Posting information about what you're researching or working on gives colleagues an opportunity to assist you with the task at hand.

Post your status

1 On the About Me page, on the Quick Launch bar, click Newsfeed.

2 On the Newsfeed page, in the Start A Conversation text box, type whatever it is that you want to share with everyone.

3 Click the Post button.

 TIP Add a picture to your post by clicking the Camera icon, which is below the Share With Everyone text box.

TRY THIS Update your status to show that you are reading *SharePoint 2013 Plain & Simple.*

View the status of a colleague

1 On your About Me page, on the Quick Launch bar, click Newsfeed.

2 On the Newsfeed page, in the I'm Following section, click the number displayed above the People label.

3 On the People I'm Following page, click the drop-down ellipsis (...) next to the name of the person whom you want to view.

4 Click the person's name.

Newsfeed ——— 1
About me
Blog
Apps
Tasks

Following   Everyone   Mentions   ···   I'm following

★ **Johnathan Lightfoot** is now following Michelle's Site.   3 ——— 2

★ **Johnathan Lightfoot** is now following **Scott Metker.**   people

People I'm following

Search people

⊛ follow multiple

I'm following (3)   My foll

A-Z ▾

Johnathan Lightfoot ——————— 4   ✕

Johnathan Lightfoot is now following
Michelle's Site.
See conversation

Dan Park

Johnathan Lightfoot is now following **Scott
Metker.**
See conversation   ··· ——— 3

Johnathan Ligh

Scott Metker
Hey, have you guy

Johnathan Lightfoot is now following
Maulik's Site.
See conversation

 TIP Notice how your Newsfeed page displays your colleague's updates sorted with the newest posts on the top.

Using your note board

When you come across a useful or interesting article, the Note Board feature in SharePoint 2013 gives you a way to make a note or comment about that content to which you can refer back. This is practical when you've saved several items as Favorites and can't quite remember why. Adding a note to an item also communicates your opinion on the topic to your colleagues. You can also add a note outside of SharePoint while browsing the web.

Add a note

1 In a library, select the check box to the left of the file or folder to which you want to add a note.

2 On the ribbon, click the Files tab.

3 In the Tags And Notes group, click Tags & Notes.

4 In the Tags And Note Board dialog box, click the Note Board tab.

5 Enter a note or comment.

6 Click the Post button.

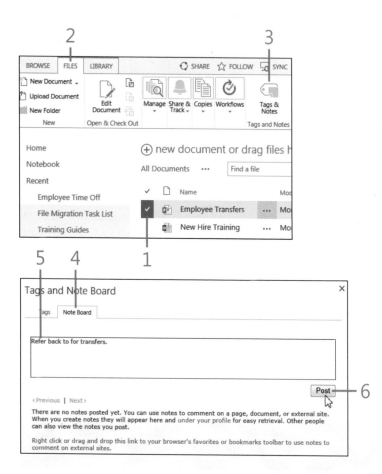

Add the notes tool to your favorites

1 In a library, select the check box to the left of the file or folder to which you want to add a note.

2 On the ribbon, click the Files tab.

3 In the Tags And Notes group, click Tags & Notes.

4 In the Tags And Note Board dialog box, click the Note Board tab.

5 Right-click the link that reads Right Click Or Drag And Drop This Link To Your Browser's Favorites Or Bookmarks Toolbar To Use Notes To Comment On External Sites.

6 On the shortcut menu that appears, click Add To Favorites.

7 In the Add A Favorite dialog box, click the Add button.

8 Back in the Tags And Note Board dialog box, click the X in the upper-right corner to close the box.

Tags and Note Board

Tags | Note Board

‹ Previous | Next ›

There are no notes posted yet. You can use notes to comment on ... nal site. When you create notes they will appear here and under your profi... people can also view the notes you post.

Right click or drag and drop this link to your browser's favorites o... notes to comment on external sites.

Open
Open in new tab
Open in new window
Save target as...
Print target
Cut
Copy
Copy shortcut
Paste
Add to favorites...
Send to OneNote
Properties

Post

Add a Favorite

Do you want to add this bookmarklet?
Bookmarklets run script and can send information to sites on the Internet. Only add bookmarklets from websites you trust.

What's the risk?

Name: | Tags and Note Board |

Create in: | Favorites ▼ | New Folder |

Add | Cancel

BROWSE | FILES | LIBRARY | SHARE | FOLLOW | SYNC

New Document | Upload Document | New Folder
New

Edit Document
Open & Check Out

Manage | Share & Track | Copies | Workflows

Tags & Notes
Tags and Notes

Home
Notebook
Recent
   Employee Time Off
   File Migration Task List
   Training Guides

new document or drag files h

All Documents ··· | Find a file

✓ | Name | Mod
✓ | Employee Transfers | ··· | Mo
   New Hire Training | ··· | Mo

TRY THIS Add the SharePoint Tags And Notes tool to your Favorites.

Using tags

Tagging documents or sites makes it easier for you and other users to find items associated with specific topics or keywords. SharePoint 2013 makes it possible to apply existing tags, also known as #tags (pronounced "hash tags"), to follow that tagged topic in your Newsfeed.

Add a tag to a document

1 In a library, select the check box to the left of the file or folder to which you want to add a tag.

2 On the ribbon, click the Files tab.

3 In the Tags And Notes section, click Tags & Notes.

4 In the Tags And Note Board dialog box, click the Tags tab.

5 In the My Tags text box, enter a Tag or Keyword.

6 Click the Save button.

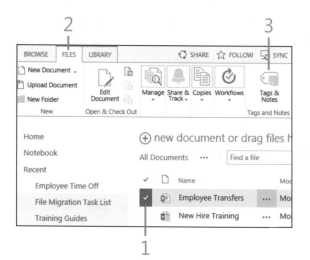

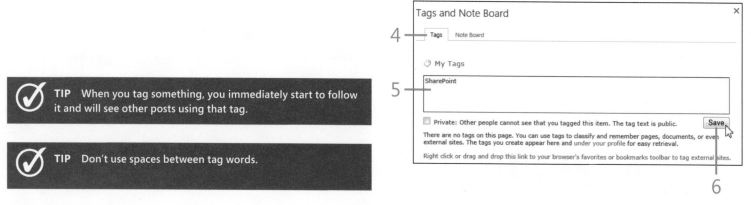

> **TIP** When you tag something, you immediately start to follow it and will see other posts using that tag.

> **TIP** Don't use spaces between tag words.

Use a tag in a post

1 On your About Me page, on the Quick Launch bar, click Newsfeed.

2 On the Newsfeed page, enter text in the Start A Conversation text box.

3 Type the hashtag symbol (#) and then continue typing to see a list of existing tags that match what you've typed.

4 In the option menu that opens, click the existing tag name.

5 Click Post.

TIP Use existing tags whenever possible so that anyone following that tag will receive an update in their Newsfeed.

TIP If an existing tag doesn't exist, continue typing and the new tag will be created after you click Post.

Using mentions

Many times when updating that status on your newsfeed or replying to a blog post, you'll reference a colleague's name. Mentioning someone in SharePoint 2013 draws attention to others and alerts those people that you've mentioned them. Newsfeeds will also be updated across the community, indicating that someone they're following has been mentioned.

Similarly, when people in your organization mention you in a post, you might want to know it occurred. If your newsfeed settings include the option to automatically receive an email when anyone mentions you in a post, you'll be notified in your Inbox. You can also view a history of all posts in which you've been mentioned.

Mention a colleague

1 On your About Me page, on the Quick Launch bar, click Newsfeed.

2 Enter text in the Start A Conversation text box.

3 Type the "at" symbol (@) and then continue typing to see a list of available colleague names.

4 In the option menu that opens, click the desired colleague's name.

5 Click Post.

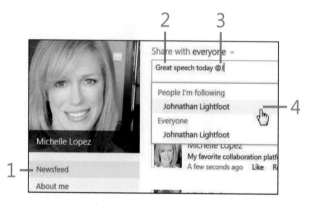

Who has mentioned me?

1 On your About Me page, on the Quick Launch bar, click Newsfeed.

2 On the Newsfeed page, click Mentions.

Using tasks

Everyone has tasks to complete on different projects, whether work related or personal. Wouldn't it be convenient to track everything in one centralized location? The My Tasks page in SharePoint 2013 does just that. It pulls tasks from various locations such as SharePoint, Microsoft Outlook, and Microsoft Project. You can add your personal tasks here as well—they're only visible to you. You can highlight important and upcoming tasks to provide a visible cue.

Create a new task

1 On your About Me page, on the Quick Launch bar, click Tasks.

2 On the My Tasks page, click New Task.

3 In the Title text box, enter a name for the task.

4 Use your mouse or tab key to move to the Due Date text box and then, on the calendar that opens, enter a due date.

> **TIP** The lock icon appears to the right of the Task name to indicate that it is private and that other users cannot view it.

Highlight important tasks

1 On your About Me page, on the Quick Launch bar, click Tasks.

2 On the My Tasks page, click the white exclamation mark (!) to the left of the important task to turn it red.

TIP By default, the red Important indicator will begin to fade and be cleared completely after two weeks. Review Important tasks often and re-click the indicator to reset the two week count down.

TRY THIS Click the Important And Upcoming view on the My Tasks page to view your tasks in a timeline.

Customizing tasks views

After the tasks assigned to you are in one centralized location on your My Tasks page, you can adjust the view options to suit your needs. You might want to only view tasks that have been edited in the last year, or revise the tasks default timeline range. You can also choose which projects or task lists to include on your page, and synchronize your tasks with Microsoft Outlook.

Edit the My Tasks settings

1 On your About Me page, on the Quick Launch bar, click Tasks.

2 On the ribbon, on the Tasks tab, click Settings.

3 On the My Tasks settings page, update any of the following options: Old Tasks Limit, Upcoming Tasks, Important Tasks, Recently Added Tasks, Default Timeline Range, Automatically Hide Empty Filters, or Projects.

4 Click the Save button.

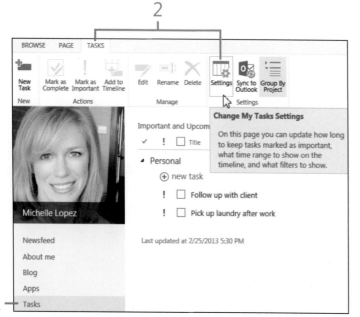

Synchronize My Tasks with Outlook

1 On your About Me page, on the Quick Launch bar, click Tasks.

2 On the ribbon, on the Tasks tab, click Sync To Outlook.

3 In the Sync Tasks With Microsoft Outlook dialog box, select the check box next to Sync Tasks.

4 Click the OK button.

3

Sync Tasks with Microsoft Outlook   ✕

Sync tasks between SharePoint and your inbox, and work with them anywhere. Your changes show up in SharePoint. Your Microsoft Outlook tasks will also show up in Tasks under Newsfeed.

☑ Sync tasks

Status:
Tasks last synced on 2/25/2013 6:04:56 PM

OK   Cancel

4

2

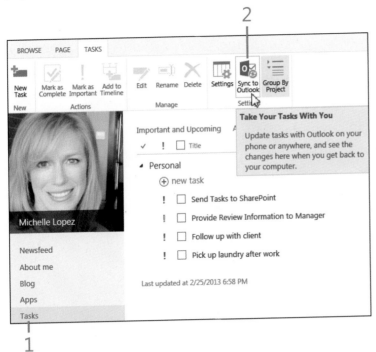

1

Searching for information

16

Even perfectly organized Microsoft SharePoint 2013 sites can grow very large over time, making it more difficult for you to find content. Additionally, when users start working with large numbers of SharePoint sites, keeping track of all of the information can become nearly impossible. Metadata, folder navigation, and site navigation are all tools to help organize information in a more practical way, but increasingly, search is becoming the first, last, and primary method employed by most users to find content.

Each major release of SharePoint featured significantly improved search functionality, particularly with respect to the user experience. SharePoint 2013 supports a seamless search experience across many different kinds of documents: Office Documents, PDF, videos, webpages, personal profiles and even previous online conversations. When searching within Share-Point, the search experience is tailored to get you the information that you need, regardless of the source or type of information.

In this section:

- Introducing the Search Center
- Creating and searching from Search Center
- Preparing your site for search
- Searching site content
- Using search refinement
- Previewing search results in Search Center
- Using advanced search
- Working with search alerts
- Setting your search preferences
- Introducing Search Administration
- Promoting search results
- Excluding content from search

Introducing the Search Center

If you've used the built-in search dialog that appears on your local SharePoint 2013 site, you've already had some experience with the SharePoint search functionality. Search Centers extend this functionality and give you the capability to tailor the search experience for the content on your site or for the audience that uses your site.

A Search Center is a special kind of SharePoint site template with which users can enter search queries and navigate search results. Each Search Center can be configured for a particular search experience (for example, optimized for searching video content). There are two Search Center templates in SharePoint 2013.

- **Basic Search Center**   The Basic Search Center supports a basic query page on which search terms can be entered and a basic results page used for displaying results. An advanced search page is also included for adding metadata to queries.

- **Enterprise Search Center**   The Enterprise Search Center includes a default query page and five pages for display of specialized results: Everything (all results), People, Conversations, Videos, and Reports. It also includes the same advanced search page as the Basic Search Center. Unlike the basic Search Center, however, you can add additional search query pages, result pages, and customized search tabs to the site.

Like most other site templates, you can customize the look and feel of the Search Center by adding or removing Web Parts from the search or results templates and even add new pages (to the Enterprise Search Center).

Most important, you can redirect your other sites to point at uniquely configured Search Centers, depending on the type of content used within these sites. You can optimize a Search Center to display only video content, certain types of documents, or only published and approved content, if necessary.

Search Centers also offer the flexibility of both hiding content from search and promoting content higher in the search rating. Hiding content can be effective for large amounts of content that you don't want your users accessing accidently. Promoted terms can be used to drive users to particularly important documents, pages, or sites when certain keywords are entered as a part of the search.

The end-user experience within the Search Center template has been greatly enhanced within SharePoint 2013, with integrated previews of Microsoft Office–based documents as well as video content directly integrated into the search results. This makes it possible for users to browse for content much more quickly. In addition, users can refine search results by using metadata to quickly home in on relevant content.

End-users also can customize their search experience within a Search Center, choosing how to open documents (online or in a client application) and picking the language of documents to return in search results. Users can even configure email alerts for when search results change.

In summary, the two most noticeable features within Share-Point 2013 search are the enhanced end-user experience and improved configurability available to administrators.

TIP The Enterprise Search Center is only available in some site configurations and licensing arrangements, so if you are unable to see this Search Center in the steps in this section, please consult your administrator.

TIP FAST search was fully integrated into SharePoint 2013, so if you are familiar with the separate FAST Search Center used in SharePoint 2010, that functionality has been merged into the Enterprise Search Center template.

Learning the SharePoint 2013 search results screen

One of the first things you'll likely think when you see the SharePoint 2013 search results page is "Wow! There's a lot going on here!" At first, the amount of information presented can be overwhelming, but many of these items are tools designed to help you to both refine and preview your search results.

As you learn the interface, you'll be able to quickly run a basic search and "home in" on relevant information by using the search tools. The preview capabilities also help with the problem of viewing a number of search results, particularly when this content consists of documents. In the past, users would need to individually open each document to determine if it contains anything of value to them. But now, with the improved preview functionality and Office Web Applications integrations, users can quickly view Office documents without having to open them from the site directly.

Although the options available in your search results might vary slightly (due to licensing restrictions and IT configuration), a typical search results page contains the following elements:

- The **Search box** shows your current query and gives you the capability to edit your search terms.

- The **Refinement** area is where you can further filter your search results based on document metadata. For example, you can click on a Result type of PowerPoint so that your results only show presentations.

- Using **search navigation**, you can switch between specialized search pages that further filter the results. This feature is only available in the Enterprise Search Center

- The **search results** shows you a listing of all site content that match the current query

- The **document preview** shows you a preview of a document by using the Office Web Apps functionality. This functionality only works for certain Web Parts.

- The **pagination** display shows you the number of pages for certain types of documents and, for Power-Point, lets you advance the previewed page.

- The **take a look inside** area shows you the first few section headers or slide titles within the previewed document.

- The **document menu** makes it possible for you to download a copy of the document.

- Using **document actions**, you can directly edit the document, follow it (receive notifications based on document changes), send the document by email, or navigate to the library containing the document.

- You can use the **open in new window** button to open the document in a new window.

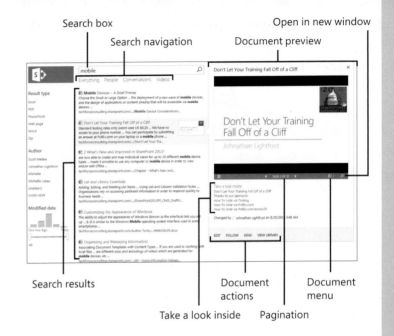

Search box

Search navigation

Open in new window

Document preview

Search results

Take a look inside

Document actions

Pagination

Document menu

Creating a Search Center

The first step toward using a Search Center is creating one. You create a Search Center as you would any other site or subsite; you start by creating a new site from a template. You can add a Search Center as a subsite directly under one of your current sites, or your administrator can create it as a stand-alone site collection.

Create a Search Center

1 From the site that you will use as the parent site, click the Settings button (the small gear icon next to the name of the logged-on user) and then, on the menu that appears, click the Site Contents link.

2 On the Site Contents page, scroll down to the Subsites section and click the new subsite link.

3 On the New SharePoint Site page, enter a title and description for the Search Center.

4 Enter a relative URL under which this site will be created.

5 Choose one of the Search Center templates.

(continued on next page)

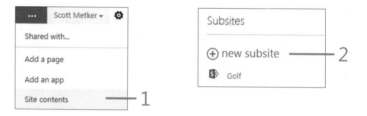

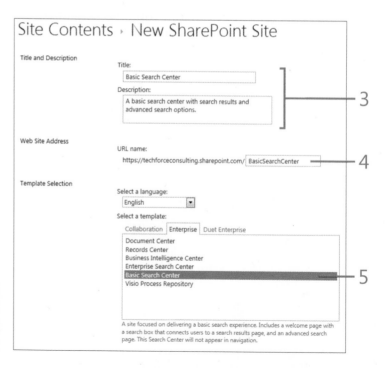

> **TIP** The Search Center templates (as well as all site templates) available for you to select are subject to both your licensing terms and the configuration performed by your IT staff. You might not have all of these templates available within your SharePoint 2013 environment.

Create a Search Center (continued)

6 Select the navigation options for the site (and the parent site).

7 Click Create.

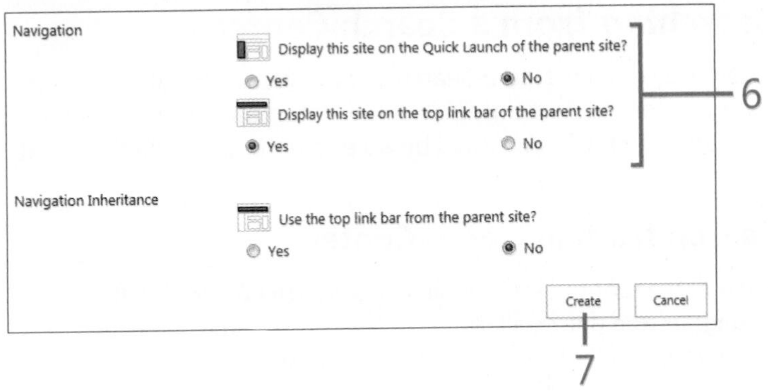

Navigation

Display this site on the Quick Launch of the parent site?

○ Yes   ◉ No

Display this site on the top link bar of the parent site?

◉ Yes   ○ No

6

Navigation Inheritance

Use the top link bar from the parent site?

○ Yes   ◉ No

Create   Cancel

7

Searching from a Search Center

After you have created a Search Center, you'll probably want to try it out for the first time. From the Home page of your newly created Search Center, you'll be able to enter a simple, free-text query similar to that which you might use with an online search provider such as Bing.com.

Search from a Search Center

1 From the root site that contains your Search Center, click the Settings button (the small gear icon next to the name of the logged-on user) and then, on the menu that appears, click the Site Contents link.

2 On the Site Contents page, scroll down to the Subsites section and click the link for your Search Center (in this example, it's Basic Search Center).

3 On the Search Center page, in the search text box, enter your search terms.

4 Click the the Search button (the magnifying-glass icon) to perform the search.

Effective search techniques

If you've made use of search within a SharePoint 2013 Search Center, you've probably already noticed how similar the experience is to working with a search engine such as Bing or Google. Regardless, the blank search window can be daunting, particularly when you are trying to search for a file that is buried under a mountain of similar content. In this case, there are options you can use that will quickly help you isolate exactly the content you need to find quickly.

The expressions that you type into the search box in a Share-Point Search Center are referred to as the Keyword Query Language (KQL); however, this is simply a complex way of describing expressions that you can add to your queries to help you focus and further analyze relevant information.

The minimalist search box that appears on a search center supports some very powerful options.

Find content containing all keywords

The simplest method for refining your search if too many items are returned is to add additional keywords to the query. SharePoint 2013 lists the keywords that you originally used at the top of the search page so that you can quickly modify and extend your original query without having to retype it.

By default, each of the search terms that you enter are all required to appear in the matching documents, so if you type three separate words into the search interface, all three words must appear somewhere in the returned documents.

Each of the three search terms must appear in any search results.

S >

proposal contoso tools

Result type

Word

Author

Scott Metker

SHOW MORE

Proposal for Contoso Marketing Tools
Contoso Marketing **Proposal**.docx ...
techforceconsulting.sharepoint.com/.../**Contoso** Marketing **Proposal**.d...

1 result

Alert Me   Preferences   Advanced Search

> **TIP** Your keywords are not required to appear in order or even together in the text. The only requirement is that each of the words must appear somewhere in the document or in the item properties.

Find content matching any of your keywords

Sometimes, in more complex queries, you want to include results that match one of two queries. In this case, you are really asking for one result "or" another, which requires the use of the *OR* keyword. Typically, when using the OR keyword, you will need to enclose multiterm expressions within parentheses to ensure that the query engine knows which terms to combine and how.

This search expression will find both documents containing *contoso* and *ediscovery* and documents containing *contoso* and *proposal*.

(contoso ediscovery) OR (contoso proposal)

My Search Site

Result type

Excel

SharePoint Site

Team Site

Web page

Word

Zip

Author

Scott Metker

smetker2

SHOW MORE

Proposal for **Contoso** Marketing Tools
Contoso Marketing **Proposal**.docx ...
techforceconsulting.sharepoint.com/.../**Contoso** Marketing **Proposal**.d...

04 - Organizing and Managing Information - Writing Comple...
and release date of the file to the file name, such as "**Contoso** - **Proposal** - May 2013.docx ... For example, if you want to find all **proposals** released in the year 2013, you have no way ...
techforceconsulting.sharepoint.com/.../04 - Organizing and Managing...

04 - Organizing and Managing Information - Author Reviewe...
and release date of the file to the file name, such as "**Contoso** - **Proposal** - May 2013.docx ... For example, if you want to find all **proposals** released in the year 2013, you have no way ...
techforceconsulting.sharepoint.com/.../04 - Organizing and Managing...

19 - SharePoint and eDiscovery - Writing Complete v1.0
that all emails containing references to **Contoso** as well as any documents assigned to this ... **eDiscovery** Queries – an **eDiscovery** query is search query that can be used to export a set ...

 TIP The OR operator can be combined with some of the other techniques in this section; thus, you can create very complex search operations that can include wildcards and phrases.

CAUTION Unlike query terms, the OR keyword must be capitalized or it will be treated as an ordinary word to search.

Search on partial keywords

By default, SharePoint searches find only exact matches for the keywords that you enter in the search box. Sometimes, you might want to search for only part of a word because it might have multiple endings. In this case, you can add a special operator to the end your partial word to match all documents containing this partial word.

This operator is called the *wildcard* operator, and it is represented by an asterisk (*). You can simply add an asterisk to the end of any partial word, and the search engine will return all permutations that match the first part of the word.

Wildcards can be added to keywords to enable partial matching.

market*

Search for complete phrases

Unlike the wildcard operator, there might be time when you know an entire phrase that is used in your document and want to only return results where your keywords appear in the exact same order in the document. In this case, you can surround your entire search phrase in double quotes. Only documents containing the entire phrase as you have entered it will be returned.

Quotes are used to match exact phrases within content.

"proposal for contoso marketing"

Proposal for Contoso Marketing Tools
techforceconsulting.sharepoint.com/.../Contoso Marketing Proposal.d...

Result type

Word

1 result

Author

Alert Me   Preferences   Advanced Search

Scott Metker

SHOW MORE

 TIP This can be a very useful tool for finding documents on a SharePoint site for which you might only have a snippet of the document (for example, if you only have part of a printout). Simply enter most of a sentence within the quotes and your search results will be quite specific.

 TIP Quotes must appear in matched pairs, so make sure that you put quotes before and after your entire phrase.

Exclude keywords

Sometimes, you have too many search results, but you don't have additional terms that you can use to refine. In this case, you might notice that your search results are being over-whelmed by a large number of documents that share an unwanted term. In this case, you can simply append a minus sign (–) to the beginning of any keyword or expression that you wish to exclude from the results.

The minus sign causes the keyword it precedes to be suppressed from the search results.

market* -contoso

Result type

PDF

PowerPoint

Word

Author

Johnathan Lightfoot

Scott Metker

Yvonne Sletmoe Wilson

SHOW MORE

Don't Let Your Training Fall Off of a Cliff
Standard texting rates only (worst case US $0.20 ... We have no access to your phone number ... Capitalization doesn't matter, but spaces and spelling do ... This slide is for display to the ...
techforceconsulting.sharepoint.com/.../Don't Let Your Tra...

Microsoft_SharePoint_2010_Plain_and_Simple
Microsoft ® SharePoint ® 2010 Plain & Simple Johnathan Lightfoot and Chris BeckettPublished with the authorization of Microsoft Corporation by: O'Reilly Media, Inc. 1005 ...
techforceconsulting.sharepoint.com/.../Microsoft_SharePoint_2010_Pl...

Mobile Devices – A Brief Primer
corporate offerings, despite the initial focus of these devices on consumer-only **markets** ... amount of change in the mobile **marketplace**, a solution built and deployed today might be ...
techforceconsulting.sharepoint.com/.../Mobile Device Considerations...

Find nearby keywords

One of the more interesting search options is the NEAR operator, with which you can return results in which two words appear near one another. For example, you might be looking for documents where a company name appears near the word "proposal." You could enter the search expression as follows:

proposal NEAR(n=4) contoso

In this case, you would find any document containing both "proposal" and "contoso," but no more than four words appear between those keywords. You can enter any number between 1 and 8 to specify how far away the terms can appear in the matching documents.

The NEAR operator is used to return results only where two keywords appear in close proximity in the text.

contoso NEAR(n=1) proposal

Proposal for Contoso Marketing Tools
Contoso Marketing Proposal.docx ...
techforceconsulting.sharepoint.com/.../Contoso Marketing Proposal.d... '

04 - Organizing and Managing Information - Writing Comple...
and release date of the file to the file name, such as "Contoso - Proposal - May 2013.docx ... For example, if you want to find all proposals released in the year 2013, you have no way ...
techforceconsulting.sharepoint.com/.../04 - Organizing and Managing...

 TIP The default spacing for SharePoint searches is a maximum of eight words between your two keywords. If you're comfortable using the default, you can drop the (n=x) part of the query and just type **proposal NEAR contoso**.

 TIP As with other operators, you must capitalize all letters when you specify the NEAR operator.

Preparing your site for search

After you've created a Search Center, you might want to ensure that users of your other sites use this Search Center instead of the default SharePoint 2013 search facility. You can configure the search box that appears at the top-level page of your site to redirect all searches to a specific Search Center. This way, you can better control the user search experience within your site.

Associate a Search Center to your site

1 On your search site, click the Settings button (the small gear icon next to the name of the logged-on user) and then, on the menu that appears, click the Site Settings link.

2 On the Site Settings page, in the Search section, click the Search Settings link.

(continued on next page)

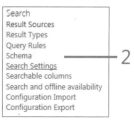

Search
Result Sources
Result Types
Query Rules
Schema
Search Settings ——————— 2
Searchable columns
Search and offline availability
Configuration Import
Configuration Export

> **✓ TIP** You can find the URL of your search results page by running a search within your Search Center and observing the resulting URL.

Associate a Search Center to your site *(continued)*

3 On the Search Settings page, enter the relative URL to your Search Center. If your Search Center is an Enterprise Search Center, append "/Pages" to the URL.

4 Enter the URL of your search results page.

5 Click OK.

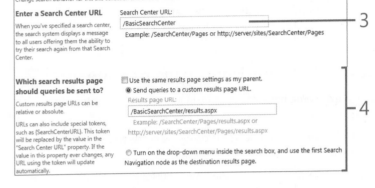

Site Settings › Search Settings

Use this page to configure how Search behaves on this site. The shared Search Box at the top of most pages will use these settings. Note: A change to these settings may take up to 30 minutes to take effect. Change search behavior for this site collection and all sites within it.

Enter a Search Center URL

When you've specified a search center, the search system displays a message to all users offering them the ability to try their search again from that Search Center.

Search Center URL:

/BasicSearchCenter

Example: /SearchCenter/Pages or http://server/sites/SearchCenter/Pages

3

Which search results page should queries be sent to?

Custom results page URLs can be relative or absolute.

URLs can also include special tokens, such as {SearchCenterURL}. This token will be replaced by the value in the "Search Center URL" property. If the value in this property ever changes, any URL using the token will update automatically.

☐ Use the same results page settings as my parent.

◉ Send queries to a custom results page URL.

Results page URL:

/BasicSearchCenter/results.aspx

Example: /SearchCenter/Pages/results.aspx or http://server/sites/SearchCenter/Pages/results.aspx

◯ Turn on the drop-down menu inside the search box, and use the first Search Navigation node as the destination results page.

4

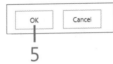

OK   Cancel

5

Searching site content

Search Centers are not the only place where you can initiate searches in SharePoint 2013. After you have associated a Search Center with your site, you can access the Search Center results directly from the search dialog on your site's Home page.

Additionally, you can perform library-specific searches directly within a document library without having to navigate to the Search Center.

Search from the Home page of a site

1 On the Home page of your site, in the search box, enter your keywords.

2 If available, click the search drop-down arrow to select the context of your search and then start the search.

3 Alternatively, simply click the Search button (the magnifying-glass icon) or press Enter to start the search.

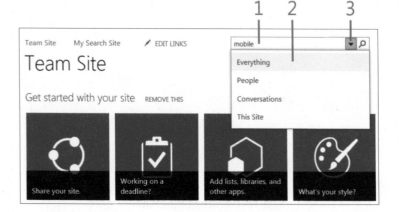

TIP The options menu in the search text box might not be available for all search configurations. If your environment does not have this option, simply proceed to the next step.

Search within a document library

1 Navigate to a document library and enter a search term in the search box.

2 Click the Search button (the magnifying-glass icon) or press Enter to start a search.

Using search refinement

Search refinement makes it possible for users to continue to filter search results after an initial query. If you've ever tried searching online within an online shopping site, you have probably already used search refinement. For example, if you search for "television" at an online electronics store, you might be presented with search options specifying size ranges such as 21–24 inches or 25–32 inches. You might see other filters with which you can select between LCD and Plasma displays. SharePoint 2013 supports the same type of dynamic filtering within search results.

One of the most powerful options within search refinement is that you only see the most relevant filters based on the query results. An example of this is the Result type refinement that shows a list of the most commonly occurring types of content that appear in your search (for example, Microsoft Word documents, PDF files, webpages, and so on). If your search results only include a few types of documents, you will not see options to filter content types that don't appear in your results. Instead, you might see a list of document authors. This saves time because only the most commonly occurring filters (within your query) are displayed.

SharePoint 2013 continues to extend the search refinement options provided in previous versions by adding additional refinement controls such as graphical date range controls and offering administrators extensive configuration options for presenting the most relevant filters to search users.

 TIP The types and kinds of refinement options can be modified on the Search Center. The refinement options can differ drastically based on the configuration.

TIP Some refinement options will only appear if a suitable number of matching documents appear in the results.

Filter results by using search refiners

1 On the Home page of a site, enter a search term in the search box.

2 Click the Search button (the magnifying-glass icon) or press Enter to search.

3 Refine the search results by clicking the refinement options.

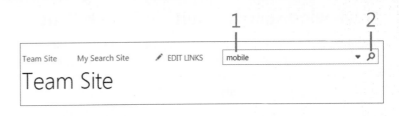

Previewing search results in Search Center

SharePoint 2013 offers a number of preview options within the search results view. For example, users can quickly preview Office documents via the Office Web Apps integration. The same is true for video results.

These features become very useful when you are trying to scroll through a large number of potentially relevant search results.

Integrated preview makes it easy for you to quickly glance at a document or video and determine if you need to investigate further without opening or downloading the full version of the document.

Preview documents

1 On the Home page of a Search Center, enter a search term in the search box and click the Search button (the magnifying-glass icon) or press Enter to start a search.

2 In the results that appear, hover the mouse pointer over any that show an Office document.

3 Navigate within the document by using the preview navigation tools.

> **TIP** Office document previews require integration with the Office Web Apps product, which might not be available in your environment. Talk with your administrator to determine if your implementation of SharePoint 2013 supports these features.

> **TIP** If you have a scroll wheel or other scrolling interface, you can hover over the preview of Word documents and roll the scroll wheel to move between pages. Microsoft PowerPoint previews expose clickable arrows with which you can move between slides.

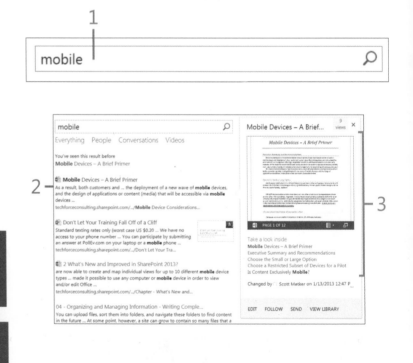

Preview videos

1 On the Home page of a Search Center, enter a search term in the search box and click the Search button (the magnifying-glass icon) or press Enter to start a search.

2 In the results that appear, hover the mouse pointer over any that show a video.

3 Navigate within the video by using the preview navigation tools.

TIP If you are on a slow network connection, the video preview might not immediately play. You will have to wait for the playback to buffer the data before preview is available.

Using advanced search

With the abundance of search options currently available in the SharePoint 2013 Search Centers, you might not find yourself needing to use advanced search. The advanced search view is still available, however, and it splits the single text field that many users currently use into a collection of text fields.

Most of the options presented, such as the ability to include entire phrases or exclude keywords from search, can also be performed from standard search text boxes. This requires remembering special symbols (or using quotes to indicate phrases). Advanced search simplifies this process.

If you want to learn more about these query options from the standard query text field, read "Effective search techniques" on page 305.

Perform advanced search

1 Within a Search Center, perform a search.

2 At the bottom of the results area, click the Advanced Search link.

(continued on next page)

1 ———

| mobile devices primer | 🔍 |

📄 **Mobile Devices** – A Brief **Primer**
Choose the Small or Large Option ... the deployment of a new wave of **mobile devices**, and the design of applications or content (media) that will be accessible via **mobile devices** ...
techforceconsulting.sharepoint.com/.../**Mobile Device** Considerations...

1 result

Alert Me   Preferences   Advanced Search

2

> ✓ **TIP** The Advanced Search link is only available within Search Centers, so you might not see the link if a Search Center has not been linked to your site. If the Advanced Search link is available, it appears at the bottom of the search results, so you will need to scroll to the end of the page to ensure the link is visible.

> ✓ **TIP** The language options available within Advanced Search will depend on the installed and supported languages available within your environment. Your options might vary.

Perform advanced search *(continued)*

3 On the Advanced Search page, enter your search terms, metadata, and language preferences.

4 Add any metadata properties to the search.

5 Click the Search button.

Enterprise Search Center

Advanced Search

Find documents that have...

All of these words: mobile

The exact phrase:

Any of these words:

None of these words:

Only the language (s): ☑ English

☐ French

☐ German

☐ Japanese

☐ Simplified Chinese

☐ Spanish

☐ Traditional Chinese

Result type: All Results

Add property restrictions...

Where the Property... (Pick Property) | Contains |

And

Search

Improve your searches with search tips

Working with search alerts

Search alerts notify you as search results change over time. Perhaps you are interested in keeping track of all documents that contain the phrase "tax audit" within your site (why you're interested in that is probably none of our business). In this case, you could generate a search alert that would email you a summary of any documents that are added or changed that match this search expression.

Search alerts do require the system to generate reports, so you are limited to receiving a daily or weekly summary of the changes that impact your search alerts. This does mean, however, that your email inbox won't fill to overflowing with every small change that might be made to a site!

Create search alerts

1 Within a Search Center, perform a search.

2 At the bottom of the results area, click the Alert Me link.

(continued on next page)

1 ⎯⎯
| mobile devices primer   🔍 |

Everything   People   Conversations   Videos

📰 **Mobile Devices** – A Brief **Primer**
Choose the Small or Large Option ... the deployment of a new wave of **mobile devices**, and the design of applications or content (media) that will be accessible via **mobile devices** ...
techforceconsulting.sharepoint.com/.../**Mobile Device** Considerations...

1 result

Alert Me   Preferences   Advanced Search

2

✓ **TIP** If you are familiar with the SharePoint 2010 RSS link on the search results page, this link has been replaced by search alerts in SharePoint 2013.

✓ **TIP** The Alert Title is a title that you can use to manage this alert in the future. Enter a descriptive value that you will recognize in the future.

Create search alerts *(continued)*

3 On the New Alert page, enter a descriptive title for the alert.

4 Choose an email address to which you want the alert to be sent.

5 Choose whether new, existing, or both types of changes will be logged in the notification.

6 Choose whether you want to receive an email daily or weekly in the event of a change.

7 Click OK.

Edit or delete search alerts

1 Within a Search Center, perform a search.

2 At the bottom of the results area, click the Preferences link.

3 On the Preferences page, in the Search Alerts section, click the Search Alerts link.

(continued on next page)

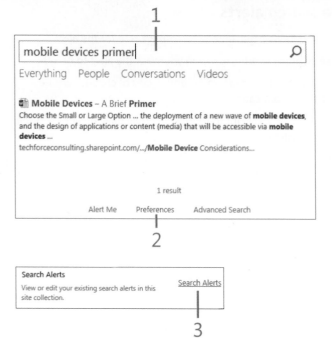

 TIP The Preferences link is at the bottom of the page, so you might need to scroll to the end of your search results to access it.

Edit or delete search alerts *(continued)*

4 To edit an alert, click the title of a search alert.

5 To delete an alert, select the check box adjacent to the alert.

6 Click Delete Selected Alerts to remove the selected alert(s).

My Alerts on this Site ⓘ

6 — ✖ Delete Selected Alerts

Alert Title

Frequency: Weekly   Delivery Method(s)

5 — ☑   Search: mobile devices primer   E-mail

4

Setting your search preferences

From within a Search Center, individual users can customize their search preferences and save these persistently. For example, users can enable or disable autosuggestion, which is a helper that completes your queries as you are writing them.

As with many new SharePoint options, you can enable or disable them if you find that they are a distraction. The primary benefit offered by the Search Center is to make it possible for users to self-administer their search preferences, without them having to talk to IT or your site administrators.

Set your search preferences

1 Within a Search Center, perform a search.

2 At the bottom of the results area, click the Preferences link.

(continued on next page)

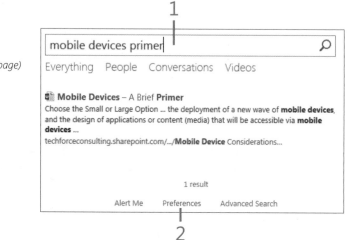

TIP The Preferences link is at the bottom of the page, so you might need to scroll to the end of your search results to access it.

Set your search preferences *(continued)*

3 On the Preferences page, choose your autosuggestion options.

4 If you want to clear your past searching history, click Clear History.

5 Select whether to open search results in the browser or by using your local client application.

6 Click the Search Languages link to choose the languages of content that will be evaluated when you use search.

7 Click the Save Preferences button.

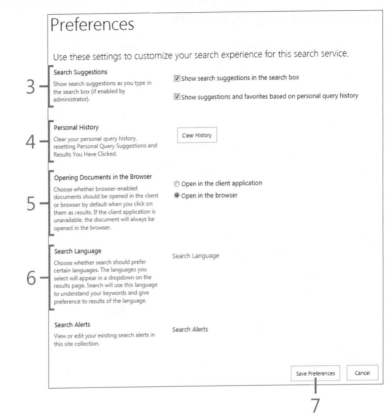

Promoting search results

If you've created a SharePoint 2013 Search Center and have begun tailoring the search options of your sites, you've probably been asked the question of how to manipulate search results. Perhaps you have a regulatory need or you just need to ensure that certain keywords always prominently feature a single result at the top of the search results.

One example might be if you want to push HR policy documents that match specific keywords to the top of all searches. You might create a promoted search result for all searches that contain the terms "vacation policy." This would give you the

opportunity to feature the formal HR Vacation Policy document as the first hit for any of these queries, regardless of the other search terms or search preferences.

This can save your user community a great deal of time if used pervasively, or this could simply represent a quick fix to promote "hard to find" documents higher in your results. Above and beyond these settings, SharePoint offers a great deal of configuration options to tune and rank your search results to help push valuable content to the top of end-user searches.

Promote search results

1   In your Search Center, click the Settings button and then, on the menu that appears, click Site Settings. On the Site Settings page, scroll to the Search section and click the Query Rules link.

2   On the Manage Query Rules page, enter a context for rule configuration. For simple SharePoint sites, choose the Local SharePoint Results (System) option.

3   Click New Query Rule.

(continued on next page)

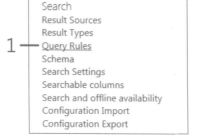

> ✓ **TIP**   The Query Matches Keyword Exactly condition is one of the simplest choices to ensure that key phrases are placed at the top of search results.

> ✓ **TIP**   Choose a descriptive name for your rule because this name will display if you later need to sort priorities of promoted results.

Promote search results *(continued)*

4 On the Add Query Rule page, in the General Information section, enter a name for your rule.

5 In the Query Conditions section, enter a query condition. For straightforward keyword promotion, enter Exact Match and enter a semicolon delimited set of terms to be promoted to the top of search results.

6 In the Actions section, click Add Promoted Result.

7 Enter the title, URL, and description that the promoted link will be given when it appears in the search results.

8 Click Save to save the Action.

9 Click Save.

Add Promoted Result ✕

Title

Mobile Training

URL

epoint.com/SEMTeamSite/Doc2/Mobile%20Device%20Considerations.docx

☐ Render the URL as a banner instead of as a hyperlink

7 ─┤ Description

Summary of Mobile Device and Training Options

Save   Cancel

8

Site Settings ‣ Add Query Rule

General Information

Rule name ─ 4

Mobile Rule

Fires only on source Documents.

▷ Context

Query Conditions

Define when a user's search box query makes this rule fire. You can specify multiple conditions of different types, or remove all conditions to fire for any query text. Every query condition becomes false if the query is not a simple keyword query, such as if it has quotes, property filters, parentheses, or special operators.

Query Matches Keyword Exactly ▾

Query exactly matches one of these phrases ─ 5

mobile training; mobile train

Remove Condition

Add Alternate Condition

Actions

When your rule fires, it can enhance search results in three ways. It can add promoted results above the ranked results. It can also add blocks of additional results. Like normal results, these blocks can be promoted to always appear above ranked results or ranked so they only appear if highly relevant. Finally, the rule can change ranked results, such as tuning their ordering.

Promoted Results

Add Promoted Result ──────── 6

Result Blocks

Add Result Block

Change ranked results by changing the query

Save   Cancel

9

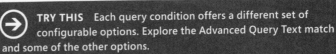

TRY THIS Each query condition offers a different set of configurable options. Explore the Advanced Query Text match and some of the other options.

Excluding site content

In most configurations, SharePoint applies security to ensure that users only see search results that they are allowed to access. However, there are cases for which you don't want to explicitly block access to documents, but you want to hide documents away from most users.

For example, you might have a new site containing informal content that is edited by a large number of users. In this case, you would not want to define a complex security model, but you might be concerned that some users would inadvertently access these pages and documents via search and think the information is finalized. In these scenarios, you can specify within SharePoint 2013 that certain site content should not be indexed, which reduces the possibility of users accidently finding these documents.

Exclude site content from search

1 From the site that you want to exclude, click the Settings button (the small gear icon next to the name of the logged-on user) and then, on the menu that appears, click Site Settings.

2 On the Site Settings page, in the Search section, click the Search And Offline Availability link.

(continued on next page)

> ⚠ **CAUTION** SharePoint search can inadvertently expose pages that contain mixed security data. If you are concerned that some site pages or lists contain data targeted at particular groups, ensure that you do not index ASPX page content within step 4 of the task that follows.

Exclude site content from search *(continued)*

3 On the Search And Offline Availability page, click No if you want to exclude the entire site from search results.

4 Alternatively, click one of the options depending on how you want to index content that appears on pages from Web Parts. Because many Web Parts contain dynamic data from other locations or expose personalized data, this might inadvertently expose user data.

5 Click OK to save your results.

Excluding document libraries and lists from search

As with site content in SharePoint 2013, you might sometimes want to hide only a specific document library or list from search, ensuring that users do not inadvertently access files via search without realizing the content is not ready for use.

Exclude document libraries from search

1 Navigate to a document library on your site and then, on the ribbon, click the Library tab.

2 In the Settings group, click the Library Settings button.

3 On the Library settings page, in the General section, click Advanced Settings.

(continued on next page)

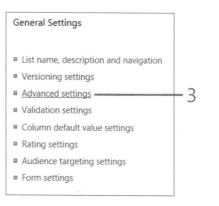

> ✓ **TIP** You will require administrative access to the list or library that you will be working with during this task. Consult your administrator if you are unable to access the advanced settings for the library.

> ⚠ **CAUTION** Hiding content from search is not a substitute for a security. If you are concerned that users should not access certain content, you should instead work with site and library permissions to ensure that only authorized personnel can access sensitive content.

Exclude document libraries from
search *(continued)*

4 On the Advanced Settings page, in the Search section, click the No option.

5 Click OK to save your settings.

Search

Specify whether this document library should be visible in search results. Users who do not have permission to see these items will not see them in search results, no matter what this setting is.

Allow items from this document library to appear in search results?

○ Yes ● No

4

5

Excluding site columns from search

SharePoint 2013 search reads not only the content of documents and pages but also the metadata (site columns) defined on list items and documents. This includes the title of the document, its file name, and the author of the document, as well as other site columns associated with the document.

If you have certain metadata that you want to ensure isn't picked up by the search engine within SharePoint, you can remove this information from the search index.

Exclude site columns from search

1 Click the Settings button (the small gear icon next to the name of the logged-on user) and then, on the menu that appears, click Site Settings.

2 On the Site Settings page, in the Search section, click the Searchable Columns link.

(continued on next page)

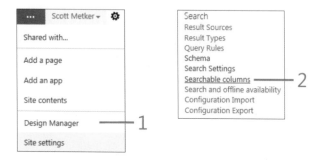

✓ TIP You can only suppress site column data for site columns defined within the current site. If your site makes use of site columns defined for a root site, you will need to navigate to the root site before performing these steps.

⚠ CAUTION Removing site columns from search will not block access to this information if a user navigates directly to a document or list item on your site. It will, however, ensure that searches that exclusively match keywords appearing in these site columns will not show these items within the results.

Exclude site columns from search *(continued)*

3 Select the check box next to the column(s) that you want to suppress from search.

4 Click OK to save your changes.

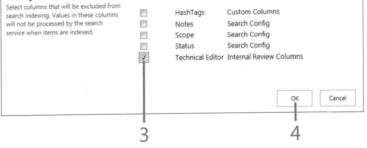

SEE ALSO For information about defining metadata (site columns), see "Creating site columns" on page 64.

Maintaining search configurations

With all of the changes that you can make to the search configuration and directly to the Search Center associated with your site, you'll be relieved to know that you don't have to enter this configuration each and every time that you set up a site.

You can export your SharePoint 2013 search configuration from a single site and import it in another site. For example, if you set up a new Search Center, you could migrate all of the promoted search results that you previously entered on another site into your new site.

Using these management tools, you can apply your site changes consistently across additional sites and help enforce continuity between sites. Additionally, they ensure that the time that you spend setting up tailored search rules is more like a reusable investment that you can take advantage of for future sites.

Export your search configuration

1 On the site for which you have configured search, Click the Settings icon and then, on the menu that appears, click Site Settings.

2 On the Site Settings page, in the Search section, click the Configuration Export link.

3 Click Save to save the export file to your computer.

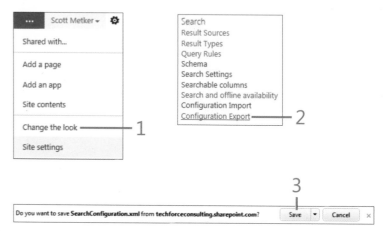

> ✓ **TIP** The default name of the export file is *SearchConfiguration.xml*. It is placed in your downloads folder unless you choose another location.

> ✓ **TIP** The search import and export process only covers the migration of the following elements: Search Schema, Query Rules, Result Sources, Result Type, and your Ranking Model.

Import your search configuration

1 On the Site Settings page, in the Search section, click the Configuration Import link.

2 On the Import Search Configuration page, click Browse and select the file that you previously exported to your computer.

3 Click the Import button to import your search configurations.

4 Refresh your browser until the import status changes from Pending Import to Imported Successfully (during import, the status will show as Importing).

Search
Result Sources
Result Types
Query Rules
Schema
Search Settings
Searchable columns
Search and offline availability
<u>Configuration Import</u> —— 1
Configuration Export

Import Search Configuration

Import Search Configuration
If you have a search configuration you'd like to import, browse for it below. Settings imported from the file will be created and activated as part of the site. You can modify any of the settings after import.

File Name : C:\Users\smetker2\Downloads\SearchConfigur | Browse...

| Import |

3   2

Search Config List ⓘ

☐	Name		Scope	Status	
	SearchConfiguration ☒ NEW		SPWeb	Pending Import	— 4

➕ Add document

Community portals and sites

17

Microsoft SharePoint 2013 includes a new site template designed for community discussions and social interaction called the Community Site template. This section discusses the administration and use of a community site.

Overview of community sites

The Community Site template is a new site template added in SharePoint 2013. It was specifically designed to enhance the social and collaborative aspects of SharePoint. Previous to the release of SharePoint 2013, a number of third-party components were required if you wanted to effectively use SharePoint for tracking informal discussions, particularly if you wanted to actively manage and retain these discussions for future use.

Previous versions of SharePoint included the discussion list, which allowed for basic discussions but did not provide for content moderation or tracking for user activity. Moderation has been added, giving site moderators the ability to remove inappropriate content, summarize answers and provide best responses, and elevate discussions by featuring them on the site. Meanwhile, you can now use badges and reputation scores to track your most prolific and accurate participants on the site.

Since the release of SharePoint in 2010, Microsoft has made social and collaborative technologies a key focus of its corporate offerings. This includes the acquisition of Skype (Voice over IP) as well as the acquisition of Yammer, a corporate micro-blogging tool. Yammer is now packaged and made available with certain license configurations for SharePoint Online and Office 365. A detailed discussion of these items is beyond the scope of this section, but these acquisitions and integrations serve to underscore the importance of collaboration to the SharePoint platform now and in the future.

The community site Home page

When you first access the Home page for a community site, you will notice a number of default Web Parts with which you can quickly track what's happening on the site. The following Web Parts and links on the Home page can be quite helpful:

- The Search box shows your current query and gives you the capability to query discussions and conversations, both in this site and across many other sites

- Using the Community Tools links, site owners and moderators can manage discussions, categories, badges, and other community settings.

- The What's Happening area shows high-level statistics regarding the usage of the site, including total members, discussions, and replies.

- The Top Contributors section shows a list of the most active contributors to the site.

- The discussion list section shows recent discussions on the site. You can use the links at the top of this section to filter the results to show recent or popular discussions as well as discussions that you have started.

- The About page link shows the About page of the site that describes the purpose of the site and any other information that the owner or moderators would like to provide for site usage (including rules and guidelines for content).

- The Members page link shows the Members page of the site that lists site members and their current usage statistics including their reputation on the site.

- The Categories page link shows the Categories page on which you can filter and show posts within site-managed categories.

Community tools   Search box

Categories page link

Members page link

About page link

Discussion List   What's happening   Top contributors

The importance of moderation

If you want your community to remain vibrant and successful, you will need to appoint one or more moderators for your site. Moderators provide continual maintenance to the site to ensure that content remains relevant and on topic.

For example, you site moderators can comb through unanswered questions, looking for content that might provide an answer. Over time, the candidate list for new site moderators can come from your top contributors to the site. Successful online communities work best when moderators and original discussion authors work together to ensure that a high percentage of questions also provide a best response. Without this feedback, users might not continue to post questions, particularly if they perceive that the community does not provide a helpful response.

In addition to helping summarize responses to questions, moderators can also provide their own responses (and mark them as the best response) that combine multiple responses from other users. Although only a single best response can be provided to a question, this combines the contributions of many authors in a single, concise reply.

Moderators can also actively manage the About page of the site. This page is provided to users of the site to read about the purpose of the site, any site activities, or any rules associated with posting content to the site.

Finally, moderators represent an escalation point for any inappropriate content, such as discussions that are off topic or even offensive. Using the Reported Posts page, moderators and site owners can review user violation reports and manage the content associated with the complaint.

Creating a community site site collection

The first step for working with community sites is to create your own site. In many companies, there might already be a governance policy in place by which you can request a new site. You should use process when requesting a new site to ensure that it falls under corporate guidelines. Alternatively, if you have a

smaller implementation without a formal mechanism for site creation (and you have administrative access to your SharePoint 2013 instance), you can create your own site collection based upon the Community Site template.

Create a community site site collection

1   On the Admin Center for your Office 365 instance, at the right end of the toolbar, click the Admin button.

2   On the menu that appears, click SharePoint.

3   In the SharePoint Admin Center, on the ribbon, click the Site Collection tab and then click New.

4   On the menu that appears, click Private Site Collection.

(continued on next page)

TIP   These steps are documented for the online version of Office 365. Your permissions and administrative layout might differ slightly if you are using the nonhosted version of SharePoint Enterprise 2013.

Create a community site site collection *(continued)*

5   On the New Site Collection page, type a title for the Community Center, a URL that will be used to access the site under your main URL, and a language for the new site.

6   Select Community Center (under the default Collaboration tab).

7   Specify the appropriate Time Zone.

8   Choose the site administrator who will have administrator rights to the site.

9   Select your storage quota and server resource options.

10 Click OK.

new site collection

Title	SharePoint 2013 Best Practices Community Site
Web Site Address	https://tforceconsulting.sharepoint.com
	/sites/ SP2013

Template Selection   2013 experience version will be used

Select a language:

English

Select a template:

Collaboration | Enterprise | Publishing | Custom

Team Site
Blog
Developer Site
Project Site
Community Site

A place where community members discuss topics of common interest. Members can browse and discover relevant content by exploring categories, sorting discussions by popularity or by viewing only posts that have a best reply. Members gain reputation points by participating in the community, such as starting discussions and replying to them, liking posts and specifying best replies.

Time Zone   (UTC-08:00) Pacific Time (US and Canada)

Administrator   Scott Metker

Storage Quota   500 MB of 7450 MB available

Server Resource Quota   300 resources of 5300 resources available

OK   Cancel

Creating a community site subsite

If you have a collection of similar SharePoint 2013 community sites that are managed by the same group of people, or if you don't have administrative access to create site collections, you can also create a discussion site as a subsite.

Create a community subsite

1 From the root site that will contain your community subsite, click the Settings button (the small gear icon next to the name of the logged-on user). On the menu that appears, click Site Contents.

2 On the Site Contents page, in the Subsites section, select the New Subsite link.

(continued on next page)

(continued on next page)

TIP If you will have a large number of Community Sites, we recommend that you implement each site as a separate site collection rather than as a subsite. Each site can be separately managed and archived. This also supports separate access and storage requirements for each site.

Create a community subsite *(continued)*

3 On the New SharePoint Site page, type a title and description.

4 Type a URL for the site, relative to the root site.

5 Choose a language.

6 Choose the Community Site template (located on the Collaboration tab).

7 Choose user permissions for the site.

If you select Use The Same Permissions As Parent Site, you will not have an automatically created Moderators group if your parent site is not also a Community Site. You will need to manually create the Moderators group if you choose this option.

8 Select navigation options for the site.

9 Click Create.

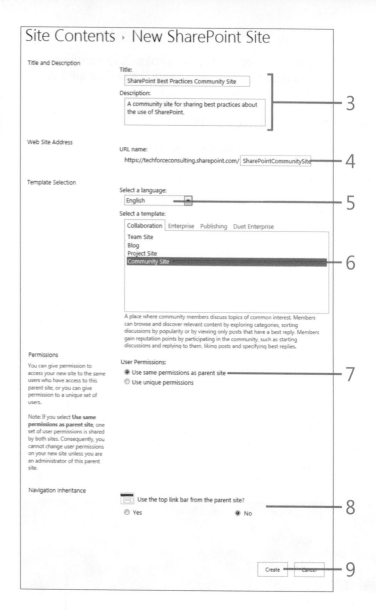

Adding moderators to community sites

After you have created a SharePoint 2013 community site site collection, you should then choose and assign an initial list of moderators to the site. Unless you are willing to undertake all moderation tasks, you should identify other moderators as early as possible. Effective site moderation is a key for user adoption, so your moderators should be ready and available prior to sharing the site with other users.

Add a moderator to your community site

1 On your community site, click the Settings button (the small gear icon next to the name of the logged-on user). On the menu that appears, click Site Settings.

2 On the Site Settings page, in the Users And Permissions section, click the Site Permissions link.

3 On the Permissions page, locate the group named [*Site Name*] Moderators, where [*Site Name*] is the name of your current site. Click the name of the group.

(continued on next page)

> **TRY THIS**   Add yourself to the site moderators group. If you are already the site owner, you will not necessarily need this access, but you can practice the steps required.

> **TIP**   If you are unable to add a user to the site moderators group, this might be because you do not have the system rights to edit this group. Contact the owner of this site or IT if you receive any access denied messages.

Add a moderator to your community
site *(continued)*

4 On the People And Groups page for your moderators group, click the New link.

5 In the Share dialog box that opens, type the first few letters of a user name or full name for each moderator. The system prompts you with partial matches as you type ahead. Select and add each user.

6 Type the text that you want to send in an email to each moderator. This should describe the reason that you're making them a moderator and any follow-up instructions that are needed.

7 Click the Show Options link to expand the dialog box and display additional information.

8 To automatically notify each moderator via email, in the expanded portion of the dialog box, select the Send An Email Invitation check box.

9 Click the Save button to complete the process, add the moderators, and send the email notification.

4

People and Groups ⟩ SharePoint 2013

New ▾   Actions ▾   Settings ▾

☐ ⬚ ☐ Name   About Me   Job Title

There are no items to show in this view of the "User Information List" list.

5   6

Share 'SharePoint 2013 Best Practices Community Site'   ✕

Add people to the SharePoint 2013 Best Practices Community Site Moderators group

Scott Metker x

I've added your to the moderators group for the SharePoint community site. Can you please help us manage community content?

SHOW OPTIONS

Share   Cancel

7   9

HIDE OPTIONS

☑ Send an email invitation — 8

Adding users to community sites

There are two primary ways that users will first access your SharePoint 2013 community sites:

- **Sharing from other users**   Site users can share an invitation to an existing community. If you want, the invitation sends an email to the user with some descriptive text.

- **Joining the site manually**   Site users can access some

of the content of your site when they first discover it. For example, they can discover an existing discussion on your site via a SharePoint search and choose to join the site after they determine the content is relevant to them.

This task describes how users can join (or be asked to join the site).

Sharing your community site

1 On the Home page of your community site, toward the right end of the toolbar, click the Share link that appears under the name of the logged-on user.

2 In the Share dialog box that opens, type of the user name or full name of the user whom you are trying to add.

As you type, the system presents a filtered list of potential matching users.

(continued on next page)

1

Sites ···   Scott Metker ▾   ⚙   ?

○ SHARE ☆ FOLLOW ✎ EDIT ▣

Search this site ▾ 🔍

Share 'SharePoint Best Practices Community Site'   ✕

👥 Shared with lots of people

Invite people to 'Edit'

They'll also get access to the 'SharePoint 2013 Plain & Simple' site and the sites that share permissions with it.

Michelle Lopez x —————————— 2

I've invited you to help participate in the SharePoint 2013 Best Practices Site. Please take a look and let me know what you think! —————————— 4

SHOW OPTIONS

Share   Cancel

5   8

> **TIP**   Depending on your site security, only certain users (for example, site owners or moderators) can use the Share link to add new users to the site.

Sharing your community site *(continued)*

3 In the list, select the appropriate user to add to the list. You can repeat this step for multiple users.

4 Type the text for an email notification to the user or users.

5 Click the Show Options link to expand the dialog box and display additional information.

6 To automatically notify each moderator via email, in the expanded portion of the dialog box, select the Send An Email Invitation check box.

7 Click the list box and select a permission group to which the user or users will be added on this site.

For example, you might add them to the Read group to give them view-only access to the site.

8 Click Save to send the email and invite the users.

Joining an open community site

1 Navigate to a community site of which you are not a member and then click the Join This Community button.

> ✓ **TIP** Depending on the settings of the site in question, there might be additional steps or the Join This Community link might not be available at all.

> ✓ **TIP** Some sites require manual moderation before you can join them.

Managing your community settings

On the Community Settings page, SharePoint 2013 owners and moderators can specify the date the group was established. This date defaults to the date your site was created, but it is intended to define when your community first started as a formal entity.

If your group existed as a formal entity prior the creation of the site, you can specify this date manually. This date is displayed on the About page of the site so that users can see how long the community has been in operation.

Manage community settings

1 On the Home page of your site, in the Community Tools section, click the Community Settings link.

2 On the Community Settings page, enter the date on which your community was established. This date is defaulted to the creation date of the site, but you can specify an earlier date if your community existed outside of SharePoint prior to the creation of the site.

3 Select the Enable Reporting Of Offensive Content check box if you want users to be able to report offensive content to moderators.

4 Click the OK button to save your changes.

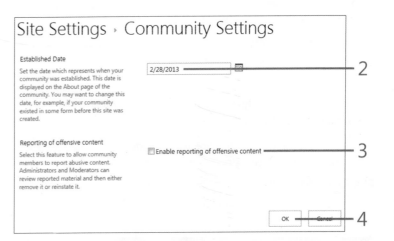

Working with categories

Within a community site, you can create categories that are used to classify discussions. Unlike tags, which are used elsewhere within SharePoint 2013, only a single category can be assigned to each discussion. As a result, you should choose broad and easily assignable categories. After all, if discussion authors have trouble choosing categories when they add discussions, the organization of content within your site will become increasingly arbitrary over time.

Non-owners and non-moderator users of your site cannot create categories, but they can browse the list of categories and view new discussions within a category. With categories, users can focus their viewpoint on discussions and conversations relevant to areas of interest.

Creating categories

1 On the Home page of your site, in Community Tools section, click the Create Categories link.

2 On the Categories page, click the New Item Link located above the list of categories.

3 On the New Category page, type a name for the category you are creating.

4 Type a description of the category.

The description displays when users hover their mouse over the category tile on the Categories page.

5 You can choose to provide a link to an image that will be used for the category tile icon in the Categories page.

6 Click the Save button to save the new category.

> **✓ TIP** If you want to use special graphic tile to represent your category, you can upload an image to the Site Assets library on the site. These tiles are displayed to users who browse the category library.

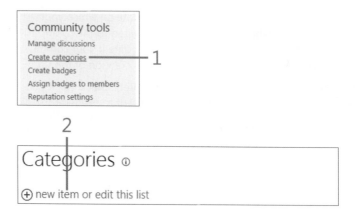

Find discussions by category

1 On the Home page of your site, in the Navigation pane, click the Categories link.

2 On the Categories page, click the Category tile representing the category you will be viewing.

You can view the description of the category before you click it by hovering your mouse over the category before you click it.

3 On the Category page for your selected category, you can filter the resulting list by clicking the Recent, What's Hot, or My Discussions links. You can find additional filters by clicking More Options ellipsis (...).

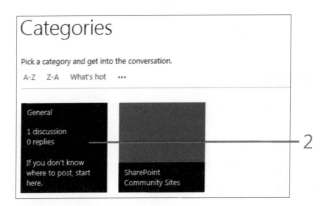

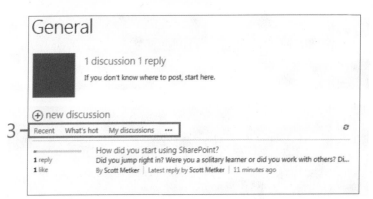

Working with badges

Badges are another new feature with SharePoint 2013. You can create new badges representing special achievements on your site, and you or your moderators can award badges to users for special achievements on the site. Badges are a form of *gamification*, which refers to using game-style mechanics and awards in a non–game-playing scenario.

One such example is Microsoft's own *SharePoint MVP* certification, which is granted to SharePoint pioneers within the Internet community, based upon the breadth and depth of their Share-Point support and evangelism.

Badges, when used properly, also help users within large communities to lend credibility to a particular reply. When a user who is assigned a badge named *SharePoint Guru* replies to a discussion, other users attach additional credibility to the response because the badge indicates that it was authored by a Guru.

You (and your moderators) should make judicious use of badges; if you award badges in a capricious fashion, you devalue the badge and the perception of content authored by all users who have this badge assigned to them.

Create badges

1 On the Home page of your site, In the Community Tools section, click the Create Badges link.

2 On the Badges page, click the New Item link.

3 On the New Badge page, type a title for your badge.

4 Click the Save button to save the new badge.

> ✓ **TIP** Badges are intended to represent positive achievements so that users can strive for particular goals. Avoid creating badges to represent negative actions. There are other methods (such as discussion moderation) for dealing with policy violations.

> ✓ **TIP** The badges that you create should be named in a way that describes the achievement in a positive light and makes the badge attractive to your community. Given the choice between badges named "Writes a Lot" and "Content Superstar," you should choose the more exciting option.

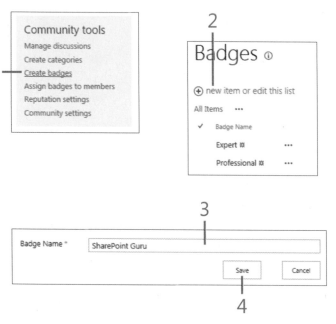

Edit a badge

1 On the Badges page, select a badge by clicking to the immediate left of the badge name.

2 On the ribbon, click the Items tab and then, in the Manage group, click the Edit Item button.

3 On the Edit Item page, edit the name of the badge.

4 Click the Save button.

Assigning badges to members

After you have created badges on your site, you can proceed to assign badges to users. When you have decided which users will receive each badge, you can begin to assign them.

Assign badges to members

1 On the Home page of your site, in the Community Tools section, click the Assign Badges To Members link.

2 On the Community Members page, you can filter displayed users via the predefined view links or the search box.

3 Locate a site member to whom you will assign a badge. Select the user by clicking to the left of the user name column.

(continued on next page)

⊘ TIP You should carefully and consistently assign badges to users based on well-defined rules. Badges help to indicate credibility to responses for your users and also help drive overall use of your site.

Assign badges to members *(continued)*

4 On the ribbon, click the Moderation tab and then, in the Gifted Badges group, click the Give Badge button.

5 On the Assign Badge page, select a Gifted Badge.

6 Click Save to assign the badge.

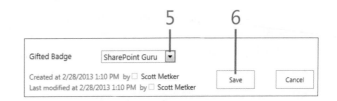

Enabling site-wide reputation tracking

You can assign reputation settings to an entire SharePoint 2013 community site that specify automated achievement levels for members based on the amount of content (discussions and replies). Reputation settings manage how members are awarded reputation scores on your sites.

The first two settings within the reputation settings determine whether ratings on the site are enabled and what type of rating ("likes" versus star-based scoring) are used for user feedback.

Using the rest of the settings, you can specify reputation tracking and fine-tune the scoring system. The member achievement point system specifies what site actions a member must take to increase their reputation score, and the achievement level points allows you to set the score thresholds for up to five achievement levels. Finally, the last achievement level representation section determines how SharePoint displays a member's achievement level (either as a small icon or as a custom text label).

Enable site-wide reputation tracking

1 On the Home page of your site, in the Community Tools section, click the Reputation Settings link.

(continued on next page)

Community tools
Manage discussions
Create categories
Create badges
Assign badges to members
Reputation settings ———— 1
Community settings

> **TIP** Ensure that your achievement level points and representation are configured to accommodate a wide enough range for your user community. If all of your site members end up at level 1 or level 5, you need to evaluate your point system and levels to determine the reason.

Enable site-wide reputation tracking *(continued)*

2 On the Community Reputation Settings page, in the Allow Items In This List To Be Rated section, click Yes.

3 Click to offer users the choice to either "like" or apply star ratings to items on the site.

4 If you want to use the member achievements point system, select the Enable Member Achievements Point System check box and enter point values for the indicated achievements.

5 In the Achievement Level Points section, choose threshold values for each achievement level.

6 In the Achievement Level Representation section, click either the Display Achievement Level As Image option or the Display Achievement Level As Text option. If the latter option is chosen, you can specify names for each achievement level in place of the default values.

7 Click OK to enable reputation tracking.

Site Settings › Community Reputation Settings

Rating settings

Specify whether or not items in this list can be rated.

When you enable ratings, two fields are added to the content types available for this list and a rating control is added to the default view of the list or library. You can choose either "Likes" or "Star Ratings" as the way content is rated.

Allow items in this list to be rated? — **2**
- ● Yes
- ○ No

Which voting/rating experience you would like to enable for this list? — **3**
- ● Likes
- ○ Star Ratings

Member achievements point system

Within the community you can allow members to collect points based on their participations.

☑ Enable member achievements point system

Specify the point values for the following activities

Creating a new post	10
Replying to a post	10
Member's post or reply gets liked or receives a rating of 4 or 5 stars	10
Member's reply gets marked as 'Best Reply'	100

— **4**

Achievement level points

As members accumulate points, they can reach specific levels as milestones of achievement. Specify the number of points required for members to reach each achievement level.

Specify achievement levels

Level 1	More than	0
Level 2	More than	2
Level 3	More than	10
Level 4	More than	50
Level 5	More than	300

— **5**

Achievement level representation

Specify whether achievement levels are represented as a series of boxes or as a textual title. You can customize the title for each level.

● Display achievement level as image ■■■■■
○ Display achievement level as text

Specify a title for each level

Level 1	Level 1
Level 2	Level 2
Level 3	Level 3
Level 4	Level 4
Level 5	Level 5

— **6**

[OK] [Cancel] — **7**

Viewing badges and reputation scores for a member

Reputation scores are another way that site members can associate credibility with users of a site. When enabled, you can view the achievement level scores for any site member next to any discussion or reply that they post on the site. However, if you know the member's name, you can simply look up the reputation for that individual on the member's page.

View badges and reputation scores for a member

1 On your community site, click the Settings button (the small gear icon next to the name of the logged-on user). On the menu that appears, click Site contents.

2 On the Site Contents page, in the Lists, Libraries, And Other Apps section, select the Community Members tile.

(continued on next page)

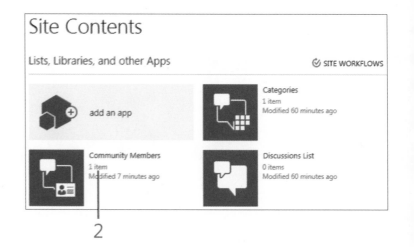

View badges and reputation scores for a member *(continued)*

3 In the member list, locate the individuals whom you are interested in viewing. View the badges for the individuals directly under their user name.

4 View the achievement level for individuals under their user names, as well (if available).

Community Members ⓘ

Top contributors   New members   A-Z   •••

Scott Metker   **2** discussions Joined Thursday at 1:10 PM
                      5 replies
SharePoint Guru   **3** best replies ———————— 3

Johnathan Lightfoot **0** discussions Joined 4 hours ago
■■■■■■   **1** reply ————————————— 4
                      0 best replies

Michelle Lopez   **0** discussions Joined About an hour ago
                      0 replies
                      0 best replies

Creating and editing discussions

Discussions are main types of content used within a SharePoint 2013 community site. A single discussion acts as a starting point for users to publicly ask a question or make a comment and for other site members to reply to the question or add their own thoughts.

When you first author a discussion, you can create a basic title to the post, categorize the discussion, and then you can attach a detailed body to the post that includes rich text, images, or even multimedia. After you have authored a discussion, you can also return and edit the original discussion post.

Create a new discussion

1 On the Home page of a Community Site of which you are a member, click the New Discussion button.

(continued on next page)

1

SharePoint Best Practices Community Site

Welcome to the community. We want to hear from you. Ask a question. Share your thoughts. Get smarter and help others.

⊕ new discussion

Recent   What's hot   My discussions   ...

There are no items to show in this view of the "Discussions List" discussion board.

> ✓ **TIP** You should generally reserve edits to your original discussion to grammatical corrections or quick corrections made immediately after your original post. Because other members can respond to your discussion, you don't want to change your original text too much, or members who follow the discussion might become confused by replies that are invalidated by your changes.

> ✓ **TIP** When you flag a discussion as a question, you make it possible for one of the replies to be selected as a best reply for the reference of other users. Moderators can also more easily find your discussion and help provide an answer if it is not addressed in a timely fashion.

Create a new discussion *(continued)*

2 On the New Discussion page, type a title for the new discussion.

3 Enter text for the body of the discussion.

4 While you are editing the body of the discussion, the Format Text contextual tab automatically appears on the ribbon. Use the tools on this tab to apply rich-text formatting to your content.

5 If you want to indicate that this discussion is a query, select the Question check box.

6 Select a category for the discussion.

7 Click the Save button to post your discussion to the site.

Edit a discussion you have created

1 On the Home page of a community site on which you have already posted a discussion, click the My Discussions link in the Discussion list.

2 Click the subject link for the discussion that you want to edit.

3 At the bottom of your discussion, click the More Options ellipsis (...) and then, on the menu that appears, click the Edit command.

4 On the Edit Discussion page, edit any of your discussion settings.

5 Click the Save button to save your changes.

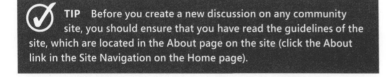

> ✓ **TIP** Before you create a new discussion on any community site, you should ensure that you have read the guidelines of the site, which are located in the About page on the site (click the About link in the Site Navigation on the Home page).

Replying to a discussion

Even if you don't have a new discussion to add to a SharePoint 2013 community site, you can contribute by responding to discussions that are already in progress. Adding your thoughts, feedback, and answers to existing questions is one way that you can enhance your reputation on a site and assist other users within your organization.

You can respond to a discussion from virtually anywhere that you can view discussions on a community site. You can reply to discussions from the Home page or from the discussions list, which is accessible by clicking the Categories link on the Home page.

Reply to a discussion

1 At the bottom of the discussion to which you want to respond, click the Reply button.

2 In the window that appears, type your reply.

3 Click the Reply button to save your reply.

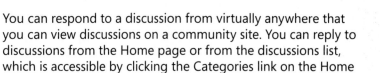

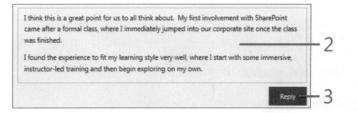

> **TIP** Before you respond to a discussion, ensure that you have read the site guidelines, which you can view by clicking the About link on the Home page.

> **TIP** You can also reply to any of the replies under the main discussion. Your response will be slightly indented and appear under the reply rather than at the end. This facilitates threads of a discussion to be grouped together so that users can engage in side-discussions while still on the main thread.

Searching for discussions

One of the ways that you can find discussions is via SharePoint 2013 search. On any community site (or from many other types of SharePoint sites) you can search all conversations to which you currently have access. Using search, you can find discussions and communities that you might not have known existed. This is one of SharePoint's most powerful features because you can discover content without requiring explicit advertisement or communication to the end-user community. Many organizations are exploring this functionality as the first steps toward informal, self-guided learning that could eventually replace formal eLearning classes for many job functions.

Search for discussions

1 In the upper-right corner of the community site (and most other site templates), click the drop-down arrow on the right end of the Search box, next to the Search button (the magnifying-glass icon).

2 On the menu that appears, click Conversations.

3 Enter the text of your query and click the Search button to start your query.

(continued on next page)

Search conversations	▼ ⌕	— 1
Everything		
People		
Conversations		— 2
This Site		

| how did you start using sharepoint | ▼ ⌕ | — 3 |

TIP The ability to search specifically on conversations might be limited based on the administrative settings within your site collection and your SharePoint farm. Contact your IT staff if you are unable to search conversations to determine if this is possible at all within your organization.

Search for discussions *(continued)*

4   Within the search results, you can hover the mouse over each conversation to display a ScreenTip that contains more detail on a discussion and associated replies.

5   Within the search results, you can filter returned results further by using the refinement options on the left side of the search results.

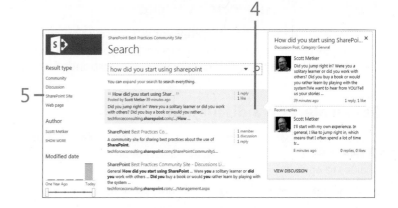

Tracking discussions in progress

Sometimes, you might find a SharePoint 2013 discussion contains a question that you are unable to answer yourself, but you are interested in tracking it in case anyone else responds. In this case, you can create an alert on the discussion that will send you a notification if someone else adds a reply.

Set an alert on a discussion

1 From the discussion list (on the Home page or from one of the site categories discussion lists), click the subject of one of the discussions to open it.

2 At the bottom of the first part of the discussion, click the More Options ellipsis (...) and then, on the menu that appears, click Alert Me.

(continued on next page)

Set an alert on a discussion *(continued)*

3 On the New Alert page, modify the title of the alert if the suggested title isn't specific enough. This title is used for future alerts notifications.

4 If you have library administrative privileges via the Manage Lists permission, you can also add additional recipients for the alert notifications.

5 Specify a delivery type for notifications.

6 Specify which types of changes to the discussion should result in a notification being sent.

7 Type additional filter for the notification.

8 Specify how often notifications should be sent.

9 Click OK to create the alert.

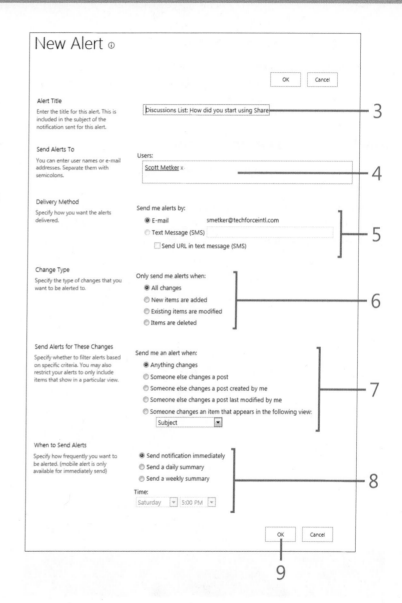

Managing replies

As a member of a SharePoint 2013 community site, you still can manage replies if you are not a moderator or owner of the site. Your editing capabilities, however, are limited to replies that you have authored or replies that belong to discussions that you have authored.

Mark a reply as a best reply

1 In the Discussion list on the Home page, click a discussion title to open it.

2 Locate the reply to which you want to assign best reply and then click the More Options ellipsis (...) located at the bottom of the reply. On the menu that appears, click Best Reply.

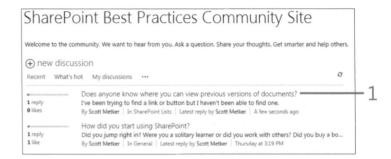

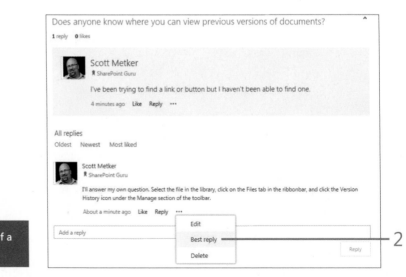

> ✓ **TIP** To mark a best reply, you must be the original author of a discussion item or a moderator or site administrator.

Remove a best reply

1 Locate a reply that has been previously flagged as a best reply. Click the More Options ellipsis (…) located at the bottom of the reply. On the menu that appears, click Remove Best Reply.

Report a reply to the moderator

1 On a reply that contains inappropriate content, click the More Options ellipsis (…) located at the bottom of the reply. On the menu that appears, click Report To Moderator.

2 In the Report Offensive Content dialog box that opens, type a note to the moderator staff about the inappropriate content.

3 Click the Report button to submit the note and a link to the flagged content.

Moderating discussions

One of the primary jobs of a SharePoint 2013 community site moderator is overseeing discussions on the site. In one case, the moderator staff should seek out unanswered questions that have become stale over time. Although not all questions must be answered by the moderator staff, it is important that they contribute to open questions when they can. This might entail writing answers to questions from scratch or simply consolidating many partial answers into a cohesive response.

Another job of a moderator is to promote important discussions and ensure that they are featured on the site. Featured discussions can be separately accessed under the featured discussions view. This provides a moderator-curated view of important content, and members of this site might find themselves monitoring the featured discussions to keep up with important discussions within the community.

Find unanswered questions

1 In the discussions list, click the More Options ellipsis (...) in the line directly under the New Discussion link. On the menu that appears, click Unanswered Questions.

TIP Your site moderators should be chosen for their subject-matter expertise in addition to their available time and capabilities with respect to the site moderator responsibilities. This is because they might be called upon to assist on difficult questions.

Mark a discussion as featured

1 In the discussion list, click the subject of one of the discussions that you want to mark as a featured discussion.

2 At the bottom of the topmost item in the discussion, click the ellipsis (...) and then, on the menu that appears, click Mark As Featured.

Reviewing posts submitted for moderation

Another responsibility of the SharePoint 2013 moderator is reviewing reported items. This can consist of discussions or replies that violate the site guidelines, corporate policies, or the limits of acceptable behavior. Effective moderation of these reported items is essential to maintain a consistency of content and proper tone within a site. Additionally, your company or organization might have rules regarding appropriate content that might need to be applied, as well.

Review posts submitted for moderation

1 On the Home page of your site, in the Community Tools section, click the Review Reported Posts link.

2 From the list of items submitted for moderation, click the post link associated with an item.

3 After viewing the item, click the Delete, Edit Post, or Dismiss Report buttons to process the request.

(continued on next page)

> **TIP** Ensure that your moderator staff have all discussed what constitutes acceptable use of the site and have all read the site guidelines, which are available on the About page on the community site.

> **TIP** If you edit a post submitted for moderation, you will still need to separately remove the moderation report to remove it from the moderation list.

Review posts submitted for
moderation *(continued)*

4 If you click Delete, you will be prompted to verify. Click OK to verify and delete the post.

5 If you click Edit Post, you will be granted access to the post where you can edit and then click Save to commit your edits.

6 If you click the Dismiss Report button, you will be prompted to verify. Click OK to verify and delete the report.

4

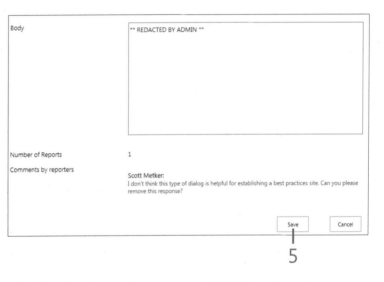

5

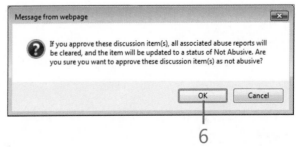

6

Automating tasks with workflows

18

With all of the different ways that you can interact with data and documents on a Microsoft SharePoint 2013 site, you might start to notice certain patterns in how you work with a site. For example, before you have a coworker review a document that you have written, you might always change a status field on the document and send out an email requesting the review.

Workflows are a way of automating multistep processes to ensure that tasks stay on track. They not only facilitate performing multiple automated steps on a document or list item, but they also make sophisticated choices possible based on user feedback and document data. With these choices available, workflows can choose separate courses of action, such as processing a document differently if an approval step is rejected versus approved. You can even choose to have activities loop, such as sending a reminder email every two days, until an action occurs or a certain condition is met.

Within SharePoint 2013, you can use workflows to reduce the amount of repetitive steps you perform when working with content and ensure consistency with respect to the way you and your team handle documents. In this section, we'll cover how to create, associate, and launch workflows on the content within your site.

In this section:

- **What are workflows?**
- **Workflows supplied with SharePoint**
- **Associating workflows with lists and content types**
- **Starting workflows on documents**
- **Checking the status of a running workflow**
- **Creating a list workflow in SharePoint Designer**
- **Editing workflows**
- **Introducing Microsoft Visio integration with SharePoint workflows**
- **Switching to the visual designer**
- **Creating workflows in Visio 2013**
- **Importing Visio Workflows into SharePoint Designer**

What are workflows?

The term workflow is broadly used to refer to a process by which various activities occur in an ordered set of steps. For example, when baking a cake, you would typically perform the following tasks, in the order shown:

1 Mix dry ingredients together

2 Add liquid ingredients

3 Bake

In this process, each of these steps occurs sequentially, which means that you must first complete one step before moving to the next. A document review (although potentially less fun than baking a cake) might follow a similar pattern:

1 Notify a reviewer that a document must be reviewed

2 Reviewer: Read and add comments to the document

3 Notify the author that the document has been reviewed

4 Author: Incorporate comments

In this example, we've also added detail about who performs certain tasks. In more complex scenarios, workflows help coordinate and organize the activities of multiple users without requiring those users to worry about the next step in the overall process. For example, if multiple reviewers are assigned to a document within a workflow, the SharePoint 2013 workflow can ensure that the next reviewer has received a copy of the document only after the previous reviewer has completed his review. This ensures that documents are not forgotten or misrouted. Workflows can also be used to send emails at certain points, which ensure that users are reminded that tasks are due. Finally, workflows can make choices based on previous steps, supporting branching or looping based on those previous steps.

How are workflows used in SharePoint?

SharePoint 2013 supports three different kinds of workflows:

- **List workflow**   List workflows are attached to lists or libraries. A user can invoke them manually on an item or they can be automatically triggered when a document is created, changed, or published.

- **Reusable workflow**   You can import reusable workflows to a site and reuse them in multiple lists or attach them to a content type.

- **Site workflow**   Site workflows are attached to the SharePoint site instead of any particular object.

Data collected during each of the steps of a workflow is also logged on the site and is available for users to review during the workflow process. Users can check the status of a running workflow, view the steps in a completed workflow, and even cancel workflows that they have started.

> **TIP**   Your workflow experience might be different based on which licensed version of SharePoint 2013 you have. Users of SharePoint 2013 Foundation use an older workflow engine based on the 2010 release of the software, and you might not have access to all of the features discussed in this section.

Workflows supplied with SharePoint

SharePoint 2013 provides a number of out-of-the-box workflows that you can use immediately within lists and libraries. The following list provides a brief overview of these workflows:

- **Approval - SharePoint 2010** This is used for basic document approval tasks. This workflow routes a document to an approver who can approve or reject the document and add additional comments to the initiator. This workflow is based upon the previous SharePoint 2010 version and runs in the SharePoint 2010 workflow engine.

- **Collect Feedback - SharePoint 2010** Collect Feedback sends a document to an individual or group for response and opinion. Those users can edit the document and/or add their comments directly to the workflow. This workflow is based upon the previous SharePoint 2010 version and runs in the SharePoint 2010 workflow engine.

- **Collect Signatures - SharePoint 2010** This workflow routes a document (limited to Microsoft Word, Microsoft Excel, or Microsoft InfoPath documents) to users for their electronic signature. This workflow is based upon the previous SharePoint 2010 version and runs in the SharePoint 2010 workflow engine.

- **Disposition Approval** Disposition Approval is used for information policy management and supports periodic review and expiration of documents within a library.

- **Publishing Approval** This is used specifically for routing publishing content for approval within a SharePoint publishing site.

- **Three-State Workflow** This workflow is a generalized workflow for routing a document through three configurable states. As the document is routed through each of the states, its document status can be updated and email notifications can be sent to designated users or groups.

> **TIP** Not all of these workflows are available on all sites. The available workflows are determined by features activated on the local site as well as your licensing model (Foundation, Standard, or Enterprise).

> **TIP** SharePoint 2013 Foundation users cannot make use of 2013 workflows.

Associating workflows with lists

One of the simplest types of workflows in SharePoint 2013 is the list workflow, which you can launch on list items or documents in a library. You use list workflows when you want to have a workflow available only within a particular list or library. You can also use them for cases in which you want the workflow to be automatically triggered when a document is created, updated, or published (because these are list-specific events).

Associate a workflow with a list

1   On a list on your SharePoint site, on the ribbon, click the Library tab.

2   In the Settings group, click the lower half of the Workflow Settings button.

3   On the menu that appears, click Add A Workflow.

(continued on next page)

> **TIP** If the workflow contains an initiation form (by which the person assigning the workflow can change certain workflow behaviors), the user will see a Next button displayed on the Add A Workflow page instead of an OK button. This Next button takes the user to another form on which workflow behavior can be changed.

Associate a workflow with a list *(continued)*

4 On the Add A Workflow page, choose a workflow to associate with the list.

5 Assign a local name for the workflow that will be displayed to users.

6 Choose the lists that will hold related workflow tasks and history.

Typically, the default values can be used, and these lists will be automatically created.

7 Choose the workflow starting options.

You can configure this workflow to automatically launch on certain events, if needed.

8 If additional, workflow-specific data is required, a Next button displays. Click the button, and enter any required information on the next page. Otherwise, an OK button is available. Click this button to save your settings.

Settings › Add a Workflow ⓘ

Workflow
Select a workflow to add to this document library. If a workflow is missing from the list, your site administrator may have to publish or activate it

Select a workflow template:
*Disposition Approval
*Three-state — **4**

Description:
Use this workflow to track items in a list.

*Denotes a SharePoint 2010 template.

Name
Enter a name for this workflow. The name will be used to identify this workflow to users of this document library.

Enter a unique name for this workflow:
Proposal WF — **5**

Task List
Select the name of the task list to use with this workflow, or create a new one.

Select a task list:
Tasks

Description:
Task list for workflow.

History List
Select the name of the history list to use with this workflow, or create a new one.

Select a history list:
Workflow History

Description:
History list for workflow.

— **6**

Start Options
Specify how this workflow can be started.

☑ Allow this workflow to be manually started by an authenticated user with Edit Item permissions.
☐ Require Manage Lists Permissions to start the workflow.

☐ Start this workflow to approve publishing a major version of an item.

☐ Creating a new item will start this workflow.

☐ Changing an item will start this workflow.

— **7**

[Next] [Cancel]

8

Associating workflows with content types

You can also associate SharePoint 2013 workflows with a particular content type. This is quite effective because workflows often operate on specialized columns that are unique to a particular content type. You might have department-specific status fields that you collect on documents such as Legal Approval Status or Medical Approval Status.

In this case, you could associate specialized review and approval workflows that automatically set values on these fields. This also simplifies administration and maintenance. Workflows associated with a content type can be invoked on items of that content type within any library in the site collection.

Associate a workflow with a content type

1   Click the Settings button (the small gear icon next to the name of the logged-on user) and then, on the menu that appears, click the Site Settings link.

2   On the Site Settings page, in the Web Designer Galleries section, select the Site Content Types link.

3   On the Site Content Types page, click the name of the content type to which the workflow will be bound.

(continued on next page)

...   Scott Metker ▾   ⚙

Shared with...

Edit page

Add a page

Add an app

Site contents

Change the look

Site settings ———— 1

Site Settings

Users and Permissions
People and groups
Site permissions
Site app permissions

Web Designer Galleries
Site columns
Site content types ———————— 2
Master pages
Composed looks

Site Settings ▸ Site Content Types ⓘ

📑 Create

Site Content Type	Parent
Document Content Types	
Basic Page	Document
3 ——— Document	Item
Dublin Core Columns	Document

✓ TIP   If the workflow contains an initiation form (by which the person assigning the workflow can change certain workflow behaviors), the user will see a Next button displayed on the Add A Workflow page instead of an OK button. This Next button takes the user to workflow-specific initiation form on which workflow behavior can be changed.

Associate a workflow with a content type *(continued)*

4   In the Settings section, click the Workflow Settings link.

5   On the Workflow Settings page, click Add A Workflow.

6   On the Add A Workflow page, choose an existing workflow to associate with the content type.

7   Choose a local name for the workflow that will be displayed on your site.

8   Enter any other settings required for this workflow and click OK to save your changes.

Site Content Types › Site Content Type

Site Content Type Information
Name: Proposal Document
Description: A content type to be used for a new client proposal
Parent: Document
Group: Document Content Types

Settings

▫ Name, description, and group
▫ Advanced settings
4 ——▫ Workflow settings

Proposal Document › Workflow Settings ⓘ

Workflows

⊛ Workflow Name (click to change settings)
    There are no workflows associated with this content type.

5 ——▫ Add a workflow

Proposal Document › Add a Workflow ⓘ

Workflow
Select a workflow to add to this content type. If a workflow is missing from the list, your site administrator may have to publish or activate it

Select a workflow template:
| Disposition Approval | —— 6
| Three-state |

Description:
Manages document expiration and retention by allowing participants to decide whether to retain or delete expired documents.

Name
Enter a name for this workflow. The name will be used to identify this workflow to users of this content type.

Enter a unique name for this workflow:
| Disposition Approval | —— 7

| OK | | Cancel |
8

Starting workflows on documents

One of the simplest ways for users to automate document processes in SharePoint 2013 is for them to manually invoke a workflow on a selected document. You can launch workflows on a document manually if they are configured for manual start and if they are associated with the current list or content type of the selected document.

Start a workflow on a document

1 From within the list that contains your target document, select the file by clicking the row.

2 On the ribbon, click the Files tab.

3 In the Workflow section, click the Workflows button.

4 On the Workflows page, if a workflow is available, it will appear in the Start A New Workflow section. Click this workflow to start the workflow.

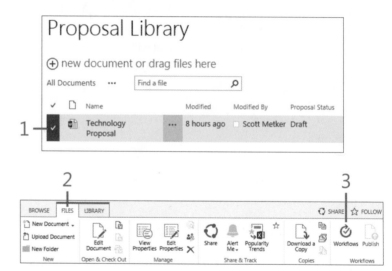

CAUTION These steps will only work if your administrator has previously linked a workflow with your document library or content type.

TIP Each workflow can have different requirements. Some workflows might prompt the user for more information and others, as configured by the administrator, might run immediately.

Checking the status of a running workflow

After you add a workflow to a SharePoint 2013 document library, a new column is created on the default view within the library. This column is named after your workflow and displays the status of this workflow on any documents in your library. For more detail, you can click the link and check the status of the workflow as well as the history of previously executed steps.

On the workflow status page, you can inspect the currently assigned tasks (there might be more than one active task if a workflow has parallel review steps, for example). Additionally, the workflow history shows all of the previous steps that have been completed in the workflow.

Check the status of a running workflow

1 Navigate to a library to which you have associated a workflow and launched the workflow on a document (see "Start a workflow on a document" on page 384). Locate the column named after your workflow and click the status field.

2 For further details on currently running tasks, click the hyperlinked title of each task or tasks displayed in the Tasks section. These represent currently running steps.

Creating a list workflow in SharePoint Designer

SharePoint Designer is an advanced tool used by high-level business administrators and developers who need to extend the out-of-the-box SharePoint 2013 functionality. If you want to create a new workflow from scratch, you will need to use SharePoint Designer.

At the time of this writing, SharePoint Designer 2013 is supported on the following operating systems only: Windows 7, Windows 8, Windows Server 2008 R2, Windows Server 2012. You can download the software directly from Microsoft or your IT staff can provide you with a download, as needed.

Create a list workflow in SharePoint Designer

1 On a list on your SharePoint site, on the ribbon, click the Library tab.

2 In the Settings section, click the lower half of the Workflow Settings icon.

3 On the menu that appears, click the Create A Workflow In Share-Point Designer command.

(continued on next page)

Create a list workflow in SharePoint Designer *(continued)*

4 In the Create List Workflow dialog box, enter a name and description for the workflow.

5 Choose the Platform Type for this workflow.

Note: the remaining instructions are written for SharePoint 2013.

6 Click OK.

7 Add new items to the workflow. For each item, do the following:

a Click a point to insert the item within the workflow.

b Select one of the insert buttons to see a list of items that can be added at the current point.

8 On the ribbon, click the Workflow tab. In the Save group, click Publish to publish your workflow on the SharePoint site.

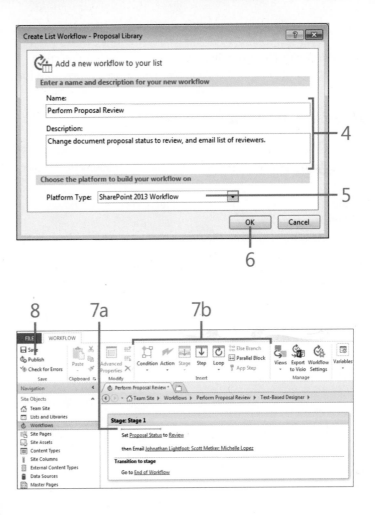

Editing workflows

Using SharePoint Designer 2013, you can also edit an existing list workflow associated with your site. This makes it possible for you to modify your workflows over time to support changing business processes.

Edit an existing list workflow

1 Open SharePoint Designer 2013 and click Open Site.

2 In the Open Site dialog box, enter the address of your site and click Open.

3 In the Navigation pane, under Site Objects, click the Workflows option.

4 Select a workflow on your site to edit.

5 On the ribbon, on the Workflows tab, click the Edit Workflow button in the Edit group.

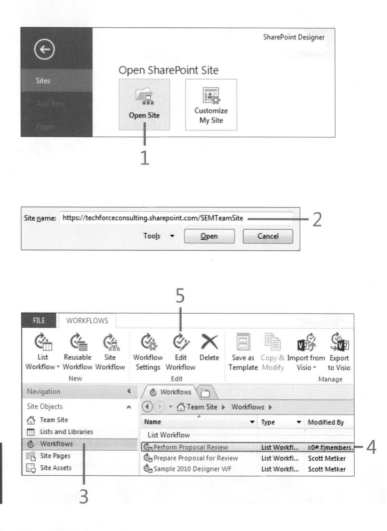

> **TIP** If you are first connecting to your site by using SharePoint Designer, you might be prompted to enter your credentials immediately after you connect to the site.

Introducing Microsoft Visio integration with SharePoint workflows

Another way of manipulating workflows in SharePoint 2013 is to make use of the visual designer, with which you can view workflows in a graphical, flow-chart–based layout that some users might find more intuitive than the text-based editor. This visual layout uses Visio 2013 and supports dragging and dropping workflow tasks onto a process diagram.

Visio visual designer

SharePoint offers a way of editing workflows by using a flow-chart look and feel, based upon integration with Visio 2013. This makes it possible for complex workflows to be displayed and edited by using simple visual designers. Here are some of the features and tools that you can take advantage of when editing your workflows:

- The Shapes pane shows the Actions, Conditions, and Components that you can add to a workflow.

- The visual designer area is where you can edit your workflows by using Visio shapes.

- You can use the Save buttons to save, publish, or validate your work.

- By clicking the SharePoint Designer Properties link that are available on each object, you can configure Actions, Conditions, and Components.

Save buttons   Shapes pane   Visual designer area

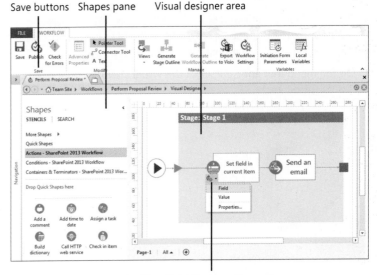

SharePoint Designer Properties

TIP The visual designer option within SharePoint 2013 is only functional if you have an installed copy of Visio 2013 (Professional Edition).

Switching to the visual designer

To switch to the visual designer, you first need to open a workflow within SharePoint Designer 2013. After you have made the switch to the visual designer, SharePoint Designer will remember your preference for the rest of your session.

Switch to the visual designer

1 From an open workflow in SharePoint Designer 2013, on the ribbon, click the Workflows tab. Then, in the Manage group, click the drop-down arrow at the bottom of the Views button.

2 On the menu that appears, select the Visual Designer option.

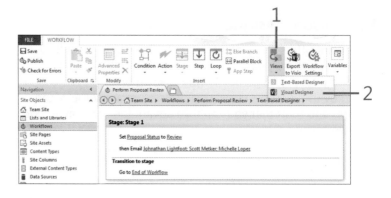

✓ **TIP** The visual designer requires that you have locally installed Visio 2013 Professional. An error message appears if you do not have the proper version installed.

✓ **TIP** You must be working with a SharePoint 2013 workflow to enable the visual designer. If you are unable to switch to visual designer on an existing workflow, it might be based upon the Share-Point 2010 workflow framework. Try creating a brand new 2013 workflow and switch to visual designer.

Creating workflows in Visio 2013

Another option for creating complex workflows is to first draft the workflow completely in Visio 2013, which scan be used to flesh out the outline of a workflow without requiring connectivity to SharePoint 2013. This can also be used to document a high-level process prior to importing the workflow into SharePoint.

Create a workflow in Visio 2013

1 Open Visio 2013 and then, in the templates search box, type **SharePoint 2013**.

2 Click the Search button (the magnifying-glass icon).

3 Double click the Microsoft SharePoint 2013 Workflow template to create a new file from this template.

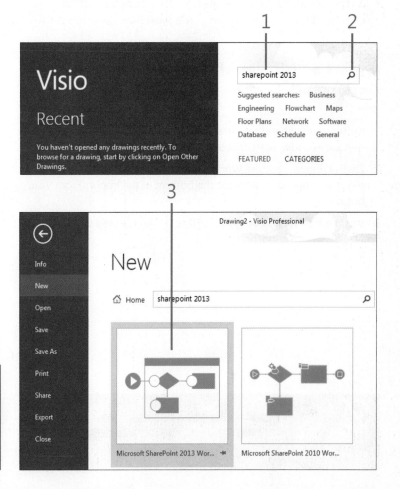

> ✓ **TIP** Plotting out workflows first in Visio 2013 can be useful if you need to document and obtain approval for workflows that are a critical part of your company's operating processes. Visio documents can be more readily exchanged and reviewed without requiring each user to have SharePoint Designer installed on their computer.

Importing Visio workflows into SharePoint Designer

Another option for users is to create complex workflows offline in Visio 2013 and import those workflows into SharePoint 2013 at a later time. However, when a Visio-created workflow is imported for the first time, you need to modify the items that refer to SharePoint site-specific data prior to publishing the workflow. For example, if the workflow modifies data on associated files, you will only be able to enter the specific columns that are modified after you have imported the workflow. This is due to the fact that the Visio application does not have visibility into the site columns defined on a particular list or library until the file has already been imported into SharePoint Designer.

Import a Visio workflow into SharePoint Designer

1 Open the SharePoint Designer 2013 window that is already connected to the SharePoint site that you will be using. In the Navigation pane, under Site Objects, click the Workflows option.

2 On the ribbon, click the Workflows tab. Then, in the Manage group, click the drop-down arrow at the bottom of the Import From Visio button.

3 Select which version of Visio (2010 or 2013) was used to create the file you will be importing.

(continued on next page)

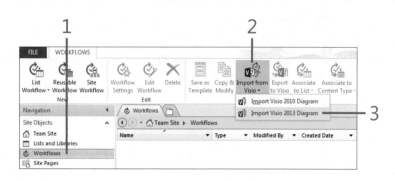

✓ TIP If you forget to modify properties on actions that are missing site-specific data, when you attempt to publish the workflow for the first time, a warning will appear showing which properties are missing.

Import a Visio workflow into SharePoint Designer *(continued)*

4 Navigate to the Visio file by using the browser.

5 Click Open.

6 In the Create Workflow dialog box, enter a local title and description for the workflow.

7 Choose the Workflow Type (List, Reusable, or Site).

8 If you have chosen to import a List Workflow, you must choose which list on this site will have this workflow associated with it.

9 Click OK to import the workflow from the Visio file.

SharePoint and eDiscovery

19

If you work within a typical company or organization, you will likely have vast amounts of content produced by your group, both formally and informally. This covers simple documents, such as contracts and invoices, as well as informally produced content such as departmental webpages, intra-office emails, and online chat sessions.

All of this information could be subject to *discovery* or *legal hold* rules at some point in the future, which dramatically changes how you create and store data on a daily basis. Your organization might be subject to these rules due to industry regulations or compliance, internal corporate policies, or due to a court case. In any of these scenarios, you will likely face two primary directives:

- Don't allow the deletion of anything relevant during an investigation.
- Find, export, and deliver all content relevant to the investigation to the appropriate authorities.

Throughout this book, we have presented ways of producing, sharing, and organizing information by using Microsoft SharePoint 2013. In this section, we will focus on ways that this information can be discovered (in the legal sense of the word), archived, and preserved.

Introducing eDiscovery and legal holds

Electronic discovery, or *eDiscovery*, is the process of finding and delivering electronic information that can be used as evidence in a court case. Tools that are used for eDiscovery scan through information systems searching for material that might be relevant to a case. After this content is identified, these tools can extract and deliver the information to representatives of the court.

What are eDiscovery and legal holds?

A legal hold occurs when a company receives a communication from legal counsel or a court that requires the organization to immediately suspend any disposal of information that might be relevant in a legal proceeding. A legal hold covers all forms of information storage used at a company, spanning both paper-based and electronic information.

In a simple example, if a company is involved in a court case involving potentially fraudulent billing to another customer (for this example, let's use Contoso Ltd), a legal hold might be issued. This legal hold would immediately block any shredding or recycling of paper-based materials concerning Contoso Ltd. In addition, this would also require that all emails containing references to Contoso as well as any documents assigned to this account (or containing certain keywords) become immediately locked down and preserved. These rules ensure that information relevant to an ongoing court case remains intact prior to a full discovery effort.

The eDiscovery Center is a special SharePoint site collection that supports legal discovery and legal holds.

eDiscovery in SharePoint

One of the challenges of legal discovery within software systems is that the discovery process typically requires both technical skills and system access reserved to IT staff, whereas the discovery process is conducted by non-technical personnel such as compliance officers or HR personnel.

SharePoint 2013 introduces a new site, the eDiscovery Center, which can be used by non-technical personnel to support these processes. Content can be preserved via a *general hold*, which preserves all content on a site, or via a targeted *query-based hold*, which uses search queries to precisely focus on specific content for preservation.

Within the eDiscovery Center site, you can work with the following items:

- **eDiscovery Case**   A case is a way of grouping all of the queries and preserved content from a particular legal case into a single site. SharePoint implements each case as a subsite under the eDiscovery Center.

- **eDiscovery Set**   An eDiscovery set is a query scenario in which a collection of query keywords is applied to a number of target sources (SharePoint sites or Exchange email servers). Typically, you would implement a number of eDiscovery sets to fully comply with a legal hold or discovery request.

- **eDiscovery Source**   An eDiscovery source is a collection of mailboxes (for Exchange integration) or SharePoint sites against which the query will be run. All matching items within the query results will be subject to the legal hold.

- **eDiscovery Queries**   An eDiscovery query is a search query that can be used to export a set of all matching documents or simply generate a report of documents matching the query.

In a typical eDiscovery session, you would create one or more eDiscovery sets to find content and issue an in-place hold. This would preserve any content matching the hold parameters from deletion or change while you prepare for further action. You would then further refine your queries (without risk of content being deleted in the meantime), preview the information, and report upon the total volume of the content. Finally, you would schedule an export of the materials and forward this information to the relevant authorities. After the legal action was completed, you would be able to close the case and release all relevant holds.

Creating an eDiscovery Center

SharePoint 2013 introduces a new type of site, the eDiscovery Center. An eDiscovery Center is a single site that can be used to organize your discovery and legal-hold activities. To work with legal holds and discovery queries, you must create at least one eDiscovery Center. This site is used to track one or many cases, which represent individual legal or regulatory actions. In this task, we will walk through the process of creating an initial eDiscovery Center in SharePoint 2013.

Create an eDiscovery Center

1 From the Admin Center for your Office 365 instance, at the right end of the toolbar, click the Admin menu.

2 On the menu that appears, click SharePoint.

3 In the SharePoint Admin Center, on the ribbon, click the Site Collection tab, and then click New.

4 On the menu that appears, click Private Site Collection.

(continued on next page)

Create an eDiscovery Center *(continued)*

5 On the New Site Collection page, enter a title for the eDiscovery Center, a URL that will be used to access the site under your main URL, and a language for the new site.

6 Click the Enterprise tab.

7 Select eDiscovery Center.

8 Specify the appropriate Time Zone.

9 Choose the site administrator who will have administrator rights to the site.

10 Select your storage quota and server resource options.

11 Click OK.

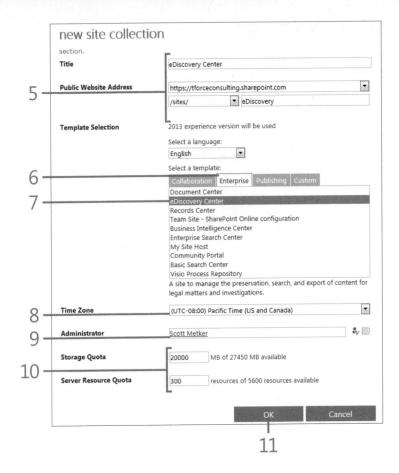

✓ **TIP** Check with your IT personnel if you have questions regarding total storage or server resources required for this site. They should have information based upon typical usages and total site sizes.

Working with eDiscovery cases

After you have a working SharePoint 2013 eDiscovery Center, you are able to create and manage cases that represent specific legal or regulatory investigation. Each case is designed to represent a single investigation and can contain all of the queries and holds encountered during the investigation. Because each case is represented by a separate subsite under the eDiscovery Center, you have independent access control for each of these cases.

Create an eDiscovery case

1 Navigate to your eDiscovery Center and click Create New Case.

(continued on next page)

Create an eDiscovery case *(continued)*

2 On the New SharePoint Site page, enter a title and description for the case.

3 Enter a URL for the site, relative to the eDiscovery Center.

4 Choose a language for your case.

5 Choose user permissions for the case.

6 Select navigation options for the site.

7 Click Create.

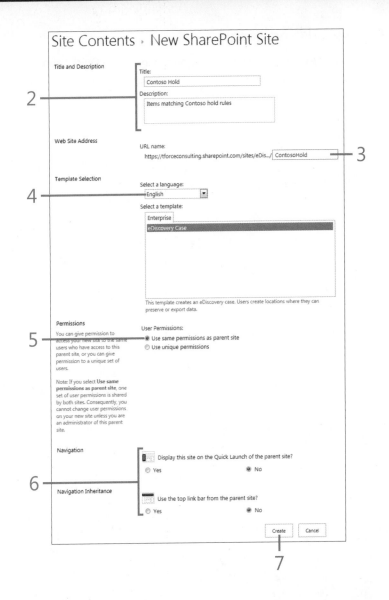

Access existing cases

1 Navigate to your eDiscovery Center and then, on the Quick Launch bar, click the Cases link.

2 Click the case that you want to access.

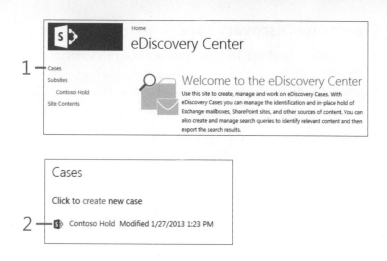

Identifying and holding content

One of the first steps for any legal or regulatory action is to ensure that data is not changed or deleted during an investigation. Within SharePoint 2013, eDiscovery Sets are used to identify content that matches search constraints and rapidly enforce a hold on that content. After the hold is put in place, you have time to explore and export relevant data during the course of the investigation.

Create a hold on a case

1 Navigate to the Home page of your case. In the Identify And Hold section, click New Item.

(continued on next page)

Create a hold on a case *(continued)*

2 On the New: eDiscovery Set page, enter a name for the set.

3 Click the Add & Manage Sources link.

4 On the Add & Manage Sources page, in the Locations section, enter one or more URLs to SharePoint sites that you want to add to the hold operation.

5 Click the Check icon next to each URL to validate the address.

6 Click OK to return to the New: eDiscovery Set page.

7 Enter your search constraints. If you leave these values blank, the entire contents of each site will be placed under the hold.

8 Select Enable In-Place Hold.

9 Click Save to trigger the hold operation.

TRY THIS You can click the Preview Results button to view representative files that will be placed under the hold prior to implementing the hold operation.

Removing an eDiscovery hold

There are a number of reasons that you might remove a current hold. For instance, the case or regulatory investigation might have completed, or you might want to replace a general hold with a more targeted hold after further details have emerged from an investigation. Regardless of the reason, If you have authorized access to the eDiscovery Case, you can disable a hold associated with any SharePoint 2013 eDiscovery Set.

Remove an eDiscovery hold

1 Navigate to the eDiscovery Case Home page and then, on the Quick Launch bar, click the eDiscovery Sets link.

2 On the the eDiscovery Sets page, click the link under the name of the set that you want to modify.

3 On the page for the specific eDiscovery set, click the Disable In-Place Hold option.

4 Click Save.

Accessing deleted content under legal hold

After content is placed under an in-place hold, users can continue to use content normally within the affected sites (this was a change from previous versions of SharePoint, which simply blocked modification or deletion of affected files). When an edit or deletion is made to that content, a uniquely named copy of the original content is placed in a special library called the

Preservation Hold Library within the same site. This library can be viewed directly by site collection administrators, and it is also used when consolidating and exporting content by using eDiscovery Queries.

Access content in a Preservation Hold library

1   On the site containing the content that's been placed on hold, click the Settings button (the small gear icon next to the name of the logged-on user). On the menu that appears, click Site Contents.

2   On the Site Contents page, click the Preservation Hold Library.

(continued on next page)

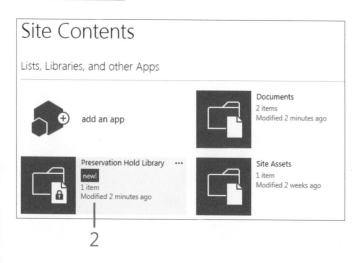

> **✓ TIP** If a file is changed multiple times, the intermediate versions are not saved. Only the version that existed at the time of the hold is preserved.

> **✓ TIP** If you are unable to locate the Preservation Hold library within a site with an in-place hold configured, this might be because you are not a site collection administrator for the site (the library is only visible to users added as the site collection administrator or granted special permissions through the web application by IT staff).

Access content in a Preservation Hold library *(continued)*

3 In the Preservation Hold Library, select an item by clicking to the left of the item's icon.

4 On the ribbon, click the Files tab.

5 In the Manage group, click the View Properties button.

6 Inspect the document properties. You can see the preservation date or even open the document for viewing. Click Close to return to the library.

4   **5**

3

6

TIP The Preservation Hold Library is maintained by SharePoint processes configured by your administrator. As in-place holds expire or are removed, the content will be removed from these libraries over time.

Sorry, something went wrong   ✕

The server has encountered the following error(s):
Initial Filing Notes_C1C3356B-27A3-49D5-99F3-15AB3A3141A92013-01-22T20-34-27.docx
This library contains items that have been modified or deleted but must remain available due to eDiscovery holds. Items cannot be modified or removed.

OK

Any attempt to delete content from this library will result in an error, as the files remain under in-place hold.

Creating an eDiscovery query

After you have created an in-place hold on content within your sites by using eDiscovery Sets, you can sift through your content at a more leisurely pace without worrying that content might disappear during the investigation.

SharePoint 2013 uses eDiscovery queries, which make it possible for users to further filter and explore content as well as

generate a full export of targeted content. This export can be sent to legal or regulatory personnel outside of your corporate network, as required.

Create an eDiscovery query

1 On the Home page of an eDiscovery case, in the Search and Export section, click New Item.

(continued on next page)

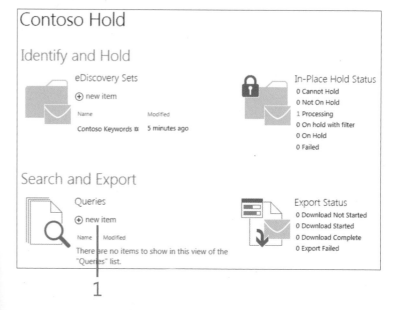

✓ **TIP** Using the Modify Query Scope dialog, you can target queries at individual sites, eDiscovery Sets, or even all content encompassed by the current case. Using these options, you can choose how much data you will search and export.

→ **TRY THIS** To further refine your query, you can use SharePoint metadata by clicking the Specify Property tab under the SharePoint query options.

Create an eDiscovery query *(continued)*

2 On the Query: New Item page, enter a name for the query.

3 Enter your query keywords and other search information.

4 Click the Modify Query Scope link.

5 In the Modify Query Scope dialog box, click the option that reflects the scope of content that you will include in the query.

6 Click OK.

7 Back on the Query: New Item page, click the SharePoint tab.

8 Click Save to save your query.

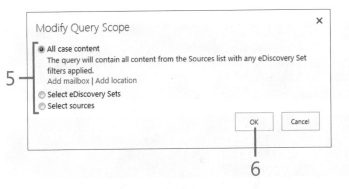

Refine your query by clicking this link and adding SharePoint properties to filter.

Exporting eDiscovery results

After you have created an eDiscovery query, you can export a report of the results or download the raw content from Share-Point. You can export eDiscovery results directly from one of your eDiscovery Case sites to a local archive. This archive could then be transferred to the appropriate legal team who could browse this content without ever requiring access to the Share-Point sites.

Export eDiscovery results

1 On the Quick Launch bar, click Queries.

2 On the Queries page, click the eDiscovery query that you want to export.

3 Scroll to the bottom for that query and click Export.

(continued on next page)

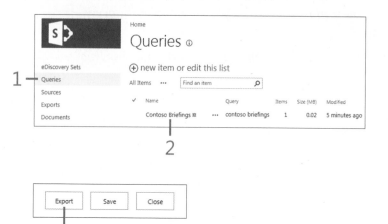

✓ **TIP** When exporting results for the very first time only on a new computer, ensure that you download a report before downloading results. An issue with the download helper can cause the pre-release version of Office 365 to fail if downloading results first.

✓ **TIP** On some systems, you might be prompted with a security warning in a pop-up message box upon export, indicating that the publisher cannot be verified. Click the Run button if it appears.

Export eDiscovery results *(continued)*

4 On the Export: New Item page, select your export options.

5 Click OK.

6 In the Export: Download dialog box, click Download Report to download a report of all findings, or click Download Results to download the actual content files that were identified. If you are prompted to sign in, click the Sign In button and enter your password.

7 In the eDiscovery Download Manager dialog box, select an export destination.

8 Click OK.

9 Navigate to your export folder by clicking the Export Location link when complete.

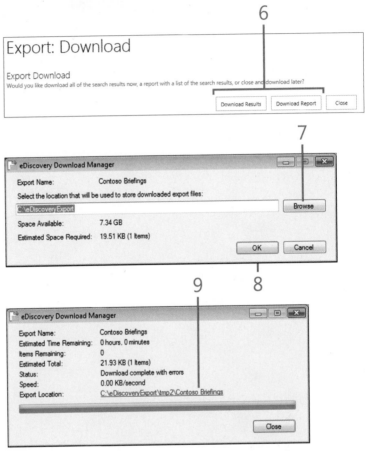

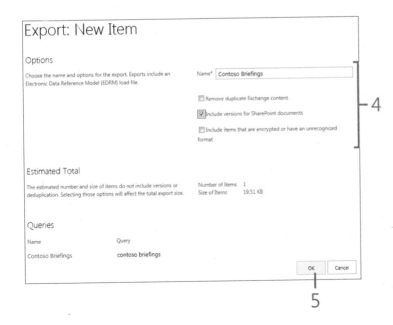

TIP Some of the export options apply to email, which you can ignore unless you will also be exporting email managed by Office 365.

Index

Symbols

About the authors

Johnathan Lightfoot is the Principal SharePoint Architect at GP Strategies. He has been involved with IT for more than 20 years, having worked in various roles, including Help Desk, Level II and III desktop support, and Windows and AS-400 server administration and development. Companies he has worked for in the past include Electronic Data Systems, Hawaiian Telcom, and Norwegian Cruise Line (yes, he actually worked on the ships). However, the best experiences he says he has had were his nine years serving in the United States Navy. Johnathan is also a Microsoft Certified Trainer (MCT) who specializes in SharePoint 2013, 2010, MOSS 2007, WSS 3.0, Office 2007/2010/2013, and Office 365 technologies, along with providing Soft Skills training for organizations. Johnathan also speaks at SharePoint and social networking events around the world.

Michelle Lopez is a Certified Microsoft Office Specialist (MOS) who specializes in SharePoint 2013, 2010, 2007, as well as InfoPath and Office technologies. She worked for 15 years at Microsoft Corporation and has dedicated the past 6 years of her career to championing SharePoint solutions to communities and companies nationwide.

Michelle is from Redmond, Washington, and currently lives in Scottsdale, Arizona, with her husband Carlos and their three young children.

Scott Metker has been an enterprise architect on Fortune 500 corporate software implementations for the past 15 years. His current role, Chief Software Architect at GP Strategies, enables him to focus on new product development and implementing software development methodologies. He has worked extensively with the Microsoft SharePoint and Dynamics platforms and currently develops commercial applications on these platforms with a focus on bringing cloud-based technologies to regulated industries such as Life Sciences.

Scott originally comes from an academic background, with a doctoral degree in electrical engineering, but he has embraced a role in private industry producing software for large enterprise and government clients. He frequently speaks at industry conferences and also teaches as an affiliate instructor at Loyola University Maryland.

What do you think of this book?

We want to hear from you!

To participate in a brief online survey, please visit:

microsoft.com/learning/booksurvey

Tell us how well this book meets your needs—what works effectively, and what we can do better.
Your feedback will help us continually improve our books and learning resources for you.

Thank you in advance for your input!